X

ENCYCLOPAEDIA
OF HOUSE PLANTS

NICO VERMEULEN
EDITED BY RICHARD ROSENFELD

ENCYCLOPAEDIA
OF HOUSE PLANTS

REBO
PRODUCTIONS

Key to symbols:

○ as light a location as possible, not always
in direct sunlight

◑ not too much light, no direct sunlight

✸ shade

⬤ little water

◑ not too much water

○ plenty of water

The amounts of light and water indicated are
the requirements of the growing season.
If there are different requirements outside the
growing season, these are given in the text.

© 1995 Rebo Productions, Lisse
Published by Rebo Productions Ltd, 1997
Text and photographs: Nico Vermeulen
Cover design: Ton Wienbelt, The Netherlands
Production: TextCase, The Netherlands
Translation: Annemarie Koelman for First Edition
Translation Ltd, Great Britain
Typesetting: Hof & Land Typografie, The Netherlands

2nd print 1998

ISBN 1 901094 08 1

Contents

Foreword

The *Encyclopedia of House Plants* is a handbook which is intended for easy use by those who like plants, whether or not they have green fingers or have much time to devote to them. And, strange as it may seem, users of this book are advised not to take it too seriously. Millions of house plants prove every day that they can stay alive even if they do not get precisely the right amount of moisture, light and heat because they are looked after by people who have other things to do besides pampering their plants. Look upon the tips as a guide rather than as instructions; they will help you to enjoy your house plants even more.

The encyclopedia takes as its starting point the question "Where do house plants like it best?". The answers are to be found in the forests of South-East Asia, on the mountain sides of the Andes and the plains of Mexico. Are these places hot or cold, damp or dry and do the plants grow in the full sun or the deep shade? The answers to these questions suggest the best locations for plants in the house and the reader will be visiting far away places in this encyclopedia.

The placing of a house plant determines whether it is going to be spindly and sickly or a picture of good health. A healthy location will usually prevent pests and diseases. If they do occur, my advice is to put the plant in a different spot. A sheltered spot outside is, for most species, an ideal place to get rid of pests and diseases.

I do not agree with the use of chemical insecticides and pesticides because they pose a grave danger for people and the environment; after all we keep house plants for pleasure. Chemicals also have only a temporary effect, and pests and diseases invariably return if the plant remains in an unhealthy position.

Because this book is written to be easy to use, you will find the plants under the names that are generally used in garden centres, even if they are out-of-date and the plants have been given new scientific names. If you only know the new name, the index will tell you where to find the plant in this book. The only exception to this is the chapter on cacti, as garden centres and nurseries do not usually put name tags on them, so I hope to have pleased cacti lovers by using

Left: *Fuchsia* 'Nell Gwyn'

the new nomenclature. It has already been introduced among keen amateurs and has the advantage that it groups together species that require similar care. The index will, of course, point you to the right page if you only know the old names.

The encyclopedia is in two main parts: foliage and flowers. The first eight chapters take a look at plants which are chiefly bought for their beautiful foliage. Chapter 9 deals with hanging plants and climbers, the foliar varieties as well as the flowering ones, and from chapter 10 onwards flowering plants are central. In the last two chapters we go outdoors and look at colourful plants for balconies and terraces.

The author

Page 9: *Helicona psittacorum*

1. Ferns

From the middle of the last century until well into this century ferns were extremely popular house plants but with the rise of central heating ferns disappeared from houses. Most species cannot tolerate dry air. Gradually it is becoming clear that dry air is also unhealthy for people so that humidification is becoming more common. Special equipment is sometimes installed. In some countries different types of central heating are being installed in place of radiators which cause dry air. In rooms that are heated by radiant heat the ambient temperature can be kept a few degrees lower without this being noticeable to the inhabitants.

To ferns, those few degrees make all the difference. Ferns grow better in a slightly cooler atmosphere because the relative humidity tends to be higher. The most modern methods of heating are therefore providing a new future for the fern. However, even if you, like most people, have standard central heating it is still possible to enjoy ferns. Put them in a cool room during the months when the heating is on and most ferns are likely to survive the winter. In Spring, as soon as the central heating is turned down, put them back in the living room.

Adiantum cuneatum

See: *Adiantum raddianum*

Left: Dicksonia antarctica

Adiantum hispidulum

If the humidity in your house is too low for *Adiantum raddianum* to grow well, you could try *Adiantum hispidulum*. This fern also likes humid air but it can tolerate drier air than *raddianum*. The fronds are made up of leaflets attached in long rows to leaf stalks which are, in turn, carried on black stalks. This gives the fern an air of transparency. If *hispidulum* doesn't thrive indoors all is not lost. Put the fern outdoors in a moist, humus rich soil in a shady and sheltered spot. There it will easily survive the winter and, as long as there is no frost, it will retain its leaves, even outside.

Adiantum hispidulum 'Bronze Venus'

Adiantum pubescens

See: *Adiantum hispidulum*

Adiantum raddianum

MAIDENHAIR FERN

The maidenhair fern immediately responds to being treated incorrectly. If the humidity of the air is too low, or if the fern has not been watered, the edges of the gossamer-like leaflets dry out. If you let the fern stand permanently in water it becomes glassy and the whole plant dies, especially in a cool room. *Adiantum radianum* originates in the warm tropical forests of South America where the air humidity is high and the temperature does not drop below 18°C (64¤F). Try, therefore, to find a place in the house which resembles a tropical rainforest as much as possible. Put the maidenhair fern in a light spot, but not in direct sunlight. In centrally heated houses provide extra humidity. Regularly spray the fern with a mist of rainwater or boiled water. Put the plant in a pot on a bed of gravel in a wide tray. Fill the tray with water to just below the bottom of the pot. But perhaps the easiest approach is to put this most beautiful of ferns in the most humid places in the house - in the bathroom or near the cooker.

Adiantum raddianum 'Brilliantelse'

MAIDENHAIR FERN

The maidenhair fern has given rise to many cultivars. The young fronds of 'Goldenelse' are golden yellow, later turning to light green. Often a golden edge remains. The vigorous cultivar 'Fragrantissimum' grows to more than 50cm (20in) high. The leaflets are blue-green and readily produce spore cap-

sules. 'Brilliantelse' is an even sturdier plant. This compact fern carries graceful golden-green leaflets on tough, glossy black leaf stalks.

Adiantum raddianum 'Brilliantelse'

Aspidium

See: *Cyrtomium*

Adiantum raddianum

Asplenium antiquum

This species from Taiwan and Japan has smaller, more pointed leaves than the bird's nest fern. The leaves often have slightly wavy edges, are more V-shaped and are also sturdier than the leaves of *Asplenium nidus*, and therefore less vulnerable. The maintenance is the same as for the actual bird's nest fern (see: *Asplenium nidus*).

Asplenium antiquum

Asplenium nidus

BIRD'S NEST FERN

The long, lanceolate leaves of the bird's nest fern unfurl from a growing point at the heart of the plant which is covered in black-brown hair resembling a bird's nest.
The thin but tough leaves form a funnel. The outer leaves of the funnel gradually die and can be cut off.
The leaves keep their good condition longer if they are kept out of direct sunlight and by regular misting with rainwater or boiled water.
Asplenium nidus likes a humid atmosphere but it can tolerate drier air. It is one of the few ferns which grows well in centrally heated rooms although it generally won't grow any taller or wider than 50 cm (20in) in these conditions. Under ideal (more humid) conditions the bird's nest fern can grow twice as big as this.
Such a large plant needs a lot of space because the leaves need to be kept completely free-standing or the edges will easily get damaged. Damage can also result from scale insects, especially when the fern

is in too dry a spot. Chemical insecticides should definitely not be used as all *Asplenium* species are very sensitive to these. Rub off the scales and paint the spots with methylated spirits. If the plant grows well it will produce spore capsules which form straight lines on the undersides of the leaves. This is characteristic of aspleniums.
There are various cultivars on the market. *Asplenium* nidus 'Frinbriatum' for instance has jagged and sometimes curly leaves but it looks sickly and is certainly no improvement on the real *Asplenium nidus*.

Asplenium nidus

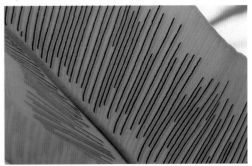

Asplenium scolopendrium

See: *Phyllitis scolopendrium*

Blechnum gibbum

In the shop *Blechnum gibbum* looks like an ordinary fern the graceful, feathered leaves forming a rosette. But if the plant is looked after well you will notice that you have, in fact, bought a tree fern. Each spring new bright green leaves appear while the old ones die off and may be pruned. Gradually a stem is formed which can be several tens of centimetres high. On the islands in the southern part of the Pacific Ocean, where *Blechnum gibbum* originates, the trunks can reach a height of 1.5m (5ft).
The name *gibbum* means "wavy" and refers to the decidedly wavy leaves of the fern. This fern tolerates more light than most others so put *Blechnum* in a light spot, possibly in the morning sun.
Keep the plant good and moist in the

13

growing season; it doesn't need much water during the winter, but in centrally heated houses it will need a regular misting to avoid red spider mite.

As long as the heating is on in the house it is best to put the plant in an unheated room where the temperature does not drop below 10°C. (50¤F)

Cibotium

BISHOP'S CROOK

Before the young fronds of *Cibotium* unfurl they are rolled up at the end of their stalk. The budding leaf looks like a staff with a hooked end, hence its Dutch common name, "bishop's crook".

Cibotium glaucum, a Hawaiian tree fern, forms a trunk as it gets older. The fronds are 1.5m (5ft) long and 50cm (20in) wide and grow higher and higher on the short trunk. *Cibotium menziensii*, also called *Cibotium chamissioii*, looks very similar and is also a Hawaiian tree fern. *Cibotium barometz* has very wide fronds of up to 2m (6ft) in length, but the plant does not grow a trunk. The Mexican tree fern (*Cibotium schiedei*) does

Cibotium

Blechnum gibbum

not grow a trunk either when cultivated, its fronds also spread out widely but the fern does not grow wider than 1 to 1.5m (3 to 5ft). A cool green house or conservatory is ideal for all tree ferns because they cannot tolerate a dry or close atmosphere. Central heating will eventually kill them. Other methods of heating such as floor and wall heating may offer a much healthier climate if the relative humidity does not drop below 50% and the air remains fresh. Tree ferns could therefore find a good home in large, light rooms such as studios. Keep the fern out of direct sunlight but give it as much light as possible. The winter temperature should not drop below 7°C (45°F) and in summer, a temperature between 15°C (59°F) and 30°C (86°F) is ideal.

Cyathea

TREE FERN

Out of more than 300 species of *Cyathea* those from the subtropics are best suited to temperate climates. The tropical species require night temperatures of more than 15°C (59°F) even in winter.

Cyathea cooperi

The *Cibotium* in a natural setting

Cyathea medullaris from New Zealand can tolerate 7°C (45¤F) at night but this means that even this robust species has to be grown in a heated room during the winter. Because the relative humidity definitely has to stay above 50%, only light and airy rooms should be considered. These tree ferns can tolerate the mild rays of the winter sun but need protection against the summer sun and plenty of water, without soaking the compost.

Cyrtomium falcatum

HOLLY FERN

Cyrtomium falcatum is a very tough fern from China and Japan which can tolerate the most inhospitable places in the house. The dark green foliage can survive even in the darkness of a lobby, but it will only thrive where there is some indirect sunlight and the relative humidity is above 50%. Even in a centrally heated living room *Cyrtomium* will bravely keep growing.

To get the most enjoyment from this plant put it in an unheated room during the winter. The temperature may safely drop down to close to freezing. In the south-west of England it will even survive the winter outside. If the plant starts to decline during the summer you can use your garden to revive it. Heel in the fern in a shady spot and bring it back into the house in September. During the winter the fern needs very little water as long as it stands in a cool spot but if it lives in a dry room it needs plenty of water, especially during the summer. The

Cyrtomium falcatum

foliage, which can grow up to 40 cm (16in) tall, needs regular misting.

Cyrtomium falcatum 'Rochfordianum' is a popular cultivar with larger prickly fronds. Less easily available are the following sub-species of *Cyrtomium falcatum: fortunei* which has matt green foliage and *caryotideum* which has fronds ending with a drooping point and leaflets with serrated edges.

Davallia bullata

MONKEY'S FOOT FERN

The rhizomes of *Davallia bullata* and the variety *Davallia bullata mariesii* are scaly rather than hairy. The fronds of this elegant fern from the Azores are 30 cm (12in) long and very finely divided. The lace-like tips of the leaflets are slightly bulbous and resemble seaweed. The leaflets are softer than those of *Davallia canariensis* and dry out more easily. Give *bullata*, therefore, a slightly higher relative humidity than *canariensis*, with a minimum of 50% but otherwise treat it in a similar fashion.

Davallia bullata

Davallia canariensis

HARE'S FOOT FERN

The rhizomes of *Davallia canariensis* eventually grow out of their pot and wrap completely round it. They are covered in reddish-brown hair which makes them look like hare's feet. To do full justice to the ornamental value of this fern, which grows to a height of about 30 cm (12in), it is best to put it in a hanging basket. In the wild it grows on trees and wraps its moisture-absorbing aerial roots around the trunk.

This gives a good indication of how best to treat *Davallia*. Grow the plant in compost that is very rich in humus with some peat moss mixed in. Do not feed at all or very little and make sure that the soil is not waterlogged. The fern benefits greatly from having its leaves and roots sprayed all over, preferably with rainwater or boiled water. Otherwise it is reasonably easy to grow and will even endure drier air and mild sunshine. Do not leave the plant in rooms where the central heating is on because it would be too dry, even though this *Davallia* comes from the Canary Islands. In the winter the fern is content with very little light and will tolerate temperatures around freezing. It is easy to propagate *Davallia canariensis* by pinning down small pieces of rhizome on damp peat moss placed on moist compost.

The rhizomes of *Davallia canariensis*

Davallia canariensis

Dicksonia

TREE FERN

Dicksonias are the most impressive of tree ferns. They mostly originated in New Zealand and Australia but because of their beauty are now on show in many gardens in tropical and subtropical countries. They eventually reach a height of several metres with a trunk as thick as that of a palm. From the top of the trunk the leaves, which are double-feathered or multi-feathered, spread out and can lightly overshadow an area of several square metres. It is quite an experience to walk under one of these ferns. *Dicksonia antarctica* will endure a few degrees of frost but, even so, should be kept indoors since drying wind is fatal. If you want to experiment with this marvellous fern make sure that you can keep it alive: do not go for it if you have to put it in a centrally heated house. It needs a light position out of direct sunlight. The air should be humid, but not chilly and there should be enough space for the leaves to develop fully. The fern, which can be grown very well in a relatively small container, should be watered moderately and kept at a moderate temperature. It should get as much fresh air as possible. In the summer the fern can be put outdoors but only in very sheltered locations and in the shade.

Dicksonia antarctica

Didymochlaena truncatula

The leaves of this bushy fern are copper coloured when young gradually turning a beautiful shiny light green. The fronds are deeply scored and the leaflets more or less oblong. Despite its great ornamental value

Didymochlaena is still relatively unknown but not because its cultivation poses any greater problems than for most other ferns. It can tolerate shade but not direct sunlight. Give it plenty of water in the summer and keep it just moist in the winter. Misting or spraying is very beneficial for the foliage because the only thing this plant cannot stand is the dry air of a centrally heated room. Put the fern in an unheated room during the winter, where the temperature should not drop below 7°C (45¤F).

Didymochlaena truncatula

Dryopteris erythrosora

JAPANESE BUCKLER/SHIELD FERN

The leaves of *Dryopteris erythrosora* have variegated late season colours when young. This fern is therefore called "autumn fern" in Holland. All through the summer new "autumn leaves" develop on this vigorous fern. It is related to the native male fern, *Dryopteris filix-mas*, which is available as a garden plant. *Dryopteris erythrosora* may be found in the company of garden plants or house plants because it is suitable for growing indoors as well as outdoors. Give it plenty of water in the summer and spray the fronds as often as possible with boiled tap water or rainwater. When the central heating is turned on for the colder months, take the fern out of centrally heated rooms. It can over-winter in an unheated room, in

Right: *Matteuccia struthiopteris*

18

the greenhouse or even outside if dug in with its pot. In the latter case this Japanese fern will lose its leaves but they will grow again in the spring.

Dryopteris erythrosora

Matteuccia struthiopteris

OSTRICH FEATHER, SHUTTLECOCK FERN

The ostrich feather fern is in fact a garden plant which will, in damp places, spread rapidly through underground rhizomes. In spring the green funnel-shaped leaves shoot up everywhere. Because this fern is so rampant not everybody likes to have it in their garden. Fortunately it is easy to keep it within bounds by planting in a large container. In the fall the dying foliage collapses over the edge of the container whilst the fertile fronds stand up proudly and glow golden-brown in the winter sun.

The ostrich feather fern is totally hardy and only needs to be kept sufficiently moist in the growing season, as it will not tolerate drying out. As long as the soil is kept moist the container can be placed in the shade, semi-shade or full sun.

Microlepia speluncae

It is best to buy *Microlepia* as if it were a bunch of flowers: enjoy it while it lasts and throw it away when it begins to die off. The soft light green fronds are thin and need a relative humidity of more than 60% to stay healthy, and this is impossible to achieve in centrally heated homes. Putting it in a cool room in winter doesn't help either, because *Microlepia* is a tropical plant and does not like temperatures below 15°C (59¤F).

If, after all, you manage to keep the plant alive, make sure that the compost is always moist but not too wet. Feed regularly, as *Microlepia* is one of the very few ferns that requires highly fertile soil, preferably incorporating some well rotted cow manure. Liquid fertilizer can also be used. Spraying and misting with rainwater is naturally very beneficial to this beautiful fern.

Microlepia speluncae

Nephrolepis exaltata

SWORD FERN

One in every forty house plants sold in Holland is a sword fern and one in every three ferns sold is a *Nephrolepis exaltata*. In millions of living rooms its deeply scored and usually curly fronds arch over the windowsill. However it is not an easy plant to keep and this perhaps explains the large turnover in new plants which are mainly bought to replace ones that have died.

Nephrolepis exaltata needs evenly moist compost, humidity of at least 50% (preferably more than 60%), and regular spraying and feeding. A fern bought in spring will usually stay healthy until October but after that its condition depends on whether you keep it in a centrally heated room or whether you can find a more humid spot for it, such as a bathroom, heated greenhouse, cool conservatory or in the kitchen near the cooker. In any of these places the sword fern can survive the winter as long as the temperature does not drop below 12°C (54¤F). Even so, the foliage may turn yellow and the leaflets sometimes drop off the leafstalks altogether. This will happen if you allow the plant to dry out or its location is too dark, or if it is undernourished. Feed regularly with liquid fertilizer at its recommended dosage. Keep *Nephrolepis* away from direct sunlight but in a light position if possible. It will, however, carry on going for an amazingly long time even in the shade. There are numerous cultivars of the sword fern on the market. Many have curly leaves: 'Teddy Junior' (crimped leaflets), 'Whitmanii' (deeply scored, curly leaves), 'Linda' (crested leaflets), 'Maassii' (wavy leaf edges). There are also cultivars with smooth leaves such as 'Cordata' (straight foliage) and 'Bostoniensis' (arching fronds up to 1m (3ft) in length).

Osmunda regalis

ROYAL FERN

The royal fern grows in damp European woods and swamps and is therefore totally

Osmunda regalis

Nephrolepis exaltata

hardy. The fronds grow to a length of 1 to 1.5m (3 to 5ft) with the leaflets regularly arranged. During the summer, fertile fronds with yellow-brown spore capsules grow from the centre of the plant.

In the garden *Osmunda* needs a very damp spot which you can create yourself. Cultivate this splendid fern in a "swamp container", a water butt cut in half is ideal. Fill it with leaf mould and water and plant the fern in it. Grown like this it may be put in the sun, although semi-shade is better. In the winter the container can safely be left outside because the royal fern is completely hardy, although it will lose all its leaves. It is a strongly growing fern which can reach a height of 1.5m (5ft). If you find this too big choose either the smaller cultivar 'Gracilis', or 'Christata' which has crested leaflets.

Pellaea rotundifolia

BUTTON FERN

The round leaves of the button fern are leathery and can tolerate considerably more dryness than most other ferns. *Pellaea rotundifolia* is a native of New Zealand

Pellaea rotundifolia

where it grows against rocks. The soil does not need to be as acid and moist as that for many other ferns. A good compost to use is a mixture of two parts leaf mould to one part grit. Never let the soil dry out completely or leave the plant standing in water.

Pellaea rotundifolia can be kept in a centrally heated room all through the year but keep it away from sunlight in the

Phyllitis scolopendrium 'Cristata'

summer. Other than that, *Pellaea* is not very demanding: a light position is fine and a dark one will be tolerated. A minimum temperature of 12°C (54¤F) is recommended. 12°C.

Phlebodium aureum

See: *Polypodium*

Phyllitis scolopendrium

HART'S TONGUE FERN

Like the bird's nest fern the hart's tongue fern has entire leaves which rise up from the soil like long, bright green tongues, but they are not arranged in the shape of a funnel. When placed outside in a windy spot the tongues will not grow longer than 10cm (4in), but in sheltered damp places they will grow to more than 50cm (20in) long. The hart's tongue fern is a native of large parts of Europe and will stand severe frosts. It grows on limestone rocks and on chalky soil and needs therefore, unlike most ferns, an alkaline compost. Add some marl or a handful of bonemeal.

The hart's tongue fern is an easy one for cool indoor rooms. The plants will tolerate room temperatures, but the air often becomes too dry, especially in centrally heated rooms. If you can provide 50% (or, better still, 60%) humidity the hart's tongue fern is a trouble-free plant in a spot away from direct sunlight. It will tolerate deep shade and is therefore very suitable for places away from windows. Always keep the soil evenly moist, but not soaked.

There are numerous cultivars of the hart's tongue fern with differently shaped leaves: 'Cristatum' has wavy edged leaves which end in an crest, 'Crispum' is strongly crimped, 'Undulatum' is a miniature form with wavy leaves.

Platycerium bifurcatum

COMMON STAG'S HORN FERN

Common stag's horn ferns grow on trees in Africa, Asia and Australia. The best known, *Platycerium bifurcatum*, is native to Australia and will tolerate the dry air in centrally heated houses reasonably well. In the wild the roots draw nourishment from moisture and humus which collects behind the fronds which arch backwards. Indoors the common stag's horn fern is best grown in a hanging basket in a mixture of leaf mould and peat moss but potting soil that is rich in humus can also be used. Water the ferns in the hollow behind the arching leaves, which are at first light green and later become papery and brown. Allow the soil to dry out slightly between waterings. If watering is a problem you can immerse the fern in tepid water every week (or every two weeks in winter). Hang the common stag's horn fern in as light a spot as possible, but not in the sun during the summer.

It is normal if the tips of the long leaves, which branch into the shape of antlers, develop brown spots; these are the spore capsules. The dust-like hairy layer on the leaves is also part of the plant and should not be dusted, brushed or washed off.

Platycerium bifurcatum

Platycerium grande

REGAL ELKHORN FERN

This fern is a native of South-East Asia and Northern Australia and is most noticeable for its backward bending fronds which branch at the top into an antler-like shape. The spores appear on different fronds which are long and hang down. But these latter ones often don't develop at all indoors, so that all you normally get is a grey, hairy cylinder of leaves. This variety, which will grow up to several tens of centimetres high, can be treated in the same way as *Platycerium bifurcatum*.

Platycerium grande

Polypodium

Polypodium literally means "with many feet". This refers to the creeping rhizomes of most of the one thousand or so species of fern that carry this name. They grow mainly in the tropics on trees, to which they attach themselves with their "many feet".
Polypodium vulgare, the common polypody, can grow in the wild in northern Europe on the ground as well as on walls or trees and is not suitable as an indoor plant.

Polypodium musifolium

However, related species from the tropics, such as *Polypodium aureum* (now called *Phlebodium aureum*), can be grown as house plants. The bluish fronds are deeply feathered and have long stalks which grow out of scaly rhizomes. The potting soil should never dry out, and this difficult fern requires a combination of high humidity and a high temperature. In centrally heated houses regular misting is a must. Fortunately the plant will tolerate low light levels such as may be found in the bathroom or kitchen. *Polypodium musifolium* is another tropical fern, from the forests of New Guinea. The leaves which resemble banana leaves, are several tens of centimetres long and have a decorative pattern of veins. This variety likes an even higher humidity and is not very often available.

Pteris cretica

WING FERN, RIBBON FERN, TABLE FERN, CRETAN BRAKE

The wing fern has a wide geographical distribution, from the Mediterranean to tropical countries. The long strap-shaped leaflets are thin and grow best in high humidity. Take this small fern out of a centrally heated room and place in a cooler room during the winter, but never let the temperature drop below 7°C (45ºF). Don't let *Pteris* dry out during the winter and water liberally in the summer, especially when the fern stands in a light spot ,which is ideal, but a slightly darker place is acceptable.
There are many cultivars of the wing fern available. *Pteris cretica* 'Parkeri' has green , compound leaves, almost hand-shaped and

Pteris cretica

slightly ribbed. The green fronds of 'Roeweri' have extremely long leaflets with crested tips. 'Mayii' also has a crest at the end of each pale yellow striped leaflet. 'Albolineata' with its silvery white band on every leaflet is very popular.

Pteris ensiformis

This fern from South-East Asia and Northern Australia has thin leaves just like *Pteris cretica*. These are not strap-shaped but more strongly feathered and sticking out above them long, thin twisted leaves, upon which spores develop, may be found. For the care of this small fern see *Pteris cretica*. There are numerous cultivars of *Pteris ensiformis* among which the two best known both have a considerable amount of white in their leaves. 'Victoriae' has a clear fishbone pattern of white in the green of the leaf or sometimes of green in a white leaf. 'Evergemiensis' is very similar, but is even whiter. And to complicate things even further, all kinds of in-between forms are available.

Pteris ensiformis

Pteris tremula

Pteris tremula has a totally different appearance from the *Pteris* forms that have been dealt with above. It is a fern which looks the way you would expect a fern to look. It has long, strongly feathered green fronds about 1m (3ft) in length. New leaves constantly develop out of the creeping rhizomes in the soil and used to be cut for use in flower arrangements. It was then called the "table fern" because the leaves were used as a table decoration. Despite its vigour, even this fern is sensitive to air that is too dry. It needs a minimum relative humidity of 50%. When the heating is on the humidity is far below this figure in centrally heated rooms. Therefore put *Pteris tremula* in a cool room in the winter with a minimum temperature of 10°C (50°F). Never let the soil dry out completely and spray as much as possible. That way you will be able to enjoy the fern's renewing greenness for a long time.

Scolopendrium vulgare

See: *Phyllitis scolopendrium*

Pteris tremula

the greenhouse or even outside if dug in with its pot. In the latter case this Japanese fern will lose its leaves but they will grow again in the spring.

Dryopteris erythrosora

Matteuccia struthiopteris

OSTRICH FEATHER, SHUTTLECOCK FERN

The ostrich feather fern is in fact a garden plant which will, in damp places, spread rapidly through underground rhizomes. In spring the green funnel-shaped leaves shoot up everywhere. Because this fern is so rampant not everybody likes to have it in their garden. Fortunately it is easy to keep it within bounds by planting in a large container. In the fall the dying foliage collapses over the edge of the container whilst the fertile fronds stand up proudly and glow golden-brown in the winter sun.
The ostrich feather fern is totally hardy and only needs to be kept sufficiently moist in the growing season, as it will not tolerate drying out. As long as the soil is kept moist the container can be placed in the shade, semi-shade or full sun.

Microlepia speluncae

It is best to buy *Microlepia* as if it were a bunch of flowers: enjoy it while it lasts and throw it away when it begins to die off. The soft light green fronds are thin and need a relative humidity of more than 60% to stay healthy, and this is impossible to achieve in centrally heated homes. Putting it in a cool room in winter doesn't help either, because *Microlepia* is a tropical plant and does not like temperatures below 15°C (59¤F).
If, after all, you manage to keep the plant alive, make sure that the compost is always moist but not too wet. Feed regularly, as *Microlepia* is one of the very few ferns that requires highly fertile soil, preferably incorporating some well rotted cow manure. Liquid fertilizer can also be used. Spraying and misting with rainwater is naturally very beneficial to this beautiful fern.

Microlepia speluncae

Nephrolepis exaltata

SWORD FERN

One in every forty house plants sold in Holland is a sword fern and one in every three ferns sold is a *Nephrolepis exaltata*. In millions of living rooms its deeply scored and usually curly fronds arch over the windowsill. However it is not an easy plant to keep and this perhaps explains the large turnover in new plants which are mainly bought to replace ones that have died.
Nephrolepis exaltata needs evenly moist compost, humidity of at least 50% (preferably more than 60%), and regular spraying and feeding. A fern bought in spring will usually stay healthy until October but after that its condition depends

1. Ferns

From the middle of the last century until well into this century ferns were extremely popular house plants but with the rise of central heating ferns disappeared from houses. Most species cannot tolerate dry air. Gradually it is becoming clear that dry air is also unhealthy for people so that humidification is becoming more common. Special equipment is sometimes installed. In some countries different types of central heating are being installed in place of radiators which cause dry air. In rooms that are heated by radiant heat the ambient temperature can be kept a few degrees lower without this being noticeable to the inhabitants.

To ferns, those few degrees make all the difference. Ferns grow better in a slightly cooler atmosphere because the relative humidity tends to be higher. The most modern methods of heating are therefore providing a new future for the fern. However, even if you, like most people, have standard central heating it is still possible to enjoy ferns. Put them in a cool room during the months when the heating is on and most ferns are likely to survive the winter. In Spring, as soon as the central heating is turned down, put them back in the living room.

Adiantum cuneatum

See: *Adiantum raddianum*

Left: *Dicksonia antarctica*

Adiantum hispidulum

If the humidity in your house is too low for *Adiantum raddianum* to grow well, you could try *Adiantum hispidulum*. This fern also likes humid air but it can tolerate drier air than *raddianum*. The fronds are made up of leaflets attached in long rows to leaf stalks which are, in turn, carried on black stalks. This gives the fern an air of transparency. If *hispidulum* doesn't thrive indoors all is not lost. Put the fern outdoors in a moist, humus rich soil in a shady and sheltered spot. There it will easily survive the winter and, as long as there is no frost, it will retain its leaves, even outside.

Adiantum hispidulum 'Bronze Venus'

Adiantum pubescens

See: *Adiantum hispidulum*

Adiantum raddianum

MAIDENHAIR FERN

The maidenhair fern immediately responds to being treated incorrectly. If the humidity of the air is too low, or if the fern has not been watered, the edges of the gossamer-like leaflets dry out. If you let the fern stand permanently in water it becomes glassy and the whole plant dies, especially in a cool room. *Adiantum radianum* originates in the warm tropical forests of South America where the air humidity is high and the temperature does not drop below 18°C (64¤F). Try, therefore, to find a place in the house which resembles a tropical rainforest as much as possible. Put the maidenhair fern in a light spot, but not in direct sunlight. In centrally heated houses provide extra humidity. Regularly spray the fern with a mist of rainwater or boiled water. Put the plant in a pot on a bed of gravel in a wide tray. Fill the tray with water to just below the bottom of the pot. But perhaps the easiest approach is to put this most beautiful of ferns in the most humid places in the house - in the bathroom or near the cooker.

Adiantum raddianum 'Brilliantelse'

MAIDENHAIR FERN

The maidenhair fern has given rise to many cultivars. The young fronds of 'Goldenelse' are golden yellow, later turning to light green. Often a golden edge remains. The vigorous cultivar 'Fragrantissimum' grows to more than 50cm (20in) high. The leaflets are blue-green and readily produce spore cap-

sules. 'Brilliantelse' is an even sturdier plant. This compact fern carries graceful golden-green leaflets on tough, glossy black leaf stalks.

Adiantum raddianum 'Brilliantelse'

Aspidium

See: *Cyrtomium*

Adiantum raddianum

Contents

NICO VERMEULEN
EDITED BY RICHARD ROSENFELD

ENCYCLOPAEDIA
OF HOUSE PLANTS

REBO
PRODUCTIONS

Key to symbols:

◌ as light a location as possible, not always in direct sunlight

◑ not too much light, no direct sunlight

✸ shade

⬤ little water

◖ not too much water

◇ plenty of water

The amounts of light and water indicated are the requirements of the growing season.
If there are different requirements outside the growing season, these are given in the text.

© 1995 Rebo Productions, Lisse
Published by Rebo Productions Ltd, 1997
Text and photographs: Nico Vermeulen
Cover design: Ton Wienbelt, The Netherlands
Production: TextCase, The Netherlands
Translation: Annemarie Koelman for First Edition
Translation Ltd, Great Britain
Typesetting: Hof & Land Typografie, The Netherlands

2nd print 1998

ISBN 1 901094 08 1

ENCYCLOPAEDIA
OF HOUSE PLANTS

2. Palms

Areca lutescens is the palm that is most frequently found on the house plant market. The palm is now correctly known as Chrysalidocarpus lutescens, but it is still generally sold under the name Areca. The leaves of the young plants are rather floppy and irregular, but they become more sturdy and regular as they grow older. Areca species are characterized by black spots which form at the foot of the bright yellow-green stem which looks a bit like bamboo with rings where the old leaves used to be. Area lutescens originates in Madagascar, where it is always warm and the golden feather palm is therefore not adapted to low temperatures. Put it in a warm spot where even at night the temperature does not drop below 15°C (59°F). Areca grows best in a very light position out of the midday sun. The potting soil should be kept as evenly moist as possible, so water regularly, but never use water straight from the cold tap as it will give the plant a shock. Mix with warm water to make it tepid or use water which has been standing for some time at room temperature..

leaves of the young plants are rather floppy and irregular, but they become more sturdy and regular as they grow older. Areca species are characterized by black spots which form at the foot of the bright yellow-green stem which looks a bit like bamboo with rings where the old leaves used to be. *Area lutescens* originates in Madagascar, where it is always warm and the golden feather palm is therefore not adapted to low temperatures. Put it in a warm spot where even at night the temperature does not drop below 15°C (59°F). *Areca* grows best in a very light position out of the midday sun. The potting soil should be kept as evenly moist as possible, so water regularly, but never use water straight from the cold tap as it will give the plant a shock. Mix with warm water to make it tepid or use water which has been standing for some time at room temperature.

Areca lutescens

Areca lutescens

GOLDEN FEATHER PALM, ARECA PALM

Areca lutescens is the palm that is most frequently found on the house plant market. The palm is now correctly known as *Chrysalidocarpus lutescens*, but it is still generally sold under the name *Areca*. The

Left: *Areca lutescens*

Caryota

FISH TAIL PALM

Caryote originates in tropical South-East Asia where the best known variety, *Caryota mitis*, grows to a height of more than 10m (33ft). The leaves have triangular, pendulous leaflets which resemble green fish tails. The palm is therefore also known as the fish tail palm. This vigorous palm will eventually will grow to a height of 2m (6ft) and a width of about 1m (3ft) so you will need plenty of space for it. It always needs a temperature of 15°C (59°F), preferably a lot higher, and regular watering.

Never let the potting soil dry out, but do not let the plant stand in water either. Use tepid water and add liquid fertilizer once a month during the summer. Pot-on only when the roots start to grow over the edge of the pot and keep the plant in a relatively small pot, if you want to keep it to a manageable size. A very light location is ideal, but don't put the palm in the full sun. Spray regularly to lessen the chances of red spider mite.

Chrysalidocarpus

See: *Areca*

Cocos nucifera

COCONUT PALM

In the time of Columbus coconut palms grew only on the Caribbean coast of Panama. But the palm turned out to be so

A fully grown coconut palm

Caryota

useful that it was transported by man to all tropical countries. Within the hard shell of the fruit is the white flesh which is rich in protein and, in the tropics, is eaten while still jelly-like. Coconut milk is a popular and healthy drink. The coconut known to the West has a hard brown kernel, but in nature it is covered with a thick skin. The fibres of this outer layer are used for various purposes and are currently available as a soil improver marketed in Holland as "cocopeat".

Cocos nucifera

In the shop you will probably buy a coconut which has just started to sprout. The nut, still surrounded by some fibrous matter, will

have been put on moist soil and left to germinate. There is not much chance that it will live for long because it is difficult to give the coconut palm favourable growing conditions, that is, a warm room and humid air. In centrally heated rooms the air is usually too dry causing the leaves to turn yellow. Only very regular spraying with luke-warm water will help the plant through the winter whilst also preventing red spider mite.

Put the coconut palm in a very light spot and protect the plant from the hot afternoon sun. Never let the soil dry out. The palm should not be allowed to stand in water.

Cycas revoluta

JAPANESE SAGO PALM

The *Cycas* is not a palm but it is dealt with here because it looks so much like one. The *Cycas* species are really ancient plants. About 200 million years ago the *Cicadaceae* were wide-spread in the Triassic period but there are now only eight species left one being *Cycas revoluta* from Japan and Taiwan. On Java this plant is grown for the edible marrow of its stem, the sago.

Cycas revoluta

Of the *Cycas* palms, *Cycas revoluta* is the one most often offered as a house plant. It has a hairy, scaly egg-shaped trunk at the top of which very regularly feathered leaves develop. When the young leaves unfurl they are soft and vulnerable, later they become hard and sturdy each with a spiny tip.

When it gets older the *Cycas* may flower. There are male and female plants. The male plant produces a cone at its centre while the female plant produces a mass of ovaries which, after fertilization, turn into orange-yellow, woolly seeds, about the size of a large bean. These lie open in the heart of the plant and it is therefore called "naked-seeded". Put *Cycas revoluta* in a warm, light spot and protect it against the fierce afternoon sun. The old leaves will gradually die off and the new ones which replace them are, each time, a bit longer than the previous ones. The leaves of very old plants can be more than 1m (6ft) long. If you manage to keep the plant alive for a very long time, it will gradually develop a small trunk. Only feed the plant when a new tuft of leaves unfurls. Do not pot-on too soon and do not disturb the top layer of soil because that is where important, fragile roots grow. Keep the compost moist, but never wet. This plant, which is not very prone to pests and diseases, may then live for a long time.

◑ ●–◐

Howea

See: *Howeia*

Howeia forsteriana

KENTIA PALM, SENTRY PALM, THATCHLEAF PALM, PARADISE PALM.

The Lord Howe Islands, which lie 500 kilometres off the East coast of Australia, have given Howeia (also often spelled: Howea) its name. The palm takes its common name from the islands' capital Kentia. The kentia palm is native to the islands and difficult to cultivate anywhere else on earth. This is of considerable economic benefit to the inhabitants since the export of the popular *Howeia forsteriana* has become their most important source of foreign currency. The tropical origin of *Howeia* is often printed on the label. Usually

Left: *Howeia forsteriana*

one buys a pot with a few seedlings of the palm. Their long leaves intertwine and form an elegant fan of foliage. To keep them healthy it is best to spray them regularly, especially in heated living rooms. In winter Howeia grows best when the temperature at night is between 12°C (54°F) and 16°C (61°F). In summer a daytime temperature between 18°C (64°F) and 25°C (77°F) is ideal. Put the kentia palm in as bright a spot as possible but definitely keep the leaves out of the hot afternoon sun. Dryness or too much sun will cause the leaves to dry out. Give plenty of luke-warm water during the summer and immerse the pot in water every week if possible. Make sure you drain the plant completely before putting it back into its ornamental pot because it does not like standing in water. Apart from the well known *Howeia forsteriana* there is the larger *Howeia belmoreana*. This palm has less foliage than *forsteriana*, but each leaf is larger and arches down elegantly. This beautiful kentia palm requires a lot of room because, if the leaf tips are often brushed against, they may turn brown.

◯ – ◑   ◯

Licuala

There are nearly 100 species of *Licuala* and they all grow in tropical South-East Asia or Northern Australia. These palms are generally small as palms go. *Licuala grandis*

Licuala

grows only to about 2m (6ft). Fan shaped leaves spread out from the top of the thin stems. *Licuala* is usually for sale as a young palm whose leaves are not unfolded into the shape of a fan, but more narrow and oblong. But even then the characteristic pleated structure of the licuala is clearly recognizable. To get the most enjoyment from this palm you need to be very skilful with plants. In the wild the *licuala* grows in a hot, humid, tropical climate but it is difficult to reproduce this in a living room. Don't let the night temperature drop below 15°C (59°F) (even in winter) and avoid allowing the root clump to become soggy. Give plenty of water, always at body temperature, especially in summer and spray with a fine mist as often as possible, especially in the dry winter months. Put *Licuala* in a light spot, but remember that as an inhabitant of tropical undergrowth it does not tolerate bright sun.

Phoenix canariensis

CANARY ISLANDS DATE PALM

On the Canary Islands, where the *Phoenix canariensis* originates, the palm eventually grows more than 10m (33ft) tall. In the

Phoenix canariensis as a house plant

winter night temperatures often drop to about 5° (41°F), which means that this palm can tolerate some cold. It is one of the easiest palms to cultivate and one of the few that can be put aside in a cool room for the winter. There the plant will suffer much less from drying heat, especially if a window is opened

Phoenix canariensis

occasionally. It is necessary only to keep the plant above freezing and to give it plenty of light.

In summer the date palm may be put outside in a pot or container but it will also grow very well indoors in a light location. Too well perhaps, because even inside the *Phoenix* will grow tall and wide with stiff leaves that have very sharp ends. This makes the palm unsuitable for a house with small children. *Phoenix* is best suited to large studios or very large living rooms.

Water freely in summer. Misting is always beneficial, but not really vital for this palm which also differs from other palms in its tolerance of the full sun.

Washingtonia filifera

DESERT FAN PALM, PETTYCOAT PALM

On the south-western tip of Great Britain large palms grow in the open air. These are *Washingtonias*, palms from the south-west of the United States where the deserts of Arizona and California cool down sharply at night. The palms protect themselves with an insulating muff of dying leaves wrapped around the vulnerable growing point Later on these leaves drop off. In northern Europe *Washingtonia filifera* tolerates the cold

Washingtonia filifera

better than the heat. In the summer the palm can be grown in the living room or outside in a container on the terrace. During the heating season, *Washingtonia* is best kept in a cool conservatory or greenhouse at a temperature of about 10°C (50°F). An unheated room is also fine; in the winter all you need to do is to make sure that the compost does not dry out completely. In the summer you need to water liberally and feed occasionally. The leaves are folded like a fan. Threads are released from the edges along the entire length of the leaf and form curls. Another variety that is sometimes available, *Washingtonia robusta*, will grow to the size of a tree even in a conservatory or greenhouse. Otherwise it looks very much like *filifera* including threads on the young leaves.

Washingtonia robusta

Zamia furfuracea

FLORIDA ARROWROOT

Like the *Cycas* the *Zamia* belongs to the *Cycadaceae* and is therefore not really a palm. About two hundred million years ago dinosaurs may have nibbled at these ancient plants for they were very common in those days. Nowadays there are between thirty and forty known species of *Zamia* and they all grow in tropical and subtropical America. *Zamia furfuracea* originates on the east coast of Mexico. The young leaves are at first

light green, later they turn olive green and are covered in rusty brown hair. In America this plant is called "soft board" palm. As the *Zamia* grows older it develops more and more pairs of leaflets. In the end every leafstalk carries twelve pairs of leaflets at an angle of about 45°. The leaf stalks can grow to be 1m (3ft) long.

In warmer regions *Zamia* can be planted outside. A few degrees of frost does not harm them as long as the tuber-like trunk remains underground (which is how it grows in the wild). Indoors the trunk is kept above the soil and the plant can be cultivated throughout the year if necessary. It is not a sensitive plant and tolerates dry air. Plant it in well drained compost preferably with some clay mixed in. Avoid damage to the brittle roots and always keep the compost moderately moist. Most *Zamia* species grow well in the semi-shade, but *furfuracea* may be grown in full sun.

Left: *Washingtonia filifera*
Below: *Zamia furfuracea*

3. Cordyline, Dracaena and Yucca

The plants dealt with in this chapter are closely related. They all belong to the agave family, Agavaceae. *The true agave will not be dealt with here, but instead in the chapter on succulents where it belongs for reasons of appearance and care.*

Cordyline *and* Dracaena *are difficult to differentiate. Experts do this by cutting into the roots and recognizing dracaena by its yellow inside and cordyline by its white inside. Even so the plants involved are sometimes classified under either of these genera. What the three genera have in common is their shape. The rosettes carry on growing upwards as the old leaves drop off. In this way a lengthening rounded stem develops. It is the architectural shape of these plants which has made them so popular in modern interiors. On top of that, they are generally very robust and survive even in unfavourable circumstances.*

Cordyline fruticosa

Officially this species is now called *Cordyline terminalis* but florists still offer it regularly under the name *fruticosa*. You probably will not find this even name on the label because generally it is only cultivars with fancy names like 'Firebrand', 'Purple Compacta' and 'Hawaian Bonsai' which are available. Plant breeders have been able to harness the small amount of red colour of the original mostly green) leaves to produce cultivars that have totally deep red or wine red leaves. Other cultivars have red, pink, yellow or white stripes. The bright green leaves of 'Red Edge' have a pinkish red

Left: *Dracaena deremensis* 'Surprise'

margin and often have cream coloured stripes as well. In 'Lord Robinson' the light parts are more accentuated and 'Kiwi' is a blaze of colour with leaves of light and dark green, yellow stripes and a pink margin.

Whether the plant keeps its colours or not depends its location. The plants can be put in direct sunlight as long as they are kept moist, but they tend to lose their intense colours. To retain their colours it is better to put them in a light spot out of the sun.

If cared for properly new leaves will regularly appear at the centre of the plant - these are the most brightly coloured. The leaves of some cultivars revert to green as the plant gets older; for example, 'Snow' which has white stripes and 'Lord Roberts' which has pinkish white stripes when young.

As the old leaves drop off a stem develops showing how the plant normally appears in the wild. If the growing point at the top of the stem is damaged the plant branches. If an old plant loses its attractiveness you can rejuvenate it by cutting out the top. Don't

Cordyline fruticosa 'Kiwi'

cut too deeply into the stem as the plant will then find it hard to sprout again.

Cordilyne is known for being exceedingly strong, but for *Cordyline fruticosa* this is not altogether the case. It is a genuine tropical species from South-East Asia, North Australia and Hawaii and it does not tolerate temperatures below about 12°C (54°F). It is best to give it a higher temperature and to keep it in the living room even in the winter. The humidity has to be as high as possible because in a dry environment red spider mite may infest *fruticosa*, especially the variegated cultivars. Water sparingly at short intervals so that the soil remains moderately moist. In winter the soil can be kept a little drier.

Cordyline rubra

This species is closely related to *fruticosa* and requires more or less the same care. The original species has green foliage and veins suffused with red. Un-named hybrids grow in gardens in many tropical countries, eventually developing several stems and becoming shrub-like. They grow to a height of about 3m (10ft). Flower shoots, with a mass of small lilac flowers less than 1cm (1/4in) across grow out of the leaf rosettes. These are followed by red-brown berries of about the same size.

Old *Cordyline* can be propagated in a very special way. Cut the stem into sections each about five to 10cm (4in) long and place them on sandy soil in a suitable container. Cover the container to create a moist atmosphere and put it in a warm spot, preferably out of the sun. After six to ten weeks new shoots will appear.

Cordyline terminalis

See: *Cordyline fruticosa*

Dracaena deremensis

Considering that *Dracaena deremensis* originates from tropical East Africa, it is surprising that it needs such a small amount

Left: *Cordyline rubra*

Dracaena deremensis 'Green Stripe'

of light. One of the easiest of house plants it can be grown in the sun but will also tolerate shade. The best place for it is in full light without too much direct sun. If watered regularly but not over-watered the plant will grow quickly. In time the lower leaves turn yellow and drop off leaving clear scars on the stem. Older plants develop a particular form with tufts of leaves growing on the bare stems. They fit perfectly in a modern interior.

Green leafed *Dracaena deremensis* has given rise to a large number of variegated

Dracaena deremensis 'Surprise'

cultivars. 'Bausei' has a simple white band down the length of the leaf. 'Roehrs Gold' has a pale yellow band on the leaf. The leaves of 'Yellow Stripe' have yellow margins and those of 'Green Stripe' are bright yellow-green. 'Warneckei' has a white band at each side of the central vein halfway between the vein and the leaf edge. On the outside of each band is a further lime green stripe. In 'Lemon Lime' and 'Surprise' the lime-green bands are wider than 'Warneckei' and in 'Lime' they are wider still.

Dracaena draco

DRAGON TREE

When you cut into the stem of *Dracaena draco*, sticky, red sap exudes. This is the so-called "dragon's blood" from which *Dracaena* gets its name, "Drakaina" being the Greek word for dragon. The dragon tree grows naturally in the Canary Islands but it is not common there. It has become rare because the red bark has been over-collected. But it is still possible to find an occasional old specimen. (The oldest specimen known, which was blown over in 1868, was an estimated 6000 years old.)

The tree does not branch until it has reached a certain height. *Dracaena draco* is single stemmed until the rosette of sturdy, pointed leaves starts to appear. After that the tree branches every time it flowers, building up a wide, parasol-shaped crown.

The authentic dragon tree is seldom available as a house plant. This is a shame because the plant grows easily and is very suitable for studios, workrooms and modern living rooms. After a while a small stem develops on which a tuft of lanceolate leaves, each about 40cm (16in) long, grows. If possible put the plant in a cool, frost-free place for the winter and water very sparingly. In the summer *draco* needs an average amount of water and prefers a light spot out of direct sunlight. The plant likes a lot of fresh air and an occasional misting, but these are not strictly necessary for it to grow well.

Dracaena fragrans

CORN PLANT

Dry cuttings of *Dracaena fragrans*, without roots or leaves, are transported all the way

Dracaena draco

from Africa or tropical America for pottingin northern Europe. The cuttings root easily. At the top end of the cutting there is often a layer of varnish which will have protected the stem against rot while rooting. The leaves of the species are green and grow up to 50cm (20in) in length. However, cultivars with yellow bands in the leaves are more commonly on offer: 'Massangeana' has yellow-green central bands, 'Victoria' has broad, bright-yellow bands along the edges. The leaves of 'Lindenii' have a greater area of yellow with green mainly along the main vein and the leaf margins. All cultivars are problem-free houseplants although the variegated forms need quite a light position, away from direct sun light. They can be kept in the living room in the summer and the winter as they like the warmth and will tolerate dry air. Below 12°C (54°F) the leaves of variegated forms develop brown patches and start to droop listlessly. Look out for these patches when you buy a plant and avoid buying those on display in the open air.

Dracaena fragrans 'Massangeana'

Dracaena godseffiana

OLD DUST DRACAENA

This Dracaena, which officially is called *Cracaena surculosa*, does not look at all like the other Dracaenas. The leaves of this West African species are fleshy with creamy-white spots. They are elliptical in shape and are carried in pairs on thin but tough stems. In the living room the plant readily produces delightfully fragrant flowers, each of which is just over 2cm (1in) wide, often followed by orange-red berries. *Dracaena godseffiana* is a robust plant which will tolerate low light levels. It only grows really well in a light position, where it will eventually reach a height of more than 50cm (20in) and even wider than that. This spreading habit is very useful if you want to combine it with other plants in a container. It needs an average amount of water, less in winter.

Dracaena godseffiana

Dracaena marginata

MADAGASCAR DRAGON TREE

This *Dracaena* is available under the name *marginata* because of the pinkish-red margins of its leaves. Plants sold under this name are really one of two other species with coloured margins, *Dracaena cincta* and *Dracaena concinna*, but they should all be cared for in the same way. All these species are very easy to grow and are therefore often used in office buildings where, even if they can't get a position near a window, they still manage to survive for a long time. However, to get the most enjoyment out of this plant, place it in as light a position as possible, even in the full sun if necessary, although a light spot out of sun will result in foliage with the best colours. The leaves will grow to about 50cm

(20in) long and 1cm or 2cm (1in) wide.
Dracaena is sometimes sold as just a leaf
rosette, but it is more common to find it
with a stem. The stems are slender and may
branch in a decorative way if the tops are
taken out. The plant will then develop an
irregular pattern of stems, each with a few
rosettes at the top. Sections of stem are
easily rooted in spring and summer by putting them in sandy peat in a propagating
tray. Cover the tray with plastic and put it in
a warm place (between 20°C (68°F) and
30°C (96°F) out of the sun. Beautiful cultivars of *Dracaena marginata* are available
on the market with 'Tricolor' being the most
popular. Its leaves have cream-coloured,
yellow and green stripes and pinkish-red
edges. The cultivar 'Colorama' has a strong
pink-red colouring, with additional yellow
and green stripes.

Dracaena reflexa

This variety is sometimes called *Pleomele
reflexa* and is rather different from the other
dracaenas. The leaves are wide and tough
but not stiff. The stem is also bendable and

this may become a problem as it eventually
causes the rosettes to hang down.
Fortunately the plant grows slowly and it
takes a long time before the stems lean over

Dracaena reflexa 'Song of India'

Left: *Dracaena marginata* 'Bicolor'
Below: Dracaena marginata

so much that they need to be cut off. *Dracaena reflexa* is an extremely easy and rewarding plant which can be kept in the living room in winter and in summer and can tolerate low light levels well. It is best to put it in a light spot, out of direct sunlight. Water sparingly, especially in winter.

The original species is hardly ever available. Most commonly found is the variegated cultivar 'Song of India', which has wide yellow margins.

Dracaena surculosa

See: *Dracaena godseffiana*

Pleomele

See: *Dracaena*

Yucca elephantipes

SPINELESS YUCCA

This is one of the easiest of house plants. The pointed, spineless leaves tolerate the full sun and also stay healthy for a long time with less light. The species originates in Central America where it can grow to a height of more than 10m (33ft) but it will not grow so tall in the living room. During the summer this *Yucca* can be placed

outside in its container. In the fresh air it grows noticeably more quickly. During the winter also the spineless yucca prefers a cool position, ideally an unheated room. The temperature may safely drop to 5°C (41°F). Water moderately during the summer and sparsely during the winter.

Yucca gloriosa

SPANISH DAGGER

This species from the eastern United States will tolerate up to about 15 degrees of frost and is sold as a garden plant as well as a house plant. It is safe to grow it as a container plant, outside during summer and inside in an unheated room during the worst of winter. If this is done an enormous panicle of round, pendulous, white flowers may develop in late summer, each flower being about 7cm (3in) long.

You can, however, keep it in a heated living room throughout the year, if necessary in a spot without much light, as it is very strong. If you want the plant to grow, you will have to put it in a light and sunny place. Water sparingly in summer, but keep even drier in winter.

Yucca elephantipes

Yucca gloriosa

4. Marantas

The Marantaceae *("peacock plants")* *grow mainly in the tropical forests of South America. The native inhabitants use the leaves of Calathea to make baskets. This is one of two explanations for the name of this plant, because 'kalathos' is Greek for 'basket'. The so-called "arrow roots"* of Maranta arundinacea *contain starch which is harvested by the native inhabitants.*

Not until the end of the last century were marantas taken out of the forests into our houses and greenhouses. They were especially prized for of their beautifully patterned foliage. In many genera variegation has been achieved through years of breeding and selection. The Marantaceae *are naturally variegated. They are so beautiful that they cannot really be improved by breeding.*

Unfortunately our living rooms only resemble tropical rainforests as far as temperature is concerned; humidity is so much lower when they are centrally heated. Marantas have a difficult time there and, only if they are grown under glass on a windowsill, or in another damp atmosphere, will it become clear how fast they can grow. And only then will it be clear that they are certainly worthy of the challenge of cultivating them.

Calathea crocata

This is the only calathea that is grown for its flowers, all the others being typical foliage plants. The leaves of *crocata* grow to about 10cm (4in) in length. They are wine-red underneath, dark red on top and form a sheath around the flower stalk, at the top of which are bracts which give the plant its decorative value.

Calathea crocata originates in the forests of Brazil where the air is nearly always close to saturation. The dryness of a living room will eventually be fatal to the plant. Putting the plant in a cool room offers no solution either as calathea species do not easily tolerate temperatures below 15°C (59°F).

You will have to take special measures if you want to enjoy their beauty. Keep the plants away from direct sunlight and try and give them a light position. *Calatheas* like evenly moist soil, slightly acid, with a lot of peat or leafmould added. Spray regularly with rainwater or boiled tap water. Put the pot on a upside down plate, or on gravel, in a wide bowl. Add water to the bowl making sure that the water level is just below the bottom of the pot so that the roots don't stand in water. The plant can also be successfully cultivated in a herbarium.

Calathea lancifolia

RATTLESNAKE PLANT

This species from Brazil is grown for its slender leaves which are narrow, slightly wavy, wine-red underneath and up to 45cm (18in) long.

The top surface of each leaf is light-green with dark-green patches. The patches are alternately large and small and form a characteristic feather-like pattern..

This species used to be called *Calathea insignis*.

Nowadays you may sometimes find 'Insignis' added to the correct name but this does not indicate a different cultivar.

Calathea lancifolia requires the same care as *Calathea crocata*. If the plant is growing well it can be propagated by tearing off young shoots, each with at least three leaves, from the base of the plant. Put them each in a separate pot in a mixture of moist peat and sand and maintain at a minimum temperature of 20°C (68°F).

Calathea lancifolia

Calathea 'Misto'

The origin of this cultivar is not known as yet. The leaves strongly resemble those of *Cala-*

Left: *Calathea crocata*
Below: *Calathea* 'Misto'

thea albertii, a species which is not on the market. The oblong leaves are dark green, with jagged light green markings across the midrib. Unlike most calatheas the leaves of this species will eventually lie horizontally. Low flower stems may develop from the base of the plant carrying flower spikes of about 5cm (2in) in length. Maintenance is the same as for *Calathea crocata*.

Calathea picturata

This species is always on offer as a plant of about 30cm (12in) in height. Indoors it will not get much taller, but if well looked after it will grow wider. The leaves are elliptical and about 20cm (8in) long and 10cm (4in) wide; they are green with a silvery pattern and the undersides are reddish-brown.
The natural species has three silvery-green lines, one along the midrib and two just inside the leaf margin.
The cultivar 'Vandenheckei' has exactly the same pattern and does in fact not differ from the species. The cultivar 'Argentea' is clearly different, however; its leaves have plain milky-green centres with wide, dark-green margins.
Maintenance is the same as for *Calathea*

Calathea picturata 'Argentea'

crocata. *Calathea picturata* and other cala-theas with large leaves benefit from the foliage being kept clean. Wipe the leaves with a damp cloth or sponge to give them back their beautiful silky sheen. This will also help the plant to grow better.

Stromanthe, whose leaves stick out hori-zontally from the stem or hang down.
This *Calathea* requires the same care as *Calathea crocata*.

Calathea pseudoveitchiana

Calathea picturata 'Vandenheckei'

Calathea pseudoveitchiana

The leaves of this plant resemble those of *Calathea veitchiana* so strongly that the word "pseudo" is used. Both varieties have large leaves and grow to about 70cm (28in) in height. The upper surface of the leaves is dark-green with three irregular light-green lines, one along the midrib and the two others as a sequence of curves just inside the leaf margin. The pattern on the underside of the leaves is even more surprising. It is reddish-brown turning to transparent light-green along the midrib and inside the margins, with the pattern of veins shining through like gauze.

Indoors you can see the upper as well as the lower surfaces of the leaves because they grow almost vertically. This is one of the characteristics which distinguishes the calathea from the *Maranta*, *Ctenanthe* and

Calathea zebrina

ZEBRA PLANT

The leaves of the zebra plant have a silky feel. They can easily grow to a length of

Calathea zebrina and other sorts.

50cm (20in). The maximum height of the plant is 1m (3ft). The leaves of the plant are bright light-green, with even lighter midribs. At regular intervals dark-green stripes radiate out from the midrib. The underside of the leaf is less clearly striped, with more light-green and red-flushed veins.

The maintenance is the same as for *Calathea crocata*, but with the zebra plant it is even more important that you spray using boiled water (or rainwater) to avoid marking the leaves by lime scale which is not easy to remove from the silky leaves. It is best not to dust the leaves or wipe them with a damp cloth. Give this species from South-East Brazil an extra warm spot of about 18°C (64°F) or more.

Ctenanthe oppenheimiana

Ctenanthe oppenheimiana can grow up to 1m (3ft) high. The leaf stalks and undersides of the leaves of are carmine to wine-red and the upper surfaces are green with wide silver coloured bands. These beautiful contrasts make it one of the most popular plants of the entire maranta family. It is also a relatively easy plant to maintain, although it needs high humidity. The minimum temperature for the plant is about 12°C (54°F) even though it originates in eastern Brazil. *Oppenheimiana*, therefore, does not necessarily need to be kept in a warm living room. In cooler rooms the relative humidity is higher. Apart from that the care is the same as for *Calathea crocata*. *Ctenanthe oppenheimiana* 'Tricolor' has splashes of creamy-white, 'Variegatus' has white and green stripes.

Ctenanthe pilosa

Only the variegated cultivar of this species, *Ctenanthe pilosa* 'Golden Mosaic', is available. The leaves are about 20cm (8in) long and 6cm (2.5 in) wide, irregularly marked with dark-green, light-green and yellow patches. The shoots have leaves at the base. Higher on the plant the leaves have bamboo-like stalks which can grow to about 50cm (20in) in length. *Ctenanthe lubbersiana*, is almost a twin of this

Ctenanthe oppenheimiana

cultivar. Both plants are from Brazil and cannot be easily distinguished by the layperson.

Maintenance the same as for *Calathea crocata*. Sponging of the leaves is very beneficial to ctenanthes.

Maranta leuconeura

PRAYER PLANT

Maranta leuconeura is an old-fashioned, well-known houseplant. In between the lateral veins of the relatively small, light-green leaves are aubergine-coloured spots: five on each half of the leaf, making ten in all. This gives rise to the Dutch common name the "ten commandments plant". There exists a subspecies, *Maranta kerchoveana*, which may be found on the market under the incorrect cultivar name 'Kerchoveana'.

The cultivar *Maranta leuconeura* 'Fascinator' is more popular than the real "ten commandments plant". The light-green leaves have lots of olive-green spots on both sides of the central vein and are surrounded by pinkish-red veins. The leaves are wine-red underneath. This cultivar is also available under the name 'Tricolor' or 'Massangeana', but these are all the same plant. Marantas have a curious habit which you can test out on *Maranta leuconeura*. During the day the leaves point downwards, but when it gets dark, they fold upwards into the so-called "sleeping position". You can induce them to come down again within a few minutes by shining a bright light at them. *Maranta leuconeura* is from Brazil and requires a constant high temperature of 15°C (59°F) or more although short drops in temperature to 10°C (50°F) won't do any harm. The humidity should remain as high as possible. This is a problem in winter in centrally heated rooms. If the edges of the leaves turn brown, the humidity has been too low. You can see how to avoid this in the section on *Calathea crocata*.

Water plentifully in summer and less in winter, but don't let the soil dry out completely. Always keep *Maranta leuconeura* away from direct sunlight but give it as light a position as possible - in the wild it grows in open places in the forest.

Ctenanthe pilosa 'Golden Mosaic'

Stromanthe sanguinea

Stromanthe sanguinea grows as a weed in Brazil around scrub and clearings in the forest and can therefore tolerate more light than the *Marantaceae* from the middle of the rainforests and may be safely put in the morning sun. It is also more tolerant of lower temperatures and can stand night temperatures down to 10ºC (50ºF).

Therefore put it in a cool room, where the humidity will be higher, because even for this robust plant dry air will eventually be fatal. The first signs of dryness are brown leaf edges. See *Calcathea crocata* for further advice on maintenance.

The leaves of *Stromanthe sanguinea* grow to a length of between 30cm (12in) and 50cm (20in). They grow on wine-red stalks and are also the same shade of red underneath. Their upper surface is plain green, often with a light stripe across the main vein. This stripe is more pronounced in the cultivar 'Stripe Star' and the lateral veins of this form turn lighter as the plant grows older.

Maranta leuconeura kerchoveana

51

5. Figs

The Ficus genus is named after the edible fig, which is grown around the Mediterranean. However, the majority of the 800 or so species of ficus grow in tropical Africa and Asia. Some of these reach gigantic proportions while others do not grow to more than a few centimetres above the ground. The banyan Ficus benghalensis, one of the largest trees on earth, grows to a height of "only" about 30m (100ft), but it is multi-stemmed and, with its prop roots, can cover an area of 200m (650ft) across. The varieties which are grown as house plants come from the tropics. Despite this they can tolerate low light levels This is because they begin their lives as lianes (kinds of woody climbing plants found in the tropics); germinating in the semi-darkness of the forest floor and growing, as young plants, at the feet of the giants of the forest, extending slowly upwards, until they outstrip their hosts. One would not expect that these plants from tropical rainforests could survive in our dry indoor climate but this unusual combination of withstanding low light and low humidity has made ficus a most popular house plant. It can even survive in the hydro-culture containers of air-conditioned offices, often at some distance from the window. Of course, there is a difference between "survive" and "thrive", but with proper care they can develop into real show-pieces at home or in the office.

Left: *Ficus benjamina* 'Foliole'   Below: *Ficus benjamina* 'Reginald'

Ficus benjamina 'Bushy King'

Ficus benjamina 'Rianne'

Ficus benjamina

WEEPING FIG

In Indonesia and other countries in southern Asia a young weeping fig will gradually climb up a host tree and eventually choke it with its strangling stems. The ficus then develops into a tree itself with a height and width of some

30m (100ft). This explains how, indoors, this plant can grow at some distance from the window. It does not need much light when young, although it will do better in a light spot, out of direct sunlight.

Being a plant from the tropical rainforests, it likes high humidity, but this is not an absolute requirement. Even in the dry air caused by central heating and air-conditioning it will survive a surprisingly long time. Spraying with

Ficus benjamina 'Starlight'

Ficus benjamina 'Golden King'

a mist fo boiled water or rainwater is very beneficial to the small leaves. It is best to use boiled water or rainwater for watering, because this ficus likes slightly acid soil and tap water would soon turn it alkaline. Make sure that the water you give the plant is at room temperatureat least, because *Ficus benjamina* is sensitive to cold. Cold water, especially if it cannot drain away easily, damages the root system and causes the leaves to drop. Leaf drop may also be the result of too cold a location, or of draught or of lack of water. Nevertheless don't water until the soil has almost dried out and make sure no water remains standing in the pot.

Ficus benjamina has given rise to many cultivars. The most widely grown are the ones described below. They need the same care as the species itself, except that the variegated cultivars need more light and higher temperatures.

'Bushy King': one of the most popular variegated forms because of its compact bushy growth.

'Exotica': the true weeping fig. Green foliage with wavy margins.

'Foliole': pyramid-shaped plant with open stems and lanceolate, green foliage. Gives an impression of transparency.

'Golden King': variegated form with a lot of green in the leaves. White marking mainly along the leaf margins. Open growing habit.

'Golden Princess': cultivar which remains smaller than 'Golden King'. Even greener, with only the odd yellow-white spot. Open growing habit.

'Hawaii': compact, variegated form with short, obliquely upward growing branches.

'Major': large-leafed, green.

'Natasha': green cultivar, compact, horizontally spreading branches with elegant, pointed leaves. The sides of the leaves turn upwards to form a V-shape.

'Reginald': golden-yellow and golden-green leaves with small, raggedy dark spots along the mid rib. Compact habit.

'Rianne': compact form with spreading branches and pointed green leaves. Looks like a bonsai.

'Rijsenhout': green-leafed cultivar with obliquely upward growing branches, giving the plant a characteristic open shape.

'Starlight': the best-known variegated form, which can also be found under the name *Ficus retusa* 'Starlight', *Ficus microcarpa* 'Starlight', or simply as 'Starlight'. The foliage is mottled green and milky-green with a lot of white. Open growing habit.

◗ – ● ◐

Ficus carica

FIG

In countries with a maritime climate the fig can live outside in a sheltered spot. It can survive about fifteen degrees of frost. The leaves will have come off by then and the

Ficus benjamina 'Natasja'

branches may be affected by frost, but the fig will sprout again in Spring. It is safer to grow *Ficus carica* in a container and to bring it indoors when there is a chance of serious frost. Put the then leafless shrub in a cool but airy spot which may be dark, and give hardly any water at all. If you want to be able to harvest the fruit, it is better give the plant a lighter place during the winter. In the Mediterranean a gall wasp pollinates the flowers by entering the closed flower structure through a tiny hole. This does not happen in northern Europe and you have to buy a self-pollinating form, such as 'Brown Turkey', if you want fruit to form. The copper-coloured fruits appear in late summer. During the winter they nestle in the axils of the fallen leaves. They only ripen during the following summer if the plant has been kept growing well throughout the season; otherwise the fruits drop off.

Even without fruits, the fig, with its deeply lobed leaves, is a beautiful plant for the living room, conservatory, balcony or terrace. The leaves are sensitive to sun when opening. In the summer the fig likes a warm, sunny spot and plenty of water.

Ficus carica

Ficus cyathistipula

This incredibly vigorous plant from tropical Africa has oblong, green leaves with brown stipules which are considered as having the shape of a tumbler, "Cyathus" being Latin for tumbler. The long, dark green leaves are rather thick, leathery and tough. They can tolerate dry air even better than other species of ficus and remain healthy even in rather dark places. Even so, light, moist and warm conditions are better.

Keep the soil fairly dry, particularly if the plant is in a shady location. Moisten the soil

Ficus deltoidea

Ficus cyathistipula

only with hand-warm water, when it feels dry. Green fruits the size of olives may develop on the ends of the branches.

Ficus deltoidea

MISTLETOE FIG

In South-East Asia the mistletoe fig can grow to a height of about 5m (16ft). The subspecies *deltoidea* remains shrub-like and reaches a maximum height of about 2m (6ft). As a house plant it is one of the smaller species of ficus and it is often for sale as a mature plant. It will already have fruits between the obovate leaves. The fruits turn from green to yellow and are about 1cm (1/4in) in size.

The mistletoe fig needs more light than most other species but it does not tolerate hot sun. Temperatures that are too high, combined with dry air, will cause the leaves to drop. This plant, which will eventually reach a height of about 1m (3ft), should be watered as soon as the soil feels dry, using luke-warm water.

Ficus diversifolia

See: *Ficus deltoidea*

Ficus elastica

RUBBER PLANT

Natural rubber was extracted from *Ficus elastica* before an alternative rubber plant, *Hevera brasiliensis* was brought into general cultivation. If the plant is cut accidentally or in order to take a cutting, white latex flows copiously from the wound. The rubber plant is slow to branch out, especially in a dark place. The reason is that in its natural habitat in India and Indonesia the plant first grows in liane fashion up a tree towards the light. Only when it has reached the top will the plant spread into a crown over its host. When the host has died, the rubber plant will start growing on its own. The plant can reach gigantic heights of 30m (100ft) to 60m (200ft). *Ficus elastica* can grow in a fairly dark spot but in that case it will not usually branch. It is possible to grow a more bushy plant by taking out the top out of the plant at the appropriate time; it is best to do this in early Spring. The top itself can be propagated after the latex has been washed off. Put the cutting in moderately moist, sandy soil and cover with plastic to keep it warm and moist underneath.

Occasionally wipe the leaves with a cloth dipped in buttermilk, if you can get it, or proprietary leaf gloss. This will remove the dust and also give the leaves a beautiful sheen. In the past the rubber plant has been the best selling ficus and, over the years, it has given rise to many cultivars:

Ficus elastica

Ficus elastica 'Tineke'

'Decora Sofia': glossy green, broad leaves arranged in a V-shape.

'Doescheri': variegated form, largely mottled yellow-green with green and greyish-green spots.

'Robusta': wide green leaves growing closely together.

'Schrijveriana': marbled leaves, yellow-green with dark green spots.

'Tineke': variegated, mainly green with grey-green and yellow on the leaf margins.

'Tricolor': variegated form with green, grey, creamy-white and a bit of pink.

Ficus lyrata

FIDDLE-LEAF FIG

The leaves of the fiddle-leaf fig grow to a length of about 40cm (16in) and the fiddle-shaped leaves are widest near the top. Indoors this ficus grows to a height of about 2m (6ft). It will branch when it gets older, or can be made to do so by taking put the top. This ficus does not need a lot of light although it will grow best in as light a position as possible out

'Abidjan': purple-brown suffused foliage.

'Belgaplant': old-fashioned, variegated cultivar. Foliage green, grey and light yellow.

'Decora': the leaves are rounder and more erect so that the pale mid-rib on the upper surface and the reddish colour of the underleaves are visible at the same time.

Ficus lyrata

of the sun. It likes higher humidity than most ficus plants. If the humidity is too low, the leaves will get brown edges. Misting and sponging are beneficial and some buttermilk or leaf gloss on the sponge will enhance the sheen of the leaves. Water only when the soil feels dry, using hand-warm water and avoid low temperatures and draughts.

Ficus microcarpa 'Starlight'

See: *Ficus benjamina* 'Starlight'

Ficus nitida

See: *Ficus benjamina*

Ficus pumila

CREEPING FIG, CLIMBING FIG

This ficus looks totally different from the species that have been mentioned earlier. *Ficus pumila* is a self-clinging creeping plant. It completely covers tree stumps in the tropical forests of Vietnam and other parts of South-East Asia, where its mature leaves reach a size of about 10cm (4in). As an indoor hanging or creeping plant it will retain its juvenile form. The leaves are only 2cm (1in) to 3cm (1/4in) in size but overlap to form a dense mat.

When you grow this ficus in a very damp atmosphere in, for example, a propagator or herbarium, you can see how quickly it can cover a large area. Spray *Ficus pumila* as often as possible. The "tray method" will also help : put the pot on an upturned saucer in a tray of water so that the bottom of the pot is just above the water level, or put the pot on wet gravel. The compost should always be damp but not too wet. *Ficus pumila* grows best in a light spot, even in the sun as long as it is protected during the hottest part of the day but it can also tolerate semi-shade. Grow *pumila* at room temperature during the summer but preferably cooler in the winter. As well as the species, various cultivars are on offer:

'Lis':	light green, lobed leaves with a dark green edge.
'Minima':	small cultivar with leaves 1cm (1/4in) wide at most.
'Rikke':	leaves in two halves, one light and one dark green.
'Sunny':	each leave has a white margin.
'White Sunny':	a white leaf margin, wider than that of 'Sunny'.
'Variegata':	strong-growing cultivar with creamy-white spots.

Ficus repens

See: *Ficus pumila*

Ficus retusa 'Starlight'

See: *Ficus benjamina* 'Starlight'

Ficus stipulata

See: *Ficus pumila*

Ficus pumila 'White Sunny'

Ficus pumila

6. Arums

There are approximately 3000 species of arum-like plants in existence and they are recognizable by their special flower formation. The flowers are closely arranged on a spadix, which is surrounded by a so-called spathe, a protective bract. Some species have a conspicuously large and coloured sheath, for instance some anthuriums and the zantedeschias. They will be dealt with under flowering plants and container plants respectively. But most of the cultivated species are kept because of their beautifully shaped and brilliantly coloured foliage.

The various arum-like plants have been put together here in a separate chapter to help you discover the similarities between them. The species which are cultivated because of their decorative foliage grow under similar conditions in the wild. They grow in tropical forests as lianes or climbers, not needing much light when they are young. They all require more or less the same care. They are tolerant of shade and dry air and this makes them ideal house plants.

Aglaonema commutatum

Aglaonemas grow in the tropical forests of South-East Asia; the species *commutatum* in the Philippines and in the north-east of Sulawesi. The leaves are about 20cm (8in) long and are naturally flecked along the veins. Breeders have eagerly used this characteristic to breed different patterns. In greenhouses the plants grow readily, but indoors it is a job to keep them alive. They should always be kept warm, although they do not like dry air and it is therefore necessary to spray frequently or to use the "tray-method" (put the plant on an upside-down saucer in a tray, and fill the tray with water to just below the bottom of the pot).

Water freely during the summer with boiled water or rainwater and regularly add liquid feed to the water. Keep moderately moist in winter. *Aglaonema* does not need much light to stay alive, but grows better in a light position. Never put it in the sun.

The best-known and most often grown cultivar is *Aglaonema commutatum* 'Silver Queen'. It has silvery leaves with patches where the green shows through. Some other cultivars are:

'Maria':	silver-green smudges along the veins.
'Albiovariegatum':	with white "frosted" leaves.
'Tricolor':	variegated with white and some pink.

◗ – ● ○

Aglaonema commutatum 'Silver Queen'

Left: *Alocasia x amazonica*

Alocasia x *amazonica*

The flower of this *Alocasia* shows clearly that it is an arum. The cream-coloured spadix is covered in flowers and surrounded by a green spathe which is all but white on the inside. However, the plant is sold for its of foliage, not its flowers. The leaves of the hybrid *Alocasia x amazonica* are several tens of centimetres long. In the juvenile stage they are glossy light green, later turning matt grey-green with prominent, thick, whitish veins.

The name of the hybrid is misleading because this plant is definitely not a native of the Amazon region. The parent plants are *Alocasia lowii* (a native of Borneo) and *Alocasia sanderiana* (a native of the Philippine island, Mindanao) where they grow in tropical, humid conditions. In our houses they prefer a warm, humid location, but the thick leaves can also tolerate lower humidity. Spray regularly with rainwater or boiled water. Wipe the leaves with a damp cloth to remove dust. In summer keep the plant out of the sun and give plenty of water and fertilizer, but make sure that the pot does not remain standing in water. Keep moderately moist in winter.

Anthurium crystallinum

CRYSTAL ANTHURIUM

Some anthuriums (also called "flamingo plants" in Holland) have striking flowers and these are dealt with under flowering plants in chapter 10. Here we are concentrating on a typical foliage plant. The juvenile foliage of *Anthurium crystallinum* is first red-brown suffused; as it gets older it grows to a length of several tens of centimetres and is dark green with a clear pattern of pale veins. In the veins as well as in the green of the leaves, small sparkling "crystals" are visible .

Anthurium crystallinum grows in trees in the tropical forests of Panama, Venezuela, Colombia and Peru and is difficult to keep in the living room. The compost should be light and rich in humus but at the same time the plant needs a lot of water. It is best grown in a propagator or in another light spot with sufficiently high humidity. Never let the temperature drop below 16°C (61°F), not even in winter, and never let the compost dry out completely.

Left: *Alocasia x amazonica*

Anthurium crystallinum

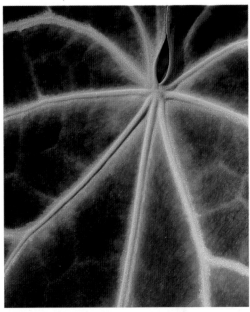

Make sure the water can always drain away freely.

Caladium bicolor

Do not be surprised when the fantastic foliage of the caladium suddenly withers inlate season. The plant is not dying; it is only entering a period of rest. Cease watering and take the root ball out of the pot as soon as all the leaves have withered. The ball contains a root tuber which can be kept dry. For storage, avoid a temperature lower than about 15°C (59°F) because the caladium is a native of the tropical forests of South America. To prevent the tuber from drying out completely put it in dampish peat.

The buds will sprout in March or thereabouts. You can then plant the tuber a few centimetres deep in a pot of fertile compost, with a lot of peat added. Wet the compost and put the pot in a closed plastic bag in a warm spot. In this atmosphere the tuber will produce new leaves. Water freely in summer and feed regularly. Make sure the air is as humid as possible. The foliage is too vulnerable to be wiped with a cloth.

Hybridization of caladium species, often with *Caladium bicolor* as one of the parent plants, has given rise to many beautiful cultivars. They are usually on the market without a

Caladium bicolor 'Candidum'

Caladium bicolor cultivar

name, with the exception of 'Candidum', a cultivar with white leaves and green leaf veins.

Dieffenbachia 'Exotica'

See: *Dieffenbachia maculata* 'Compacta'

Dieffenbachia maculata

COMMON DUMB CANE

Dieffenbachias have been in cultivation for a very long time because of their decorative foliage. Spontaneous hybridization has occurred as well as a lot of deliberate breeding and this has made total chaos of the nomenclature. *Dieffenbachia maculata* is often one of the parent plants of the many cultivars. According to some plant experts *Dieffenbachia maculata* and *Dieffenbachia seguine* are so closely related that they should in fact be regarded as belonging to the same species. However, there is one obvious difference: the leaves of *maculata* are more oblong than those of *seguine*. They also look more fragile and is more sharply pointed.

In the market place, the cultivars are currently grouped according to whether they have larger or smaller leaves. The small-leafed cultivars are classified under *maculata,* for instance:

Dieffenbachia maculata 'Camilla'

'Candida' foliage yellow to cream-coloured with green spots and a green leaf margin.

'Camilla': foliage colour varies from yellow through cream to white, without spots, but with a green leaf margin.

'Compacta': (also called 'Exotica') at the foot of the plant the foliage is dense; irregular green markings on a yellow to cream background.

'Mars': irregular dark green, light green and yellow markings.

Dieffenbachia is a fickle plant. Some people can keep it thriving for years, others kill it off in a few months. The problems that a dieffenbachia may encounter and cause it to die off are:

- The tips of the leaves were drooping when the plant was bought. Such plants may not have been hardened off properly and hence cannot at first withstand dry air.
- The plant was bought on the street during the cold season (temperatures below 15°C (59°F)). If the plants collapses and withers within a few days take it back to the supplier.
- Withered or mis-shapen leaves or brown spots indicate a disease: bacteria, viruses or fungi.
- Avoid draught and cold at all times. Temperatures should never drop below 15°C (59°F).
- Never let the plant the plant dry out completely.
- Water liberally with luke-warm water (at at least room temperature) but never leave the pot standing in water.
- Oil fumes, from fires or lamps, are very detrimental.
- Never place dieffenbachias in the sun, but they like a light position. In a dark position the leaf markings fade
- If the air is too dry the leaf edges will turn brown.

Dieffenbachia seguine

The large-leafed cultivars are usually included among this species. A trunk-like stem develops, like that of a banana, with large leaves which don't usually conceal the foot of the plant. Some of the cultivars are:

'Alix': a compact form with pale feathery markings along the green mid-rib. Leaf margin green.

'Amoena':	green to bluish-green foliage with yellow to white spots along the lateral veins.
'Tropic Snow':	the most popular large-leafed cultivar. Similar to 'Amouna', but the spots more light green to white.
'Tropic Sun':	even lighter in colour than 'Tropic Snow', compact.
'Wilson Delight':	pointed, ovate green leaves with clearly white veins.

Dieffenbachias are poisonous. Foliage and stems contain calcium oxalate in the form of needle-like crystals which can lodge in the mucous membranes. They cause a strong burning feeling, swelling and inflammation and if swallowed can cause serious inflammation of the stomach and intestines. The very bitter taste of the plant will usually stop children and pets from eating it. However should this happen, make them drink a lot of water and consult a doctor as soon as possible. Dieffenbachias that have grown too big can be cut off about 20cm (8in) above ground level. They will then send out new shoots. Make sure not to get any of the poisonous sap on the skin or in the eyes.

Dieffenbachia seguine 'Tropic Snow'

Monstera deliciosa

SWISS CHEESE PLANT

The Swiss cheese plant is a liane from Panama and southern Mexico, where it climbs up to 20m (65ft) high. The leaves of a young plant are heart-shaped. When the liane is grown in a light and not too dry spot, the new leaves will get deeply cleft margins. In ideal circumstances the leaves will get bigger and develop oval holes. *Monstera* is an easy house plant which will grow in the semi-shade and tolerates dry air reasonably well. If the leaves become dull they can be made shiny again by wiping them with a cloth dipped in buttermilk, if available, or proprietory leaf gloss.

A light, humid location out of the sun is ideal. Water liberally in summer, with hand-warm water and regularly add some liquid fertilizer. Water less in winter.

The name 'deliciosa' refers to the delicious fruits that used to be cultivated in Central-America and England. The taste is reminiscent of banana as well as of pineapple. In the living room the plant will rarely flower and it is not a good idea to experiment because all parts of *Monstera deliciosa* are poisonous except the ripe fruits. For the symptoms of poisoning, see *Dieffenbachia seguine*.

Monstera deliciosa

Philodendron erubescens

BLUSHING PHILODENDRON

Philodendron erubescens has thin, red-flushed stems that need support. so the growing plants are often tied against a moss stick. In their natural environment in Colombia they climb trees.

In the house *Philodendron* is a robust plant which does not need much light, especially if it is one of the forms with green leaves. A light position out of the sun is better. Water moderately in summer with luke-warm water

Right: *Philodendron erubescens* 'Golden Erubescens'

and less in winter. Temperatures should never drop below 15°C (59°F). Philodendrons are poisonous: for actions to take in case of poisoning, see *Dieffenbachia seguine*.

Some popular cultivars of *Philodendron erubescens* are:

'Emerald Queen': green stems and green leaves

'Emerald King': same as 'Emerald Queen' but all parts larger.

'Red Emerald': wine-red stems with long, pinkish-red bracts and dark red veins on the undersides of the glossy green leaves.

'Golden Erubescens': red stems and bracts. The pointed leaves are yellow-green to strikingly golden-yellow.

Philodendron 'Imperial Red'

The origin of this compact cultivar is unknown as is the case with many cultivars of philodendron. It does not show any inclination to climb but will eventually spread out sideways to become a sturdy pot plant. It has reddish-green leaves, about 30cm (12in) long. The leaves of a related cultivar 'Imperial Green' are even larger, glossy green, and have reddish bracts.

Regularly wipe the leaves with a damp cloth to remove the dust. Some buttermilk or leaf gloss on the cloth will help to make them shiny again. Spraying and misting are beneficial to the health of the plant as long as soft water is used (boiled or rainwater), of at least room temperature. Philodendrons are very sensitive

Philodendron 'Imperial Red'

to being watered with cold water and to their roots being kept wet. Use loose, fertile compost; water moderately and feed regularly in summer.

Philodendron pertusum

See: *Monstera deliciosa*

Spathiphyllum

The thirty-six known species of *Spathiphyllum* grow in the damp soil of tropical forests in Central and South America, and also in South-East Asia where the humidity is always high. Despite that they are strong house plants which can give a green accent to a dark place in a room where other plants would wilt through lack of light. In such a spot you will have to make do with the green, lanceolate leaves, because the plant will only flower if kept in a lighter spot.

Keep the *Spathiphyllum* away from direct sunlight because it will burn the leaves. They first start to curl backwards and gradually turn yellow, becoming vulnerable to red spider mite. Less sun and higher humidity in time get rid of the red spider mite. It also helps if you put the plant in the shower and rinse it with luke-warm water.

Like so many arums the *Spathiphyllum* does not like 'cold feet'. When watering always use water of at least room temperature (preferably rainwater or boiled water). Avoid draught or temperatures below 15°C (59°F). Only the species *Spathiphyllum wallisii*, a native of Panama and Costa Rica, can tolerate lower temperatures and then not below 10°C (50°F). Most of the cultivars found on the market have *walissii* as a parent or can be treated as if they have. The differences are hardly visible to the amateur: a little green line on the bract or a difference in the position or the shape of the foliage can be enough reason for the breeders to give a plant a new name. Well known cultivars are: 'Adagio', 'Ardito', Castor', 'Cupido', 'Euro-Giant', 'Fiorinda', 'Mauna loa', 'Mozart', 'Pallas', 'Petite', 'Prelude', 'Sensation' and 'White success'.

Apart from these there are true species. They are slightly more vulnerable than the wallissii-hybrids and are rarely on offer. This is a shame because there are gems among them such as *Spathiphyllum patinii*, which remains very

Right: *Spathiphyllum* 'Mozart'

Spathiphyllum patinii

Syngonium podophyllum

GOOSEFOOT PLANT

The *Syngonium* is closely related to the philodendron. The more than thirty species grow in the warm forests of Central and South America. *Syngoniom podophyllum*, the most cultivated species, is a native of Panama and Costa Rica. Maintenance is the same as that of philodendron; a shady position if necessary, but preferably a light one out of the sun. Water sparingly in summer with water at least at room temperature. Never leave the plant standing in water. Give little water in winter. The temperature should be a minimum of 15°C (59°F), in summer as well as winter.

Syngoniom podophyllum is usually on sale as a young plant. It will spread out and hang down unless you give it the support of a moss stick. Give the plant loose, humus-rich soil and feed regularly in summer.

Syngonium podophyllum has given rise to many cultivars. 'White Butterfly' is the best-known one, but others are:

'Emerald Gem': Arrow-shaped, fleshy green leaves.

'Emerald Gem Variegated': Arrow-shaped, thin foliage with a white and light grey pattern of spots. A compact plant.

small. Flower stems of about 30cm (12in) in length rise up between the lanceolate, green leaves. They carry a spadix with net-like markings, surrounded by a white spathe which is flushed with green along the central vein. The minimum temperature requirement is 15°C (59°F) and this species likes a bit more light but can otherwise be treated like any other spathiphyllum.

Below: *Spathiphyllum wallisii*

Right: *Syngonium podophyllum*

7. Foliage plants

People who like flowering plants usually buy them on impulse. They come across a plant with beautiful flowers, buy it, take it home, and find a place where the flowers can be displayed to advantage.

People who like foliage plants generally have a totally different approach. They are the architects and planners of their interiors. The plant is not an isolated object, but an important addition to the interior, where it can become part of a beautiful still-life created with a feel for form, colour and light. Plants define the atmosphere of a house. What a difference it makes when they are taken away!

Different types of plant are suited to different types of interior. Stately plants, such as the banana, Pittosporum and the Norfolk Island pine seem to belong in a stark modern interior. Begonia, croton, Aspidistra and Coleus heighten the intimate atmosphere of a more classical interior.

Consider your visit to the garden centre as an architectural adventure. It may result in just the finishing touches you need whether your interior is classic or modern.

Araucaria excelsa

See: *Araucaria heterophylla*

Left: *Codiaeum variegatum* 'Rina'

Araucaria heterophylla

NORFOLK ISLAND PINE

The Norfolk Island pine likes a cool climate. The species is a native of Norfolk Island, north of New Zealand in the pacific Ocean. There it can grow to a height of more than 50m (160ft). The young plants that are kept in the house grow slowly. If looked after well they add a layer of side branches each year. complete with fresh green needles which hardly prick at all.

Put the Norfolk Island pine in as light a place as possible, but out of the sun. Even in a rather dark position the plant will survive for a remarkably long time, although it will then grow even more slowly. Keep the plant dryish and only pot-on when absolutely necessary because *Araucaria* hates it. After potting on in humus-rich soil (preferably leaf mould and sand), do not feed for at least two months. Feed only sparingly after that.

Mist or spray the plant regularly, or put it outside in the rain, but only when it is about 7°C (45°F) or more. The Norfolk Island pine will get through the winter best at 7°C (45°F) or more, but should not be in a heated room where the air would be so dry that the lower branches would turn yellow and drop off. This is a natural process but once branches have

Araucaria heterophylla

73

dropped off they will never grow again and the lower part of the plant eventually becomes bare. In warm, dry air this happens more quickly.

To recuperate, the plant, still in its pot, may be dug in outside in a shady spot.

Aspidistra elatior

CAST IRON PLANT

It is hard to kill an aspidistra, a vigorous plant from China which tolerates any climate and any location. Light frost won't harm it, neither will dry, hot rooms, nor smoke or otherwise stale air. Forgotten to water it? No problem. The thick rhizomes, from which the long leaves rise directly, can only be killed by leaving them sitting in water, because this will make them rot. The leaves do not like the full sun.

In time the rhizomes will fill the pot and this is a good time to re-pot. It is also a good time to split the root ball. You can offer the extra plant to someone who is unable to keep any house plant alive. The species has sturdy, green leaves.

There are quite a number of cultivars with

Aspidistra elatior 'Milky Way'

yellow or white spots or lines on the leaves. 'Milky Way' is the best-known with cream-coloured spots; 'Variegata Ashei' has white

A begonia growing wild in Costa Rica

lines whereas 'Variegata Exotica' has a more irregular pattern of lines.

Aspidistra elatior 'Minor'

See: *Aspidistra elatior* 'Milky Way'

Begonia

There are about one thousand species of begonia and they are widely spread throughout the tropics, especially in Central and South America and in Asia. Some are typical inhabitants of damp forests, often with spreading roots or rhizomes. Others grow higher up in the mountains. They survive adverse periods by withdrawing underground as a root tuber. In this chapter only begonias that are cultivated for the ornamental value of their leaves are included. Other species will be dealt with in the chapter on flowering plants.

Begonia boweri

MINIATURE EYELASH BEGONIA

This Mexican begonia is in fact called *Begonia bowerae* but is usually offered under the incorrect name 'boweri'. White flowers flushed with pink adorn the plant; however, that is not the reason why it is sold. Its decorative value lies mainly in its light green leaves which have black and brown spots and are edged with white hairs. Some cultivars have been developed from the species which is itself rarely on offer. You can usually find

Begonia boweri 'Tiger'

'Tiger' which has olive-green leaves with light green spots. The undersides of the leaves and the brittle, juicy stems, are wine-red.

Give it a light but not too sunny location in a heated room. Water regularly with hand-warm water, so that the compost stays always moist but never soaking-wet. Do not spray because this may encourage mildew and give as much fresh air as possible, avoiding draughts or cold air, and a temperature of preferably at least 15°C (59°F). Pot on every half year and regularly give liquid feed. Always leave the plant in the same position in relation to the light.

Begonia Rex hybrids

Begonia rex originated in Assam. The varieties available are all hybrids of this plant with one of the countless other Asiatic begonias and may be found on the market under the collective name of *Begonia Rex* hybrids. Their leaves are up to 30cm (12in) in length and their great weight can cause the plant to topple over. Re-pot into a large or heavy pot as soon as you obtain the plant. Never plant it more deeply than it was before, because that may cause rotting.

The leaves are often brilliantly marked and

Begonia Rex hybrid

have a beautiful sheen. The patterns are mainly built up of the colours pink, carmine, silver, green and red-brown. The plants are imported in mixed batches so that that you can choose the colour combination that you like from those on offer.

If a leaf breaks off it can be used as a cutting. Put the leaf on damp compost and cut through the veins in a few places with a sharp knife. Cover with plastic and put in a warm spot, out of direct sunlight. After a few weeks new plants will have developed where the cuts were made and you can pot them on individually. (See *Begonia boweri* for care instructions).

Brachychiton rupestris

BOTTLE TREE

In the dry areas of Queensland, Australia, grow gigantic trees with swollen stems which store water for the dry season. Plants in the juvenile form of these colossal trees are on sale as house plants. Their swollen stems are often strangely twisted, giving them an oddly amusing appearance. The plant can tolerate dry air very well.

Young plants often have single, strap-shaped leaves nearly 20cm (8in) long at the same time as compound leaves with three to nine oblong lobes.

There is not much else positive about this plant. The distance between the leaves is large and the stems become lanky, which means that *Brachychiton* is soon too big for the living room. It is better to grow this plant as a container plant, keeping it outside in a sunny

Brachychiton rupestris

spot in summer, and inside at a minimum temperature of 12ºC (54ºF) in winter. Hardly water at all in winter, moderately in summer.

Codiaeum variegatum 'Excellent'

Codiaeum variegatum

CROTON, JOSEPH'S COAT

Croton should in fact be dealt with in the chapter on euphorbias because it belongs to the *Euphorbiaceae*. But most lovers of house plants know it as one of the most popular decorative foliage plants, as is evident from the large numbers sold, especially some years ago.

Unfortunately it is not an easy plant to keep healthy for a long period of time. The temperature should never drop below 15°C (59°F), the location should be evenly warm, and there should never be any draught. This, combined with a great need for high humidity, poses a clear problem; how to keep a croton alive and well in winter when the central heating is on. It is possible to achieve this by spraying frequently, by wiping the leaves with a damp cloth or by using the "deep tray method". This means putting the plant on an upside-down saucer in a tray filled with water. The water level should remain below the bottom of the pot. Gravel can be used instead of a saucer. Always keep the compost moderately moist and feed regularly in summer. Put this marvellous shrub in a very light spot out of the bright sun. It can tolerate morning or evening sun but in a dark location

the croton will loose its colour. Numerous cultivars, which are usually looked upon as different species, have been bred from the subspecies *Codiaeum variegatum pictum*. The one which is sold most is the large-leafed cultivar 'Excellent' whose leaves have a narrow portion at the tip. The leaves which form first are reddish and dark green, the leaves that form later are yellow and green. Other large-leafed cultivars are:

'Rina':   red and yellow veins in large, elliptical green leaves.

'Norma':   large, green and yellowleaves.

'Petra':   irregularly blotched leaves, with green, yellow, orange, red and purple

'Nervia':   long, pointed leaves with a very wide mid-rib and lateral veins in a fishbone pattern. The red or yellow of the veins forms a strong contrast to the light green and purple of the rest of the leaf.

'Mrs. Iceton': A particularly elegant cultivar with foliage curved slightly backwards. The leaves are light red, orange or yellow near the leaf stalk and become green or purple towards the tip of the leaf.

Codiaeum variegatum

These small-leafed cultivars are evidently becoming more popular:

'Goldfinger': it has strap-shaped yellow and green leaves.
'Pictum': also yellow and green, but in a pattern of spots.
'Punctatum': shrubby, with very narrow green and yellow freckled foliage.
'Aucubifolia': yellow and orange freckles on green foliage.

Coffea arabica

ARABIAN COFFEE PLANT

Coffea arabica originally came from Ethiopia, but was first cultivated in narrow terraces which may still be found in the mountains of the Arabian country of the Yemen. Later the Dutch smuggled the un-roasted fruits and established the plants in the Dutch Indies and later in South America where most coffee is cultivated nowadays.

It is worth trying to grow coffee on a windowsill. You need fresh, un-roasted coffee beans to do this and these are sometimes on offer pre-packed. The seeds need warmth from below to germinate (20-25°C (68-77°F)) and like to grow in moist air. The seedlings develop glossy green leaves. They grow best in a warm, airy atmosphere, in a light position, out of the bright sun and in moist, fertile soil. On plantations coffee plants flower after a few years and in greenhouses it is quite possible to get flowers and fruit. But in the house you will have to make do with coffee out of a packet.

Coleus Blumei-hybrids

FLAME NETTLE, PAINTED NETTLE

In spring and summer, flame nettles, with their richly patterned foliage, give a fine show in garden centres. There is an enormous variety of colours; light green with chocolate-brown, green with bright red veins, orange-brown with a green edge, green with a yellow centre, purple-red to near black. The hybrids are usually anonymous: just choose the colours that you like. Put the flame nettle in a sunny spot, but protect it from the bright afternoon sun in summer. Water liberally and try and give these plants from South-East Asia a high humidity. Flower stalks will eventually appear, but they do not increase the decorative value of the plant. It is best to prune the plant back hard when it starts to flower, so that it

branches and bushes out again. The hot dryness of centrally heated rooms causes leaf drop and disease. Either throw the plant away in late season or keep it in a cool room (between 10°C (50°F) and 16°C (61°F)). In the spring you can take tip cuttings of the sap-rich upper part of the stems. They will root in water and can then be potted.

Corynocarpus laevigata

NEW ZEALAND LAUREL

This tree from New Zealand is very suitable for light, cool rooms when it is a young plant. A centrally heated room is too warm and too dry for *Corynocarpus* and red spider mite may attack. Misting and wiping with a damp cloth may help to avoid this. If there is no cool, light room available the tree can be treated as a container plant. Put it in a cool room in winter (minimum temperature 5°C (41°F)) and keep it rather dry. In summer put it outside in a pot or container and see that the soil is kept moderately damp.

Right: The beans of *Coffea* photographed in the original area of coffee cultivation, the Yemen
Below: *Coleus* Blumei hybrid

As well as the species, which has oval green leaves, the variegated cultivar 'Variegata' is sometimes obtainable. 'Variegata' has lighter green foliage, with cream-coloured blotches, especially at the tips of the leaves.

Corynocarpus laevigata

Cupressus macrocarpa

INDOOR CYPRESS

This plant from California grows into a tree about 25m (80ft) in height. Its cultivar 'Goldcrest' is available as a house plant. In warm, heated rooms it will grow lanky. It is better to put it in a cool room in a spot that is as light and airy as possible. Water liberally in summer, less in winter. The indoor cypress can also be grown as a container plant. The container only needs to be brought inside if

Cupressus macrocarpa

the temperature drops below minus 10°C (14°F). If grown in the open ground it is even more tolerant of frost. In places with a mild climate this plant is available as a garden plant.

Cyperus albostriatus

See: *Cyperus diffusus*

Cyperus alternifolius

UMBRELLA PLANT

Ribbon-shaped leaves spread out at the top of the long, green, round stems of this *Cyperus* from Madagascar. When the plant is growing well, the stems become sturdy and as tall as a person. Strong growth can be achieved by cultivating the plant in a large, water-tight tub. Put the plant in fertile soil in the tub and then fill it with water. The soil may be completely under water. Put the tub in a light, even sunny, place with some extra humidity, for instance near the cooker or in the bathroom. If the air is too dry, red spider mite is very likely to attack the plant. If that happens put *Cyperus* in the bath or outside (if the temperature is above 10°C (50°F)) and rinse the leaves.

In time the roots will completely absorb the excess moisture from the muddy soil. The creeping rhizomes can be split. If they are too matted and intertwined to be split then pieces can be cut off and planted in fresh wet soil.

It is also possible to propagate this plant by snipping off the tips of the stems. Keep the umbrella and about 10cm (4in) of stem. Trim back the leaves of the umbrella to a few centimetres and put the clipped umbrellas upside down in water or on muddy compost: they will soon root.

As well as the original species the cultivar

Cyperus alternifolius 'Zumula'

'Zumula' is very popular these days. The stems remain shorter, the ribbon-shaped umbrella leaves are longer, and the flower stalks with oval spikelets rise up from between the leaves at a young age.

Cyperus argenteostriatus

See: *Cyperus diffusus*

Cyperus diffusus

This species originates in South Africa. It has thin stems with short, but relatively wide ribbon leaves on top. The plant does not grow higher than about half a metre and is therefore particularly suited to people without much living space. Maintenance is the same as for Cyperus alternifolius.

Cyperus diffusus

Cyperus papyrus

PAPYRUS

The Egyptians used this plant to make paper long before the birth of Christ. It grows in the hot swamps of Africa and needs a warm spot in the house, at least 16°C (61°F), but preferably warmer. The thread-like umbrella leaves, which grow on triangular stems, do not tolerate dryness well. The dampest place in the

kitchen or bathroom is therefore best for this species. The true papyrus can only be propagated in this country by splitting. Maintenance is otherwise the same as for *Cyperys alternifolius.*

Cyperus papyrus

Fittonia argyroneura

See: *Fittonia verschaffeltii argyroneura*

Fittonia verschaffeltii

PAINTED NET LEAF, NERVE PLANT

The green leaves of this creeping plant are interlaced with a network of red veins. The veins of the subspecies *argyroneura* are silver-white. In the shop this plant is usually named *Fittonia verschaffeltii* 'Argyroneura'. There are other true cultivars with different white marking or different sized leaves.

The species grows in the tropical forests of Colombia and Peru where it covers the forest floor. In the living room high air humidity is required. It is best to keep the plants in an indoor greenhouse or a herbarium, where they will spread fast in all directions and minute yellow flowers on spikes will appear. The temperature should never drop below 15°C (59°F), in summer or winter. Water moderately during the winter, liberally during the summer. Put the plant in a light spot, for example near an east or north facing window, but protect it from the bright sun.

Fittonia verschaffeltii cultivar

Hemigraphis alternata

RED/FLAME IVY

The silvery green foliage of this perennial has a metallic sheen and purple-red tips, at least when *Hemigraphis* is grown in a light spot. If not, these decorative characteristics fade and you are left with plain green foliage, which is wine-red underneath. The species grows naturally on the floors of the tropical forests of India and Java and will not, therefore, tolerate full summer sun. See *Fittonia verschaffeltii* for maintenance.

Hemigraphis alternata

Hemigraphis colorata

See: *Hemigraphis alternata*

Fittonia verschaffeltii argyroneura

Hypoestes phyllostachia

POLKA DOT PLANT, FRECKLE FACE

The olive-green foliage of this species has pink freckles. This was not enough for the plant breeders, who have developed various different colours through hybridization. The cultivar 'Splash', for instance, has considerably larger freckles, as if splashed with pink paint. The foliage of 'Pink' is predominantly pink, with green veins and some green spots. The foliage of the cultivar 'White' is white apart from the veins. It is little wonder that these decorative plants are often bought on impulse but keeping them healthy indoors is a different matter. See *Fittonia verschaffeltii* for maintenance.

Hypoestes sanguinolenta

See: *Hypoestes phyllostachia*

Ledebouria socialis

There are about sixteen species of this bulbous plant from South Africa. They are all closely related to the hyacinth. The flowers are

Ledebouria socialis

elegant, coloured green and purple, but all these species are grown for their spotted foliage. The leaves of *Ledebouria socialis* are about 10cm (4in) long and silver-coloured with green spots. The plant needs to be put in full sun to keep its markings. Water moder-

Hypoestes phyllostachia

ately in summer, hardly at all in winter. In winter it is best kept in a greenhouse or conservatory at a minimum temperature of 5°C (41°F), but *Ledebouria* will also survive the winter on the windowsill of a cool room.

Leea guineensis

This plant from tropical Africa is grown for its decorative foliage. The species has green foliage but when the leaves first unfold they are deep red. The plant mostly on offer is the cultivar 'Burgundy' (also called 'Bourgondia'). The stems and the undersides of the leaves are deep red. The rest of the foliage is dark green.
The winter will cause problems for leeas kept in the living room. They only keep their foliage if the temperature remains above 15°C (59°F). In a centrally heated living room the air humidity is far too low. You will therefore need to take special precautions such as putting the pot on a layer of gravel in a wide tray. Pour water in the tray to a level just below the bottom of the pot. Misting and the use of a humidifier will also help. Water liberally with luke-warm water in summer, regularly adding fertilizer, but keep the plant drier in winter. Put in a light spot but out of the bright summer sun.

Murraya paniculata

ORANGE JASMIN

Murraya paniculata is a popular shrub in tropical gardens. The plant flowers several

Murraya paniculata

times a year with deliciously fragrant flowers, followed by orange-red berries. This evergreen shrub will also flower in temperate climates, but only in a greenhouse or conservatory. In a living room the conditions are less favourable. If kept indoors try to make the humidity as high as possible and put the shrub in bright light; protect it from the hot summer sun, though. Water and feed liberally in summer. In winter there is not enough light in most rooms, so place the plant in a particularly light room during that period. Choose a cool place (minimum of 10°C (50°F)) and water sparingly.

Musa acuminata

DWARF BANANA

The dwarf banana is a few tens of centimetres high when for sale in the garden centre, but it soon grows into a large plant of at least 2m (6ft) high and nearly as wide. The name "dwarf banana" is generally given to *Musa nana*, but that species is assumed to be synonymous with *acuminata*. The leaf of the living room banana is beautiful when it unfurls. It is green with a bluish hue and

Right: *Leea guineensis*
Below: *Musa acuminata*

mottled with purple-red. Cultivars have been developed that are especially suitable for growing indoors, because they stay smaller. 'Dwarf Chyla', 'Puerto Rican Dwarf', and 'Dwarf Orinoco' are some of them, but even these grow very big given time. If the plant outgrows its allocated space you can rejuvenate it like the banana farmers do. Cut off the pseudo-stem at its base and wait until side shoots develop. Leave only the strongest one to grow on. Bananas need a lot of light in summer as well as winter, and you need to water and feed them liberally in summer. The warmer the better, but avoid the bright afternoon sun in summer. Keep the plant at a temperature above 10°C (50°F) during the winter. Other species of banana need a much higher temperature to get through the winter. *Musa acuminata* can be placed outside during the height of summer in a warm, even sunny, spot, but definitely out of the wind, asthe wind will cause the leaves to fray and end up in tatters.

Musa nana

See: *Musa acuminata*

Pachira aquatica

Pachira aquatica grows near the mouths of rivers and on wet banks in Central America and northern South America. Despite having a

Pachira aquatica

thickened stem the plant needs plenty of water during the growing season. If well watered it will grow very quickly. The top can be cut out, if so wished, to give the plant a more bushy growth. Put the pachira in the full sun, but not during the hottest part of summer, or else in as light a spot as possible. Keep moderately moist in winter and at a minimum temperature of 15°C (59°F).

Peperomia caperata

EMERALD RIPPLE

The leaves of *Peperomia caperata* can be silver-green, bi-coloured, dark green or reddish, depending on the cultivar. They are nearly always offered for sale without name labels. All cultivars have one characteristic in common, the foliage is very "lumpy" because of the deeply impressed veins. Stalks with minuscule flowers often rise above the foliage. They look like tails, hence the Dutch common name "rat's tail". Emerald ripple has fleshy foliage that can tolerate dry air well. Keep the plant indoors, in summer as well as winter, in a light spot, but out of the bright sun. Water moderately, or immerse the pot in water and

Right: *Peperomia*
Below: *Peperomia caperata*

drain well. The compost should be loose and rich in humus. Do not immerse the pot again until the soil has nearly dried out and keep even dryer in winter.

Peperomia clusiifolia

BABY RUBBER PLANT

The fleshy leaves of this peperomia are completely smooth, glossy and full of sap. The green-leafed form will even grow in front of a north facing window, but the variegated form 'Variegata' needs more light. In the sun the green and creamy leaves develop a good colour and the edge becomes more distinctly red. Protect the plant against the bright afternoon sun in Spring and Summer. Maintenance is otherwise the same as for *Peperomia caperata*.

Peperomia clusiifolia 'Variegata'

Pittosporum tobira

JAPANESE PITTOSPORUM, TOBIRA

The soft-yellow flowers of tobira smell delicious, but the plant is sold for its foliage. The leaves of the cultivar 'Variegatum' are grey-green with cream-coloured markings on the edges. *Tobira* can be grown as a container plant. Put it outside in the summer and in a cool, light room in the winter. This foliage plant can also

remain indoors, but make sure it gets the best available light as otherwise the shrub will lose many of its leaves. Another species that is often on offer is *Pittosporum tenuifolium*, from New Zealand. There are also variegated form of this species available. They are easily distinguishable from *Pittosporum tobira* by their very dark leaf stalks and young shoots. Water moderately in the summer, somewhat less in the winter. *Pittosporum* species tolerate dry air and the two species that have been dealt with here will even survive ten degrees of frost. In some coastal regions they are used as wind screens, because they are able to tolerate salty air.

Pittosporum tobira 'Variegata'

Pogonatherum paniceum

Pogonatherum paniceum has become very popular in a short time. The thin, flexible stalks carry light green foliage which drapes elegantly over the edge of the pot. This low-growing species of the grass family originates in South-East Asia and Australia, where it is humid and

Pogonatherum paniceum

warm. Therefore do not put the plant over a central heating radiator, but in a more humid place in the light. Avoid dryness and bright sun, because they will cause the leaf tips to turn yellow. Water regularly and feed occasionally, so that the plant keeps growing winter and summer. Eventually the compost will get exhausted. You can then divide the plant and pot up the pieces in fresh, standard potting soil.

Rademachera sinica

This shrub from China (hence the name sinica) and other parts of South-East Asia requires a large watering can because a lot of moisture evaporates from its leaves. The plant should definitely never dry out and needs to be grown at room temperature. Therefore it should be watered regularly and hand-warm water should be used.

Put this plant, which will grow several tens of centimetres tall and wide, in a light spot, out of the sun so the foliage won't burn. In very favourable conditions this foliage plant can develop large sulphur-yellow flowers, but this happens very rarely when grown indoors. As well as the species, which has green foliage,

there is a cultivar, 'Kaprima', which has golden-green foliage and is cared for in the same way.

Rademachera sinica

Sansevieria trifasciata

MOTHER-IN-LAW'S TONGUE

Sansevieria is looked upon as an old-fashioned plant but in fact it grows very well

Sansevieria trifasciata 'Golden Hahnii'

in the modern living room with its dry climate. You can hardly find a tougher house plant than *Sansevieria trifasciata* from Nigeria. All the common green species, including the cultivar 'Laurentii' (with yellow-edged foliage) and the low-growing cultivars 'Hahnii' and 'Golden Hahnii' (the with pale yellow leaf edges), are impossible to kill. You can put them safely in the sun. Water them moderately and only re-pot when the fleshy roots have cracked the old pot. These are the simple rules for the maintenance of mother-in-law's-tongues. The rather unpleasant common name is also very old-fashioned and perhaps the time is ripe for finding a new one. The best way to propagate *sansevieria* is by division of the roots. It is also possible to take leaf cuttings. Cut pieces about 5cm (2in) long and let them root in sandy soil. Variegated forms will lose their yellow margin if propagated like this.

Scilla violacea

See: *Ledebouria socialis*

Selaginella

There are about 700 species of this plant, but the plants mainly on offer are cultivars of *Selaginella martensii* and *Selaginella kraussiana*. The former originates in Mexico, the latter in South Africa. Both can tolerate lower temperatures than those from the tropical forests. It is therefore possible to put them in a cool room in the winter (5°C (41°F) or more) and they will not be in danger of drying out near the central heating. That certainly would happen if they were kept in a warm, centrally heated room.

The potting soil should never dry out and the water should be able to drain away freely. Keep these plants, which resemble moss, out of the sun, but in a light position.

Selaginelle lepidophylla strongly resembles the rose of Jericho (Anastatica) whose leaves curl up in dry conditions. *Selaginella lepidophylla* is a native of deserts from Arizona to Peru and their leaves also curl up in dry conditions. It can be looked after in the same way as the other species of *Selaginella* mentioned above.

Selaginella apoda is a maverick. The fine leaves grow as ground cover in the eastern United States where it can be tens of degrees below zero. Even so, do not put this creeping

Selaginella kraussiana

plant outside because it is likely to dry out. In the regions where it originates it spends the winter under a thick layer of snow.

Soleirolia soleirolii

MIND YOUR OWN BUSINESS, BABY'S TEARS

Baby's tears forms a mat of minuscule leaves that creep along the soil on thin stems and hang down over the edge of the pot. The plant originates in Corsica. In the house baby's tears grows best in a cool room, for instance a bedroom. High humidity is beneficial for growth but not absolutely necessary.

Soleirolia is not very demanding in other ways either. The lighter its position, the more water it will need. Never let the plant dry out and keep it away from the hot afternoon sun in the summer.

There are three forms of baby's tears available. The species itself has green foliage. That of the cultivar 'Variegata' (also known as 'Argentea' and 'Silver queen') is grey-green and that of 'Aurea' (also known as 'Golden Queen') is golden-green.

Solenostemon scutellarioides

See: *Coleus Blumei* hybrids

Sparmannia africana

AFRICAN HEMP

The large, light green, downy leaves of African hemp are a pleasure to behold.

When you buy a new plant it is usually rather limp as a result of having been grown too fast. At home African hemp (which is a member of the same family as the common lime) becomes more sturdy but still grows rapidly.

The plant can easily reach a height of about 2m (6ft) in one summer and can also spread considerably. It is best to put the plant in an unheated room during the winter. It will even tolerate a few degrees of frost, but then it will lose its leaves. The African hemp is one of my favourite plants.

The foliage will only become large and beautiful if the plant is put near a north facing window. Never put it in the sun because the leaves will burn.

In summer *Sparmannia* grows enormously, either indoors or if planted in its pot in a sheltered and shady spot in the garden. It will easily grow up to 2m (6ft) in one season. Late

Soleirolia soleirolii

in the growing season it can tolerate a few degrees of frost if left outside, but eventually it will have to be brought in and put in a cool room. If it is grown in the living room, it will lose some of its leaves in winter, so it is better to put it in a cool spot. It does not matter if the leaves drop off, because in spring the dormant buds on the stems will sprout, even if the stems have gone woody. If you want to rejuvenate the plant, it is best not to cut back all the stems at once, but to prune a few stems

at the time close to ground level. The stumps will draw strength from the other stems and sprout again.

Water liberally during the growing season, re-pot regularly and give liquid fertilizer. Hardly water at all in the winter.

Strobilanthes dyerianus

PERSIAN SHIELD

This plant from Myanmar (which used to be called Burma) has brilliantly coloured foliage in its natural state. It has grey-green veins and margins and shimmers with purplish-pink between them.

The leaves are just over 10cm (4in) long. If the plant becomes too big, you can pinch out the tops. The plant needs to be given a light position to develop intense colouration. Avoid direct sunlight. Water liberally during the growing season and feed occasionally. Keep moderately moist in the winter and at a temperature of at least 10°C (50°F).

Sparmannia africana

Strobilanthes dyerianus

8. Ivies and related species

The ivy family, the Araliaceae, *is named after the native ivy of Northern Europe. This easy-to-grow climber adheres to walls and trees with clinging roots and covers them in a blanket of green. It is, however, an exception. The majority of the approximately 800* Araliaceae *grow in the tropics and do not have clinging roots. Most of them wind around tree trunks like lianes.*

Well known house plants, such as the scheffleras, belong to the family but do not look like climbers. They are sold as sturdy foliage pot plants. When the supporting sticks are taken out their real growing habit shows. Young plants especially will lean over precariously. As for maintenance, all Araliaceae *have two things in common: they do not need a lot of light and they will only grow well if the air humidity is high.*

Aralia elegantissima

See: *Dizygotheca elegantissima*

Aralia japonica

See: *Fatsia japonica*

Dizygotheca elegantissima

The narrow-leafed *Dizygotheca elegantissima* has fragile leaves which are bronze coloured when young and in time turn to deep green. In its natural habitat in New Caledonia *Dizygotheca*, which plant experts these days call *Schefflera elegantissima*, grows into a 15m (50ft) high tree. As it gets older its leaves become much wider. You don't need to worry about the rate of growth of the plant in the living room. It will find it hard enough to stay

alive because the air humidity is often much too low. The plant does not like temperatures below 15°C (59°F). Mist and spray as often as possible or put the plant on a upside down saucer in a tray of water, making sure that the water does not reach the bottom of the pot because *Dizygotheca elegantissima* does not like to stand in water. In a dry atmosphere the plant is very vulnerable to red spider mite. Put it in a light position but not in the bright sun during summer.

Dizygotheca elegantissima

x Fatshedera lizei

TREE IVY

x *Fatshedera* was raised in the French nursery of Lizé Frère at Nantes in 1912 by cross breeding *Fatsia japonica* 'Moseri' and *Hedera hibernica* (a type of ivy). The result of this strange cross-breeding is the tree ivy. The stems grow straight up without branching. They hardly cling and therefore need to be given support. Otherwise it hardly needs any care. x *Fatshedera* is a problem-free house plant which tolerates warmth, withstands dry air reasonably well, does not need a lot of light, and, if grown outside, even survives more than ten degrees of frost.

x *Fatshedera* is seldom inclined to branch. You can make it bushy by pinching out the tips regularly. Propagation is best done in late summer, using cuttings from the green stems, just below the tip, or by using the tip itself as a cutting. Cut straight through a leaf node, snip of the two leaves above the node but leave the third and cut off the stem about one centimetre above this third leaf. Put the cutting in moist, sandy soil, under plastic.

There are a few cultivars on the market. 'Pia' has wavy leaf edges, 'Variegata' is green with creamy blotches. The latter cultivar grows better in a light location.

x *Fatshedera* 'Pia'

Fatsia japonica

FALSE CASTOR-OIL-PLANT

Fatsia japonica can remain outside in the open ground or in a pot in places where the temperature never drops more than a few degrees below zero. In Holland *Fatsia* is a good container plant and is especially rewarding as a house plant. The leaves are palmate, about thirty centimetres across and spread out widely. They are very well suited to a light, modern interior. Never put the plant in the sun. It likes a light position although it will tolerate a less light one. Give a lot of fresh air and keep the air humidity as high as you can. Keep it cool in the winter if

Fatsia japonica

possible. Wiping the leaves with a damp cloth is very beneficial to *Fatsia*. Give plenty of water but make sure the pot does not stand in water.

Fatsia can be propagated in exactly the same way as x *Fatshedera*. If the parent plant loses its looks put it in the garden in spring and see how many winters it survives.

Hedera helix

COMMON IVY

Ivy used to be one of the most popular outdoor as well as indoor plants. The ivy has made a come-back as a wall plant after a decline during the years when everything had to be "tidy". It protects walls, gives breeding and hiding space to birds and saves a lot of energy. The insulation capacity of a wall increases by about 30% when an ivy grows against it.

Indoors the ivy has never again gained the great popularity it used to enjoy. At the start of this century it was used indoors in all kind of ways: as a hanging plant, as a climbing plant or as a complete living room screen. The fact that the plant can tolerate such a lot

Hedera helix 'Pin Oak'

of shade added to its uses. You can still grow ivy indoors but in a dark spot rather than near a window over a radiator, which would be much too dry. This dryness is the reason

Hedera helix

why ivy is grown much less as an indoor plant than it used to be. In dry heat ivy runs a great risk of attracting red spider mite or scale insects. When the central heating is on put *Hedera* in an unheated room, never in the sun at other times.

Because the roots of ivy grow near the surface it can be kept in a shallow pot. The soil dries out quickly which is an advantage because ivy does not like to stand in water. Only give water when the soil feels dry again. The best method is to immerse the pot completely and drain off well afterwards. That way the plant will get enough water and there is less chance of pests. It is safe to use tap water because *Hedera* likes alkaline soil. In spring and summer you can feed with bonemeal or another alkaline fertilizer .

There are hundreds of *Hedera* cultivars which differ from each other in the size and shape of their leaves. The leaves are green or marked with yellow, white, light green or even reddish-pink blotches and vein patterns. There are also cultivars, such as 'Congesta' and 'Erecta', which have stiffly upright growing stems and leaves arranged in regular rows. In the end these cultivars also droop like other types of ivy.

Hedera helix 'Erecta'

Hedera canariensis

CANARY ISLAND IVY

The difference between this ivy and the common ivy is most clearly visible in the stems and leaf stalks which are reddish and covered in fine hairs. The maintenance is the same as that of *Hedera helix,* except that *canariensis* requires more light and a higher temperature. Especially the variegated form *Hedera canariensis* 'Variegata' likes a light position out of the sun.

Polyscias balfouriana

DINNER PLATE ARALIA

The ornamental plant which is sold under this name is officially called *Polyscias scutellaria* 'Balfourii'. It is a popular house plant which is usually sold as a rooted stem cutting. The species originated in the Far East but these days it is a common plant in the tropics, where *Polyscias* is used as a hedge.

In dry air the edges of the leaves turn unsightly and brown. This spoils the decorative value of the white margin. Spray as often as possible and put the plant, which does not require a lot of light, in as humid a position as possible, for example, in the kitchen, bathroom or a moderately heated room. Never put it where the temperature drops below 12°C (54°F). Water freely in summer, sparingly in winter.

The cultivar 'Balfourii' has round leaves with a white margin. There are other cultivars with round foliage; 'Fabian' has no white in its leaves but has a bronze colour, 'Pennockii' has pale-yellow leaf veins.

Polyscias fruticosa

This *Polyscias* has deeply scored foliage. It grows from a rooted stem section which makes the plant look like a bonsai. If looked after well it becomes bushy with lots of new, sap-rich foliage. This species requires a high relative humidity. If the temperature and humidity are too low the leaflets will drop off the leaf stalks. Only try to grow this plant if you can provide a warm and humid

Right: *Polyscias balfouriana*

atmosphere. Plenty of spraying can prolong its life span. Water liberally in summer, preferably with rainwater.

Polyscias fruticosa

Polyscias guilfoylei

WILD COFFEE

Growers take advantage of a peculiarity of *Polyscias guilfoylei* to produce an interesting decorative effect. The plant occasionally produces a group of thin shoots. When this occurs, they are bent into hoops and fastened with elastic. Eventually they loose their resil-

Polyscias guilfoylei

ience and stay in a hoop shape even after the elastic has been cut. You can continue to produce rings by bending the shoots. They grow quickly and are easily trained into the desired shape. For maintenance see *Polyscias fruticosa*.

Polyscias scutellaria 'Balfourii'

See: *Polyscias balfouriana*

Schefflera arboricola

This liane from Taiwan is currently one of the most popular house plants. The stems grow in their pots supported by sticks rather than by. The stems become sturdier as they get older but will always benefit from support. In the wild the species grows in mountainous forests where the temperature is never very high. Put *arboricola* therefore in a light but not too hot location and certainly not in the sun. A temperature between 16°C (61°F) and 18°C (64°F) is ideal. Do not let the temperature drop below 12°C (54°F) in the winter, because that will cause the palmate leaves to drop off. (The plant may, however, sprout again all over after its leaves have fallen off). Because *Schefflera* needs high humidity it is beneficial to spray it with a fine mist as much as possible,

Schefflera arboricola 'Trinette'

sponge the dust off its leaves regularly, and put the plant in a humid place, for instance on a bed of wet gravel. It is best if the compost does not get too wet because that causes the roots to rot. Make sure the compost is nearly dry before watering again. The water should be at least at room temperature. There are a large number of cultivars of *Schefflera arboricola*. The following are the ones that you are most likely to come across: 'Compacta' (a green form, possibly a juvenile form of the real species), 'Nora' (a tall green cultivar with fine leaflets), 'Renate' (with green leaflets which are divided (pinnate), sometimes twice (bi-pinnate) as far as the main vein), 'Gold Capella' (with golden-yellow blotches but only on the bottom leaflets), 'Trinette' (yellower than 'Gold Capella' on more narrow leaflets) and 'Henriette' (with yellow and white blotches along the leaf margin).

Schefflera elegantissima

See: *Dizygotheca elegantissima*

Tupidanthus calyptratus

Plant experts know this species as Schefflera pueckleri but the plant trade has not accepted

Schefflera arboricola 'Gold Capella'

this name yet. To add to the confusion the plant looks like the well known *Schefflera actinophylla*. The plant is a tree from South-East Asia which in temperate regions grows into a large, bushy house plant with dark green, palmate leaves on long leaf stalks. Just like other scheffleras this vigorous grower can be pinched out to make it become more bushy, but it is very difficult to propagate the pinched out tops Re-pot the plant every year and give liquid feed regularly; maintenance is otherwise the same as for *Schefflera arboricola*.

Tupidanthus calyptratus

9. Hanging and climbing plants

It is surprising how many house plants were originally climbers (for instance philodendrons, see the chapter on arums) or hanging against trees. Others, which are now cultivated as hanging plants, covered the forest floor. They all have one characteristic in common: they grow well under a leaf canopy. There are similarities in conditions between our living rooms and the forest. Even in the windowsill plants get much less light than they do outside. Further away from the window the light decreases rapidly and only those plants that are satisfied with a glimmer of light can grow there. The average living room is relatively dark so that it is best to put even the hanging and climbing plants from the forest in as light a spot as possible, but not in the hot summer sun.

Aeschynanthus lobbianus

LIPSTICK VINE

Aeschynanthus means "with flowers that are ashamed of their crimson blush". There are over 100 species. They grow on trees in South-East Asia. Give them an airy compost, rich in humus. Grow them in a basket hanging in a very light place but out of the bright summer sun. Water abundantly in summer with hand-warm, decalcified water and spray as often as possible. Water sparingly in winter. The temperature in winter can drop to about 15°C (59°F). When the buds appear, put the plant back in a warmer location. Feed regularly during flowering. The species from Java, *Aeschynanthus lobbianus*, is best known. It has crimson flowers which grow out of deep-purple calices. *Aeschynanthus radicans* from Malaysia looks exactly the same as do the numerous cultivars that are on offer: 'Ara' has leaf edges that are more clearly red, 'Mira' has

rather pointed leaves, 'Altair' has broader foliage and so does 'Mona Lisa'. *Aeschynanthus speciosus* from Malaysia lacks a cup-shaped calyx, but it has large, strikingly luminous flowers, with the colour running from orange to yellow.

Aeschynanthus 'Mira'

Alsobia dianthiflora

See: *Episcia dianthiflora*

Antigonon leptopus

CORALLITA, CORAL VINE

This climber from Mexico trails along the ground if it can not find any support. This member of the Polygonaceae family has become naturalized in many tropical countries. In our region it is an exceptionally rare plant for the greenhouse or conservatory. Cultivate it in the full sun and water plentifully in summer. In winter the temperature can drop to about 10°C (50°F) and the coral vine should then be given much less water.

Left: *Passiflora mollissima*

Antigonon leptopus

Apios tuberosa

Apios americana

See: *Apios tuberosa*

Apios tuberosa

This papilionaceous climber grows from a root tuber which was once an important source of food for the native North American. The plant climbs about 3m (10ft) each season and flowers profusely in summer. However, the flowers have a rather modest colouring and therefore rather inconspicuous. This may explain why *Apios tuberosa is* rarely available. The foliage dies off in winter but the tubers are totally hardy as long as they are kept fairly dry. The winters in north-west Europe are too wet for the plant and it has to be cultivated in a greenhouse, conservatory or in a large container which can be put outside in a sunny spot during the summer. Water plentifully in summer but make sure that the water can easily drain away.

Aporocactus flagelliformis

RAT'S TAIL CACTUS

The stems of the rat's tail cactus are covered in golden spines which bend under their own weight and hang down. They are at the most 1cm (1/2in) across but can grow tens of centimetres long. If cared for well they will flower every spring with crimson-pink flowers each about 10cm (4in) long.
In winter they need, just like most other cacti, a period of strict rest. Only water when the 'tails' start to shrivel up and hang the plant in a light, cool spot (between 5°C (41°F) and 15°C (50°F)). Only when small reddish-pink dots appear in spring (these are the buds!) should you gradually water more. Hang the plant in a warm and very light place but protect it from burning sunshine in early spring. Later the cactus can tolerate the full sun and appreciates plenty of fresh air and misting. Dry air is sure to cause red spider mite to attack. If that happens hang the plant outside in the semi-shade during summer and the red spider mite will disappear (photo on page 000).

Asparagus densiflorus

This very robust house plant can tolerate sun and semi-shade, and low temperatures down to a minimum of about 5°C (41°F). Plenty of water is fine but no harm is done if it dries out once in a while. Even dry indoor air is not fatal. If there is not enough humidity or a shortage of water the linear leaves will turn yellow and drop off. This also happens during the dry season in South Africa from where the plant originates. Give a bit more water if the leaves are starting to drop off and the plant will recover easily. There are pale root tubers in the soil which serve as a moisture buffer. These will eventually appear above the surface and this is a sign that it is time to re-pot. The plant can then be divided and cut back hard.
The pendulous stems are thin and the long long leaflets drop off sooner or later. The leaves also bear little hooks, so anybody who likes a clean house or is impatient should give this plant a miss.
The best known cultivar is *Asparagus densiflorus* 'Sprengeri' which has loose, pendulous stems covered in green, linear leaves. Nowadays another cultivar called 'Meyeri' is more and more often available. This plant produces long, cigar-shaped plumes that first grow erect and later hang down under their own weight. This cultivar can tolerate more shade than the parent species.

Asparagus densiflorus 'Meyeri'

Asparagus myriocladus

See: *Asparagus umbellatus*

Asparagus umbellatus

The foliage of this asparagus from the Canary Islands appears to be as soft as down. In reality the true leaves are little thorns and the phylloclades feel rather stiff. Give this plant a slightly higher humidity than normal, for instance by putting it somewhere cool in winter. It can tolerate a light frost. Maintenance is otherwise the same as for *Asparagus densiflorus*.

Asparagus umbellatus

Bacopa 'Snowflake'

Don't be ashamed if you have never heard of this plant, because it is very new. It could well be that it will win over the hearts of plant lovers and that we will see it more often in the future. Bacopas are originally marsh plants from tropical and subtropical regions. However the cultivar 'Snowflake' will grow very well in a hanging basket. Give it a light location, preferably outside in summer, where it can hang in full sun, as long as the soil never dries out.

Hang the plant indoors during the winter, in a cool, airy spot, otherwise there is a great risk of fungal infestation. The temperature is not very important, but in a light position in a

Left: *Aporocactus flagelliformis*

heated room you will have to watering liberally. The plant will hardly need any water at all in winter if kept in a cool room, minimum temperature of 10°C (50°F).

Cuttings can be taken in August or September. Snip off stems and root them in an airy, moderately damp soil mixture. In spring the cuttings will soon cover the pot or basket with greenery and lovely white flowers.

Bacopa 'Snowflake'

Basella rubra

In South-East Asia basella is eaten as a green vegetable and the leaves are prepared like spinach. For cultivation, heat is necessary. The seeds only germinate above 18°C (64°F) and the plants themselves prefer a similar temperature for growth. At the height of summer this climber can go outside in a roomy container but if grown indoors or in a greenhouse it will keep better.

The small, bladder-shaped flowers develop into crimson-red berries, which contain the seed. This can be collected as soon as the berries shrivel up. Be careful because the juice stains and is used as a dye in Asia. Sow in spring, in loose, sandy soil. The plant can survive the winter but sowing it afresh gives better results. As well as the species with reddish foliage there is the variety Basella rubra alba which has green foliage.

Chlorophytum capanse

See: *Chlorophytum comosum*

Chlorophytum comosum

SPIDER PLANT

This is one of the easiest house plant to keep. The grass-green leaves grow in the sun or shade, in warm or cool rooms (at a minimum temperature of 5°C (41°F)), humid or dry, and it causes no problem if you occasionally forget to water. The thick roots of this South African plant contain a reserve. The spider plant grows at its best in very light, even sunny, positions, where it will flower regularly with little white flowers. Later numerous new tufts of leaves which can be detached and potted develop on the flower stalks. In the past the species *comosum* and *capense* were distinguished but they are so much alike that only the name *comosum* applies nowadays. The species itself has green foliage. It is more common to find variegated cultivars on offer. The most widely available is 'Mandaianum' which has white stripes down the middle of the leaves. The cultivar 'Variegatum' is green along the mid-rib and has white margins.

Chlorophytum sternbergianum

See: *Chlorophytum comosum*

Left: *Basella rubra* 'Rosebud'
Below: *Chlorophytum comosum* 'Mandaianum'

Cissus

The real cissus, *Cissus antarctica* (kangaroo vine), is a well-known, very robust climbing or hanging plant from Australia. It can tolerate dry air very well, although regular spraying will decrease the chances of infestations of red spider mite. In a light spot out of the sun it will grow at a tremendous rate and will cover a frame up to more than 1m (3ft) high in one season.
Cissus striata grows a bit more slowly. It is a very decorative hanging plant with stems suffused with red and quinnate leaves. The species originates in Chile and will thrive in a light, not too sunny spot indoors.
Cissus rhombifolia (Grape ivy) can tolerate much less light and should definitely not be placed in the sun. Self-clinging tendrils carry the dark green foliage, which benefits from regular spraying. This species from tropical America has given rise to the very popular cultivar 'Ellen Danica', with larger leaflets which are deeply scored.
Water *Cissus* species moderately in the winter and summer; they can be kept in the living room during the winter but they will keep better if you put them in a cool room (with a minimum temperature of 5°C (41°F)) and give very little water.

Cissus striata

from the island of Ternata in the Moluccas where the photograph was taken. The species grows throughout South-East Asia. The plant winds its way through the bushes. *Clitoria* is an easy plant to look after in warm, sunny rooms. It can be grown from seeds which need a minimum temperature of 20°C (68°F) to germinate. The seedlings can be put outside in midsummer in an large pot with loose, nutritious compost. They will grow faster in a greenhouse, conservatory or on a sunny window. Unfortunately this beautiful climber is not often available.

Clitoria ternata

The respectable plant expert Linnaeus thought this flower looked like a clitoris. It was known

Clitoria ternata 'Butterfly Pea'

Columnea hirta

The foliage and stems of this hanging plant from Costa Rica are completely covered in short hairs. The young shoots grow upwards at first but soon start to droop under their own weight. In late season or winter the orange-red flowers appear which may turn into white berries if the plant has been looked after well. This can only happen if the flowers have not dropped off prematurely. Flower fall occurs if the plant is watered too much during flowering. If not watered enough the foliage turns yellow; moderate moisture is what *Columnea* requires over this period. Give it a high relative humidity if possible (for instance by spraying) and hang it in a light place, but definitely out of direct sunlight. Give the plant a few months rest after flowering by keeping it drier, (at a slightly lower temperature but never below 12°C (54°F)), and cut back the long trailing stems. They will branch in spring and after a few months flowers will develop on the newly formed stems. *Columnea hirta* is the original parent plant of cultivars such as 'Sanne'. *Columnea hirta* 'Variegata' has light green foliage with creamy-white markings.

Columnea hirta 'Sanne'

Columnea 'Hostag'

The origin of many *Columnea* hybrids is not known but this does not make them any less beautiful. 'Hostag' flowers profusely with orange-red blooms on pendulous stems which are densely covered in foliage which is mainly yellow, with a green edge. This cultivar requires more light than the green-leafed species but even so it should not be put in the sun. For further details of maintenance see *Columnea hirta*.

The fruit of *Columnea hirta*

Columnea microphylla

GOLDFISH PLANT

'Microphylla' means small-leafed and this species from Costa Rica does indeed have small leaves. The round leaves are thinly spread and carried on red stems, which can grow to more than 2m (6ft) in length. This gives the plant a "see-through"appearance which disappears during flowering when the newly formed stems are covered in orange-red flowers. Even more than with other species of *Columnea*, it is important to prune *Columnea microphylla* after flowering. Otherwise maintenance is the same as for *Columnea hirta*.

Convolvulus mauritanicus

See: *Convolvulus sabatius*

Convolvulus sabatius

In Italy and North Africa the woody stems of *Convolvulus sabatius* creep along the ground. Here it is grown as a attractive hanging plant which can tolerate some frost but will have to

Left: *Columnea* 'Hostag'

Below: *Convolvulus tricolor* 'Blue Titt'

come indoors in the winter. In the summer it requires a sunny spot outside and moderate watering. The stems flower very profusely, like a waterfall, with purple-blue flowers which are each a few centimetres in size. It is best to put

Below: *Convolvulus sabatius*

it in a very light position in a cool room in winter. Shorten the shoots considerably. If this is done in spring, the cuttings can be propagated by putting them in moderately damp compost. It is also possible to propagate from seed.

Convolvulus tricolor

Convolvulus tricolor blooms from late June onwards with flowers of three colours. They have a yellow centre, with a white band outside and surrounded by purple. They can be grown in the garden as annuals but, because the stems eventually start to droop, it is better to cultivate them in a spacious basket.
Sow in March or April but only hang the plants outside when the danger of frost is over. You can also put the plant in a very sunny spot by the window. *Convolvulus tricolor* requires average watering and, if looked after well, will flower well into September. Collect the seeds to sow in the following year. The species has given rise to numerous cultivars with different colours in the outer band: 'Blue Ensign': bright blue, 'Cambridge Blue': light blue, 'Crimson Monarch': carmine, 'Lavender Ro-

sette': lavender-pink, 'Royal Ensign': dark blue.

Dipladenia

See: *Mandevilla*

Epipremnum aureum

See: *Epipremnum pinnatum*

Epipremnum pinnatum

In the forests of South-East Asia *Epipremnum pinnetum* coates the trees with its climbing stems which carry enormous leaves. They each reach a length of about 1m (3ft). The house plant is a juvenile form of this liane, and it grows leaves of about 10cm (4in) on soft stems that can climb if supported. But the plant is usually cultivated as a hanging plant.
Despite its tropical character the plant can tolerate dry indoor air fairly well, although it benefits greatly from spraying and misting. Keep the plant away from direct sunlight but give it as light a position as possible. In the

Left: *Columnea microphylla*

Below: *Epipremnum pinnatum* 'Marble Queen'

cultivars with variegated foliage, the less green there is the more light the plant needs for optimum growth. Even so, the species will survive in a dark spot but do give plenty of water in the summer. In winter the plant can be put in a cool room, not below 10°C (50°F) where it will need little water. If kept in the living room you will have to carry on watering as normal throughout the winter. You will usually buy one of the following cultivars:

'Aureum': green foliage with yellow spots.

'Golden Pothos': golden-coloured foliage with a touch of green.

'Marble Queen': white to creamy-white foliage with green blotches.

Episcia dianthiflora

This hanging plant from Costa Rica would undoubtedly be very popular if it were not so difficult to cultivate. Fairy-like flowers, a few centimetres in size, open between the velvety soft leaves. The petals are deeply feathered like those of pinks (dianthus), hence the name. Water *Episcia* moderately and keep the foliage dry, otherwise mildew might attack. Make sure the plant gets fresh air but avoid draughts and rapid changes in temperature. Getting it

Episcia dianthiflora

through the winter is the real problem because the plants need more light than nature provides at that time of year. So hang the plant under a strong lamp. Propagate by putting stem cuttings in moderately moist compost in spring.

Gloriosa 'Rothschildiana'

GLORY LILY

Unless you have a greenhouse or conservatory it is best to buy *Gloriosa virescens* 'Rothschildiana' in summer while it is in flower. Every leaf ends in a tendril with which the plant will cling to a stick in the pot. You can also grow *Gloriosa* against wire mesh or string on the windowsill, a method which make the exotic flowers stand out particularly well. 'Rothschildiana' originates in Uganda in the heart of tropical Africa. So give *Gloriosa* a warm position but keep it away from direct sunlight. Grow the plant in loose, fertile soil. Water liberally without ever letting excess water settle in the bottom of the pot. If you have a conservatory or greenhouse you can grow *Gloriosa* from tubers which are bought in spring. Wait until the growing points show signs of life and then put them in large pots or containers at about the end of April. Heat the container from beneath and the tuber will soon sprout. The stem is at first leafless and it will only climb when the leaf tendrils start to cling. Until then you can tie it to a support, if you like. Bring *Gloriosa* indoors in September. When the foliage has died the newly formed tubers can be stored dry at room temperature. Make sure not to damage the growing points. As soon as they start to sprout the tubers can be put back in the soil.

Ipomoea purpurea

COMMON MORNING GLORY

From May onwards you can buy potted morning glories in flower with their growing shoots twined around supporting sticks.

The large, funnel-shaped flowers bloom for one day only (hence the Dutch common name "dayflower"). However, healthily growing plants will produce new flowers every day so that you can enjoy them for several months.

Right: *Gloriosa* 'Rothschildiana'

Indoors the plants can be kept through the winter but it is definitely easier to re-sow in spring. Common morning glory can be grown as an annual in the garden where it will easily climb 2m (6ft) high. It can also be grown in pots but will then grow less vigorously. After the last frost the pots can go outside.

Common morning glory can also be grown very well on a windowsill as long as it gets plenty of water, fertile soil and a chance to climb. If you harvest the big triangular seeds in late season you can sow them indoors in March or April, or outdoors from mid-May. Then you will get another year of flowers.

Ipomoea quamoclit

CYPRESS VINE

This maverick among the *Ipomoea* species is sometimes on offer as a container plant. The climbing stems carry deeply scored foliage and produce fiery-red flowers. The flowers and foliage are less overpowering than those of other species, rendering it a suitable plant for the keen amateur. Maintenance is the same as for *Ipomoea* purpurea.

Ipomoea purpurea

Ipomoea tricolor 'Heavenly Blue'

Ipomoea tricolor

This species is often sold under the name *Violacea*, which is another species that is not in cultivation. *Ipomoea tricolor* grows even more rapidly than *Ipomoea purpurea* (up to 4m (13ft) high) and the flowers are bigger. The plant requires a lot of water and nutrients and this explains why it is so seldom offered as a pot plant. In a large pot or container with fertile black soil and a lot of water this *Ipomoea* will reach for thestars.

Ipomoea quamoclit

The most often available cultivar is *Ipomoea tricolor* 'Heavenly Blue' which has strikingly large blue flowers with pale centres. For maintenance see *Ipomoea purpurea*.

Ipomoea violacea

See: *Ipomoea tricolor*

Isolepis cernua

See: *Scirpus cernuus*

Lobelia erinus

In spring you can buy one of the many cultivars of *Lobelia erinus*, usually under the name "hanging lobelia". The stems grow over the rim of the pot like a curtain and they flower for months on end as long as you remember to water and to feed them regularly. If you neglect to do so, the stems become woody and bare and this South African plant goes into a resting period. Just cut back the stems drastically and give the plant enough water and fertilizer and you will be surprised how rapidly it recovers. *Lobelia erinus* grows well in pots on the terrace and is very suitable as a low-growing plant in window boxes or hanging baskets. But it will also flower exuberantly in a sunny and airy spot on the windowsill or in the conservatory. It is possible to keep the plant through the winter but it is easier to re-sow in spring.

Mandevilla 'Aphrodite'

There are more than 100 species of *Mandevilla* but the best known ones are often for sale under the name *Dipladenia*. These are usually hybrids with pink flowers. *Mandevilla spendens* is very likely to have been one of the parent plants. Superficially the large flowers

Lobelia erinus

look like those of oleanders but the flowers of mandevillas are found amidst climbing stems. These stems can only develop well if they can climb to at least 1m (3ft) high. The flowers are produced on new wood. Give these climbers from tropical America a sunny and airy position (outside or in a conservatory). Water liberally and feed the plant regularly. If you do so it will flower until you have to bring it inside to avoid the first night frosts. Keep the plant in a light and cool place during the winter at a minimum temperature of 10°C (50°F) and prune back the soft shoots in early spring. Re-pot as little as possible. The best way to propagate is by taking cuttings from the stems in the spring while they are sturdy but still green.

Mandevilla boliviensis

The large, white flowers of *Mandevilla boliviensis* look like something out of a fairy tale. Despite their attractiveness you do not come across this climber very often. It originates in Bolivia and Ecuador where the stems can climb to 4m (13ft) high. In colder climates the plant can easily reach 2m (6ft) when grown in a pot but it can be kept smaller. From spring till late season new

Mandevilla boliviensis

clusters of flowers will keep appearing between the shining green leaves. For maintenance see *Mandevilla* 'Aphrodite'.

Mandevilla 'Aphrodite'   Right: *Mandevilla laxa*

Mandevilla laxa

CHILEAN JASMINE

Mandevilla laxa comes from Argentina and is different from the other mandevillas. The white flowers smell more sweetly than those of other species and look like large jasmine flowers.

They are produced in summer and grow in clusters from the climbing stems. The plant can easily tolerate a few degrees of frost although it will then drop its leaves.

In more severe frost often only the roots will survive. So, except in regions with extremely mild weather, you will have to bring the pots indoors in winter. For further maintenance see *Mandevilla* 'Aphrodite'.

Mandevilla suaveolens

See: *Mandevilla laxa*

Mikania apiifolia

See: *Mikania ternata*

Mikania dentata

See: *Mikania ternata*

Mikania ternata

The stems and leaves of this hanging plant are totally covered in hair giving a wine-red glow to this velvety soft Brazilian plant. It likes a warm, humid location.

Try to ensure a high humidity without spraying, because spraying causes the hairs to turn a rather unsightly grey colour and become sticky.

You can safely put the plant in a sunny spot, where the colours will be at their best. But it can also survive in darker spots. Water evenly in summer and moderately in winter.

In winter it needs a cool place with a minimum temperature of 10°C (50°).

Passiflora

PASSIONFLOWER

Passionflowers have a very complicated structure. They usually have five sepals and five petals, which are difficult to distinguish, five stamens, three stigmata and around these a circle of filaments which looks like a "crown of thorns". Because the flower was thought to display various signs from the Passion of Christ the plant was called passionflower.

Passionflowers originate mainly in the warm parts of America. Some species can survive northern European winters outdoors, but most have to be brought into a greenhouse or a cool room for the winter.

All species can be cultivated in large pots in sun or semi-shade outside, or in a greenhouse or conservatory. They can also be grown indoors if put in a very light spot. The plants are rampant climbers and hold on by means of tendrils.

They need a lot of space. The shoots can be trained and pruned as necessary. Give plenty of water in the growing season and water hardly at all when the plant is resting. Too much feeding will stimulate the production of foliage at the cost of flowers. The winter temperatures which are necessary for optimum development of the plant are given separately for each species.

Passiflora x alato-caerulea

This plant is a cross between *P. alato and P. caerulea*. The flowers are at most 10cm (4in) wide with white sepals and mauve petals. Minimum winter temperature is 5°C (41°F).

Mikania ternata

Passiflora antioquiensis

This species originates in Colombia. The flowers do not face upwards like those of most other species but hang down. They have a strikingly long flower tube. The pinkish-red flower is more than 10cm (4in) wide. Winter temperature at least 5°C (41°F).

Passiflora antioquiensis

Passiflora caerulea

COMMON/BLUE PASSIONFLOWER

This bestknown passion flower can be grown as a garden plant against a wall as well as a house plant. When young it is susceptible to

Passiflora caerulea

frost but when it grows older it can survive severe winters although it will drop most of its leaves. When grown as a house plant *Caerulea* is tied to a wire ring. It can be kept in the living room during the winter if it is not too

Passiflora x *alato-caerulea*

hot. It is better to put it in a cool and light spot, where it should be watered sparingly. If grown in a pot it should be given a temperature of at least 5°C (41°F). The true passionflower has given rise to beautiful cultivars, which require the same maintenance. 'Constance Elliot' has white flowers, those of 'Star of Mikan' are pink with a purple corona.

Passiflora edulis

PASSION FRUIT, PURPLE GRANADILLA

This species is cultivated in all the warm regions on earth because of its edible fruits. Superficially it looks like *P. caerulea* but the filaments of the corona of *edulis* are mostly white, with a purple to blue ring around the centre of the flower, they are much longer and clearly curled at the ends. The plant needs a minimum temperature of 12°C (54°F).

Passiflora foetida

The scientific name means "smelly passionflower" and refers to the unpleasant smell emitted by the stems when they are damaged. The flowers are 5cm (2in) wide. They are white with a pink centre and are followed by edible fruits which have antler-like projections. The plant needs a minimum temperature of 12°C (54°F).

Passiflora foetida

Passiflora mollissima

BANANA PASSION FRUIT

This species from South America has beautiful light pink flowers which hang down and can develop fully even in a northern climate. The plant grows fantastically well in large containers and can produce a handsome display outside on a terrace or balcony. It needs a minimum temperature of 5°C (41°F).

Passiflora edulis

Passiflora subpeltata

This passionflower from tropical America has relatively small flowers (5cm (2in)) but they are so elegant that it would be good to see them more often. Unfortunately this species (with white, reflexed petals and an unkempt corona) is not often obtainable. It requires a cool, light position and a minimum temperature of 10°C (50°F).

Peperomia rotundifolia

The small leaves of *Peperomia rotundifolia* grow on stems of a few tens of centimetres in length which hang over the edge of the pot. They can be put in the sun (preferably with some protection on hot summer afternoons) and they only grow well in bright light. It is better to water too little than too much because stagnant water is fatal for this species. Use hand-warm water. The stems will easily root in humus-rich compost.

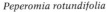

Peperomia rotundifolia

Philodendron scandens

HEART LEAF, SWEETHEART PLANT

The twining stems of the climbing philodendron search for the light even if grown a few metres away from the window. New,

Passiflora subpeltata

123

heart-shaped leaves keep opening at the tips of the stems. You can allow the stems to hang down or train them against something; they do not cling or barely cling by themselves.

Philodendron scandens can tolerate deep shade, heat, stale air, smoke and dryness. Just make sure that the pot is never allowed to stand in water. Use water at room temperature when watering and you will be able to enjoy the "eternal green" of this rewarding plant.

Philodendron scandens

● ◗

Plectranthus

Plectranthus is usually sold without any indication of species. There are many hybrids around. The habit of growth can help you to choose a plant. Some are typical hanging plants such as *Plectranthus madagascariensis*, *P. oertendahlii* and *P. verticillatus*, others can climb high against wires or sticks such as *P. forsteri* and *P. fruticosus*.

The variegated hybrids are the most popular. The hanging species can stay in the living room during the summer and the winter. They require average light levels and quite a high relative humidity. Always keep the soil moderately moist. The climbing species are best grown in containers. In summer put them

outside in the fresh air, in sun or semi-shade, and water liberally. In winter put them in a cool place and water sparingly.

Plectranthus

○–◑ ◐–○

Pyrostegia ignea

See: *Pyrostegia venusta*

Pyrostegia venusta

FLAME FLOWER/VINE, FLAMING TRUMPETS

This plant is really a climber suitable for a warm greenhouses where it can reach a great height and will flower beautifully from late-summer onwards. The plant is rarely available, but if you manage to get hold of a cutting or seedling, and do not have a conservatory, try growing it by a sunny window. Put the plant in a large pot with airy, fertile compost and water freely in spring and summer. Try to keep the humidity as high as possible such as one would find in its native region, South America. Keep it at a minimum temperature of 12°C (54°F) in winter and water regularly so that the leaves do not drop off. In spring the

Right: *Pyrostegia venusta*

plant can be cut back hard. It is a very suitable plant for training.

Rhipsalidopsis gaertneri

EASTER CACTUS

Christmas cactus and Easter cactus are often confused with each other. *Rhipsalidopsis gaertneri* is a typical spring flowering plant, full of orange-red flowers around Easter, at least if it does not get spoiled. I inherited my green fingers from my mother, who specialized in growing the Christmas cactus. This is her recipe for success: put *Rhipsalidopsis* in a cool room during the winter and keep it totally dry until the buds appear. Then put it in a heated room and gradually give it more water. Once the buds are half-grown keep the plant in the same position. (The buds grow towards the light and break themselves off if they suddenly have to grow in a different direction.) Keep watering moderately after flowering and make sure not too feed too much. Plants that are overfed flower poorly or not at all. If the soil looks useless the plant will probably flower well. Stem segments can be broken off. Let them dry for a few hours and then plant them shallowly in some compost: they will soon root.

Rhipsalis baccifera

See: *Rhipsalis cassutha*

Rhipsalis cassutha

MISTLETOE CACTUS

Rhipsalis cassutha is actually a cactus although this is hard to spot. It is a primitive species that does not grow only in America (like most other cacti) but also in Africa and Sri Lanka. The long stems do not have spines but a few bristles. It produces small white flowers in the winter followed by white berries in the spring. Provide a resting period in late season. Water hardly at all till the buds are visible. Then water more and hang the plant in a warm, light place. Never let the temperature drop below 10°C (50°F) and protect against direct sunlight in summer.

Rhipsalidopsis gaertneri

Rhipsalis cassutha

Rhodochiton atrosanguineum

PURPLE BELL-VINE

This Mexican climber has quickly become

Rhodochiton atrosanguineum

popular with a small group of very keen house plant amateurs in just a few years. They sow this perennial in pots every year to see it flower throughout the summer. It is possible to keep *Rhodochiton* through the winter but easier to re-sow indoors during March or April and put it outside in its pot in mid-May. It is possible to grow this climbing plant indoors if it is given a sunny but airy position. Give plenty of water and feed regularly. It will then carry on climbing and producing new flowers: aubergine-coloured tubes dangling from Bordeaux-red calices.

Saxifraga stolonifera

MOTHER OF THOUSANDS, STRAWBERRY GERANIUM

A feature of this plant is that young plantlets hang down on thin, red threads between the round leaves of the main- or mother-plant. They can be detached from the parent plant and put in a pot. This decorative hanging plant can also flower. Tiny flowers appear on slender stems, 30cm (12in) to 40cm (16in) long. The flowers have two long petals at the bottom and three red-spotted mini-petals pointing upwards at the top. Hang this plant in a light and airy position out of direct sunlight. Give average amounts of water and quite a high humidity. Saxifraga stolonifera originates in Japan and China. It can be kept cool in the winter and is, in fact, hardy and

Saxifraga stolonifera 'Cuscutiformis'

can be grown as a creeping plant in the garden in a semi-shady spot.

Scindapsus aureus

See: *Epipremnum pinnatum* 'Aureum'

Scindapsus pictus

In the wild the slender stems of *Scindapsus* attach themselves to the trunks and branches of trees. The heart-shaped leaves are about 10cm (4in) long and sheath the stems as if they were stuck to them. The cultivar 'Argyraeus' is the one which is nearly always on offer as a house plant. This cultivar is a juvenile form and hardly climbs. It can be tied up or grown as a hanging plant. It is important to give *Scindapsus* the highest possible humidity by growing it against a moss stick or on a bed of wet gravel. Spraying or misting are beneficial, but make sure that this is done with boiled water or rainwater for tap water will spoil the beautifully patterned foliage. The leaves feel like chamois leather and are not suited to being wiped with a damp cloth. The plant can tolerate quite a lot of shade but not direct sunlight and needs an average amount of water. Use hand-warm water and always keep the plant indoors.

Scindapsus pictus 'Argyraeus'

Scirpus cernuus

Nurserymen sometimes try to make Scirpus grow upright by letting a tuft of leaves and stems grow through a tube. As soon as they grow out of the tube however, they droop again and this, incidentally, looks rather odd.
Treat Scirpus as if it were a marsh plant. It should definitely never dry out if placed in a sunny position. If it can be put in a more shady spot it needs an average amount of water and it is not at all harmful if some water remains on its tray or in the outer pot. In time the plant can be rejuvenated by dividing the root clump. Make the environment of the plants as humid as possible.

Scirpus cernuus

Selenicereus grandiflorus

QUEEN OF THE NIGHT

In tropical countries, such as the Galapagos Islands, Queen of the Night grows in gardens. In temperate climates it needs to be kept frost-free in the winter if we are to be able to admire its enormous flowers. They can grow up to 30cm (12in) long. The plant puts all its energy into flowering for one night, during which it will hopefully be pollinated, for instance by bats. Put this large plant in a cool room in the winter (at a minimum of 10°C (50°F)) and water very little. In spring and summer you can water and feed liberally (for a cactus). Protect it against the hot afternoon sun. Only the older stems will produce flowers which it is well worth staying up to see.

Sedum morganianum

BEAVER-TAIL, BURRO'S TAIL

Right: *Selenicereus grandiflorus*

128

The cylindrical leaves of *morganianum* hang down on long stems. They are bluish and covered in a waxy layer to protect them from the sun's rays. You can safely hang this Mexican plant in the sun. It does not even matter if you occasionally forget to water it. However if the young leaves shrivel you know the plant is not getting enough water. The old leaves eventually drop off but, because new shoots develop all the time, you can rejuvenate the plant by cutting off the old "tails". You can also carefully pick off leaves to use them as cuttings.

Sedum morganianum 'Burrito'

Streptocarpus saxorum

FALSE AFRICAN VIOLET

This is one of the most beautiful of the streptocarpusses. It has creeping stems which hang down when they have no soil to support them. The velvety-haired leaves arch over the edge of the pot. And as if that were not enough, slender stalks sometimes appear between the leaves carrying one or two lilac to carmine-red flowers with a white eye which hover about 20cm (8in) above the plant. This is a beautiful sight. You do not even have to do much to achieve it. Hang the plant in a

light spot out of direct sunlight and water regularly, preferably with water at room temperature. The compost should never remain soaking wet, because with all

Streptocarpus saxorum

streptocarpusses this leads to root rot -- and they do not have many roots in any case.

Surfinea

Surfinea is the fancy name for petunias that have been propagated from cuttings. They have one unusual characteristic, they are truly hanging plants. The average petunia mainly grows sideways and arches elegantly over the edge of the pot. *Surfinea* has pendulous stems which are covered in flowers. *Surfinea's* are therefore particularly suitable for hanging baskets on terraces, outdoors in summer, or even indoors. Maintenance is very simple: plenty of water and light in the growing season with occasionally some liquid feed.

Thunbergia alata

BLACK-EYED SUSAN

Sowing *Thunbergia alata* is child's play. Push

Right: *Surfinea*

the big, brown seeds in a large pot in March. About six weeks later you will be enjoying the first flowers. They are orange with a deep-violet throat which looks like the pupil of an eye. This is how the plant got its name "Black-eyed Susan".In its native South Africa, Black-eyed Susan is a rampant climber. In temperate climates it can grow outside as long as night temperatures do not drop below 10°C (50°F). If grown in the open ground the stems will twine up to a height of 2m (6ft) around sticks, string or wire netting, and will become co-vered in flowers. In pots it will grow less fast but it will still flower for months on end.

If you do not want to sow, you can buy *Thunbergia alata* already in flower from April onwards. Put the plant in a light spot but not in the hot midday sun. A lot of water evapo-rates from the leaves, so it is necessary to water liberally, especially if you put the plant in its pot outside during the summer. Check regularly for red spider mite and spray often to avoid attacks from this pest. Put the plant outside if red spider mite or its webs occur. Bees will pollinate the flowers and big round fruits develop. When these are ripe they burst open and seeds fly around. This characteristic makes Black-eyed Susan an ideal plant for children. They can collect the big seeds, keep them for a few months, and sow them in

spring. In this way they can experience at first hand how seed-bearing plants reproduce from seed. Sometimes the seeds produce plants which have flowers of a new colour. Some of these are cultivated and available under names such as *Thunbergia alata* 'Alba' (white flowers with a dark throat). There are also forms with plain flowers without a dark pupil.

○ - ◑ ○

Thunbergia erecta

The unbelievably beautiful flowers of *Thunbergia erecta* bloom in Western Africa, where this climber originates. In northern Europe they are unfortunately hard to come by; you will have to search to find this gem. You could ask your supplier to try to order you one. *Thunbergia erecta* is a perennial which does not flower until a year after sowing. Treat it as a container plant and help it through the winter by putting it in a light, cool place (at a minimum temperature of 12°C (54°F) and watering it sparingly. Cut it back in spring but not too drastically because that will make it produce fewer flowers. It is better to train the stems against wire mesh or sticks to create a fresh-green screen using a pot as large as 1.5m (5ft). This in itself is a splendid

Left: *Thunbergia alata*   Below: *Thunbergia alata* 'Alba'

Thunbergia erecta

sight. Water copiously during the growing season and feed occasionally. *Erecta* needs to be hardened off at the end of the season by ceasing to feed it and gradually giving less water. Plants that are kept outside need to be brought indoors when the night temperature drops below about 10°C (50°F).

Thunbergia grandiflora

BLUE TRUMPET VINE

The blue to purple flowers of *Thunbergia grandiflora* are up to about 8cm (3in) long and wide. Until recently they only flowered in special collections of tropical plants. These days this climbing plant from India is on offer as a house plant but it is in short supply. To keep *Thunbergia* flowering it has to be kept growing vigorously. This is only possible if it is cultivated in a large pot or container in a conservatory or in the open ground in a greenhouse. Make sure the humidity is high and give it as warm a place as possible. But keep it out of the hot afternoon sun. This evergreen climber can be kept through the winter in a light location with a minimum temperature of 12°C (54°F). Take tip cuttings

Thunbergia gregorii

in spring and let them root in a warm spot (about 25°C (77°F)) in damp compost.

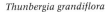

Thunbergia grandiflora

Thunbergia gregorii

Thunbergia gregorii is usually grown as an annual (see *T. alata* for method of sowing) but in very mild climates this unruly twiner from Africa can survive the winter outside when it loses its leaves and stems.

It will take some effort to keep *gregorii* alive as a pot plant through the winter but it is worth trying. Make sure that the stems stay alive as much as possible. This is not too difficult if the plant is kept at a temperature of 12°C (54°F) to 16°C(561°F) and is given enough water and light.

In summer this twining plant produces bright-orange flowers. It is possible to keep it inside by a sunny window but there has to be a fair amount of space available. Water copiously during flowering but give less when flowering diminishes.

Tolmiea menziesii

PICK-BACK/PIGGYBACK PLANT

From the centre of each leaf of *Tolmiea* a young plant grows. Snip away the "mother-leaf" as much as possible and put the "child" in damp, sandy soil where it will root rapidly. After rooting, pot the new plant in fertile soil, water liberally and give plenty of feed and light (preferably filtered sunlight). It will grow very rapidly outwards and eventually hang over the edge of the pot. In less favourable circumstances *Tolmiea* grows more slowly but it does not easily die. It is a very strong plant which can survive about fifteen degrees of frost if grown outside in the open ground. It can therefore also be grown as a garden plant. It is usual to buy one of the cultivars rather than the species, for example 'Maculata', 'Variegata' or 'Taff's Gold'. All three are variegated forms with light green foliage having cream-coloured to pale-yellow spots.

Tolmiea menziesii

Tradescantia

SPIDERWORTS

Tradescantia is one of the easiest hanging plants to cultivate. Long shoots hang down untidily over the edge of the pot. If they touch the soil they root readily and can be used as cuttings. The plant can be kept in the living room in the summer and the winter. The markings, especially of the variegated forms, will sharpen up if the plant is kept in the sun. Make sure to give enough water to avoid drying out. You can also hang the plant out of the sun in a light spot or in the semi-shade where it will need less water. Do not take any notice of the name given to a particular plant. The true species are usually not in cultivation or they are available under incorrect names. There are countless variegated forms with beautiful patterns of lines along the leaves. Choose the one you like best but remember that the stronger the variegation the more light the plant will require.

○ – ◐ ◑

Tradescantia fulminensis

Tradescantia zebrina

See: *Zebrina pendula*

Tropaeolum majus

NASTURTIUM

The nasturtium is a garden annual but it is also suitable for cultivation in the house. The true species seeks support and climbs up to a height of 1.5m (5ft). Without support it creeps or trails with long stems. Dwarf strains like 'Tom Thumb' have a bushy growth but also hang elegantly down over the edge of a pot.

Sow indoors in March, or outdoors in April to May, directly in a pot, container or window box. Give enough water when they are growing but never feed them. The plants flower a lot better in poor soil. Indoors *Tropaeolum majus* will only stay healthy if kept in the most airy place available. It is really better to put it outside in a sheltered spot in the sun or semi-shade. Instead of *Tropaeolum majus* you could choose to grow a canary creeper (*Tropaeolum peregrinum*). These are true climbers and have orange-yellow, fringed flowers. The leaves look like miniature fig leaves.

○ ○

Tropaeolum majus

Zebrina pendula

SILVERY INCH PLANT, WANDERING JEW

This species is so closely related to *Tradescantia* that it is called *Tradescantia zebrina* nowadays. Maintenance is the same as for the ordinary *Tradescantia*. 'Pendula' means hanging and refers to the leafy stems which are tens of centimetres long and trail over the edge of the pot. If given enough support they will creep upwards.

The foliage has particularly beautiful markings of olive-green and purple but the main part of the leaves of this species consists of wide, silvery stripes with a metallic sheen. Hang *Zebrina* ("the stripy one") in a light spot to enjoy its sheen and to keep the colours at their best.

○ – ◐ ◑

Zygocactus truncatus

CHRISTMAS CACTUS

A cactus that will flower indoors in winter has got to become popular. *Zygocactus* (also called *Schlumbergera)* is indeed sold great deal. It is a native of Rio in Brazil where it grows in trees. We grow the Christmas cactus in pots on the windowsill or in hanging baskets which can hang in front of a window (away from direct sunlight). Grow the plant in loose, peaty soil. It needs to be watered regularly in spring and summer and make sure that no water remains unabsorbed. Watering should be decreased gradually in late summer. As winter approaches hang the plant in a cool, light room (at a minimum temperature of 12°C (54°F) and do not bring it into the warmth until the flower buds appear. Keep watering sparingly even during flowering.

The Christmas cactus can tolerate the winter sun, but it needs some protection from the summer sun.

Zygocactus truncatus

10. Flowering plants

One refers to flowering plants as those which are cultivated especially for their flowers. Most foliage plants also produce flowers, but are they bought for their foliage.

The atmosphere in a house full of flowering plants is very different from one that is filled with foliage plants. Foliage plants create a cool atmosphere with an emphasis on form whereas a living room full of flowering plants tends to be warm and cosy. Even a rather cool and dark room can be livened up by flowering azeleas, calceolarias, clivias and hortensias which grow very well in such a climate. In warm and light rooms there are much greater possibilities. Most of the flowering plants that are dealt with in this chapter like warmth and light but not usually direct sunlight. If you want to fill a south-facing windowsill with flowers, you can find suitable species in this chapter as well as in the chapter on cacti, succulents and euphorbias.

Abutilon x hybridus

Countless hybrids of abutilon species are available under the collective name *Abutilon x hybridus*. They may have white, yellow, orange or red flowers or any shade in between. If these plants are kept growing well during the summer, by giving them plenty of water and feed in warm weather, they will eventually grow to about 2m (6ft) in height.

It is safe to put them in a sunny spot if they are grown outside. The sun is only harmful if they do not get enough water. The leaves will then curl up from the edge and drop off. If kept indoors they need protection from the sun when it is at its hottest. In winter the plant

Left: *Abutilon striatum* 'Thompsonii'   Below: *Abutilon* x *hybridus*

likes a light, cool position in a frost-free greenhouse or an unheated room. The best way to help them through the winter is to keep them at a temperature between 10°C (50°F) and 16°C (61°F), although some hybrids can tolerate a few degrees of frost when kept outside. Give very little water. Leaf-drop is normal. Prune in early spring leaving sufficient growing points on every branch. Plants that have been pruned sprout more vigorously in spring. Abutilons are sensitive to red spider mite, white fly, aphids and scale insects. An airy but draught-free location helps them avoid attacks from these pests.

Abutilon megapotamicum

This abutilon has red and yellow flowers and stamens which are sometimes purple. These colours give rise to its Dutch common name "Belgian flag", which is red, yellow and black. The bell-shaped flowers hang down like lanterns between the velvety green leaves. The stems on which the pointed leaves grow can easily be trained to produce a screen of flowers. *Abutilon megapotamicum* originates in Brazil but it can tolerate about ten degrees of

frost if grown outside in open ground. Do not put this to the test with pot-grown plants. Bring them indoors before the first night frost. Care is otherwise the same as that of *Abutilon x hybridus*.

Abutilon pictum

See: *Abutilon striatum*

Abutilon striatum

This species, which is officially called *Abutilon pictum*, has yellow-orange flowers with conspicuously thick veins, darker than the rest of the flower. *Abutilon striatum* is a sturdy shrub which can be successfully cultivated as a container plant (kept outside during the summer in a large pot and kept dry during the winter in a frost-free, light spot). The species soon grows too big for the living room. It is the cultivars which are usually available. 'Thompsonii' is particularly popular because of its yellow-green, mottled foliage. The mottling is caused by a "mosaic virus". Unfortunately the attractive effect does not

Left: *Abutilon megapotamicum*

Below: *Abutilon striatum* 'Thompsonii'

occur if the plant is propagated from seed as the virus is "cured". It is better, therefore, to propagate abutilon cultivars from cuttings. These should be put to root in compost or water at about 20ºC (68ºF).

Acalypha hispida

RED-HOT CAT'S TAIL, CHENILLE PLANT

Acalypha is particularly noted for its long tassels, densely packed with flowers, which makes them look like reddish, hairy tails. At first they grow obliquely upwards from the leaf axils, later bending over and hanging down. They can grow up to 50cm (20in) in length.
Put the red-hot cat's tail in a warm, light spot, even in direct sun light and always water liberally. This plant, which originates in Indonesia, should never be allowed to dry out completely or to remain standing in water.

Achimenes

HOT WATER PLANTS

In spring, the counters in plant outlets are full of colourful *Achimenes* hybrids. They show a

Acalypha hispida

mass of pretty red, pink or purple flowers. Choose whichever colour you like best -- the care is the same for all. Put *Achimenes* in a light spot but definitely out of direct sunlight. It likes a warm place because it is a native of tropical America. Water evenly in the growing

Achimenes

season with hand-warm water making sure that the root ball never dries out. Do not spray hot water plants but humidify the air as much as possible. In late season the foliage dies down, at which point hot water plants are usually thrown away because they are thought to be dead. In fact they only entering a resting period for the winter. Cease watering and put the pot somewhere cool (at a minimum temperature of 10°C (50°F)) and even dark if need be. In spring, when the growing points start to show signs of life, the rootstocks can be re-potted in fresh compost. This is a good time to divide the root ball. Gradually give more water and put the plant back in a light, humid spot and it will flower again.

Allamanda cathartica

GOLDEN TRUMPET

Deep inside the Brazilian interior people decorate their houses with a evergreen plant from the forest which we call *Allamanda cathartica*. Its beauty has now been discovered by lovers of conservatory and container plants. If grown in a very large pot the shoots climb quite quickly. If kept indoors *Allamanda* grows more slowly and often remains bushy. To flower profusely the plant needs plenty of sunlight, preferably direct, an average amount of water and occasional feeding.

Amaryllis

The "amaryllis" which is bought in the shops is not an actual amaryllis, although it looks like one; it is officially called *Hippeastrum* and is a bulb species from South Africa which is naturalized on the Azores and the British Channel Islands. The true *Amaryllis* is obtainable only from bulb specialists. Plant the bulb in spring with its nose above the soil. Give an average amount of water and food while the bulb has its strap-shaped, green leaves. Halfway through the summer, during its leafless period, water moderately and do not feed. Always give it the warmest possible place on a terrace or in a conservatory or greenhouse. In late summer the leafless bulb may produce a sturdy flower stalk but this does not usually happen until a year later. It will certainly produce leaves in late season. The plant needs a light, frost-free place in winter and very little water. Re-pot as little as possible.

The *Hippeastrum* varieties, well known in the

Allamanda cathartica

Amaryllis belladonna

living room, nearly all originate in the mountainous regions of South America. Most of them are offered for sale as winter flowering bulbs. The bulbs should be planted in late summer, one-third under and two-thirds above the soil. Keep the pot in a light, cool place (about 15°C (59°F)). A higher temperature will make the bulb flower sooner but for a shorter period. Water liberally during the growing and flowering period and feed regularly. Cut off the flowerstalk after flowering and keep watering and feeding as long as the foliage remains green. High temperatures are very important during this period. Stop watering and feeding as soon as the foliage starts to die down. Put the plant away in a cool spot

Hippeastrum (amaryllis)

and start watering again as soon as leaves and buds appear. The many available cultivars of wild *Hippeastrum* are usually offered without specific names. The flowers of the cultivars are larger, fiery-red, pink, salmon-coloured, orange or white, sometimes multi-coloured, veined or "picotee" (with a thin coloured band along the edge of each petal).

○ – ◑ ◑ – ○

Anigozanthos

KANGAROO PAW

All the eleven species of kangaroo paw originate in the dry regions of western Australia. They were discovered and imported as a curiosity for our living rooms and used to be taken from their natural habitat to such an extent that their survival was threatened. Nowadays they are in common cultivation, but nice varieties and hybrids are few and far between. The kangaroo paw is likely to remain a rare plant because it is not easy to grow in the living room and will usually die in its first year, even if the directions for its care are closely followed. Give plenty of light, preferably direct sunlight. Water liberally during the growing and flowering periods but keep the plant quite dry during the winter at a

Anigozanthos

minimum temperature of 5°C (41°F). Give humus-rich compost, for instance leaf-mould, and water with rainwater or boiled water.

Anthurium

Hundreds of species of *Anthurium* grow in the tropics in damp forest soil or hanging in trees. They like high humidity and high temperatures and usually require a tropical greenhouse to keep healthy. Two species appear to be suited to the climate of our living rooms. These are *Anthurium andreanum* (originally from Colombia) and especially *Anthurium scherzerianum* (originally from Costa Rica).

They have been in cultivation since halfway through the last century and over the years many cultivars have been developed. They are usually on offer without specific names. Anthuriums belong to the *Araceae* family. The spathe is the most striking part of the plant. Over the years plant breeders have bred a considerable number of cultivars with good colours. Usually the spathe is red, orange, pink or white but nowadays there are also spotted forms.

Anthurium Scherzerianum-hybrids (flamingo

Anthurium Scherzerianum-hybrid

flowers) can be recognized by their convex and almost round spathe and their relatively slender, often slightly curved, spadix.

Anthurium Andreanum-hybrids (tail flowers)

Anthurium andreanum 'Lady Jane'

have a slightly fatter, shorter and straighter spadix while their spathe is more heart-shaped and clearly pointed as well as nearly always strikingly glossy as if lacquered. The flower structures are often used as cut flowers. As a house plant, andreanum needs a higher humidity and temperature.

Anthurium Scherzerianum-hybrids can grow very well in living rooms. Put them in a light but not too sunny spot. They can tolerate "ill-treatment", but treat them well by giving them loose, humus-rich soil and watering regularly but not too much. Use rainwater or boiled water at room temperature. Put the flamingo flower in a light place but preferably not in the bright summer sun.

Aphelandra squarrosa

ZEBRA PLANT

Aphelandra has double decorative value. In the summer yellow flowers bloom between warm yellow spathes. In the rest of the year the variegated foliage steals the show. It is quite a difficult task to keep the plant healthy and it needs a high level of care. Never let it dry out otherwise the foliage will turn brown or drop and pests may attack. Water with soft water or rainwater at room temperature or warmer. Put this plant from Brazil in a warm, light place but definitely out of direct sunlight. Make sure the humidity is as high as possible and spray often. If you manage to do all of this you will see new buds appearing in the following year.

Begonia Elatior-hybrids

WINTER FLOWERING BEGONIAS

Nine out of ten begonias that are on offer belong to the Eliator hybrids. These are a cross between tuberous begonias and the winter flowering *Begonia socotrana*. They develop into full, round plants which flower for a long time. The flowers will even open in winter as long as the plant is kept in a light spot, but placed elsewhere the buds will drop off.

The buds will also drop off if you keep the plant too cold or too warm (below 10°C (50°F) or above 20°C (68°F)), if you do not water enough or if you change the plant's position during flowering. Mark the pot or put a match stick in the compost so that you can always return the plant to exactly the same position. Always keep the soil mildly moist using water

at room temperature and feed regularly because its abundant flowering will soon exhaust the plant. Put it in a light position preferably with morning and evening sun but never in the full midday sun. You can keep Eliator in a heated room throughout the year as long as the temperature does not change rapidly and there is no draught. If you discover a white powdery haze on the foliage throw the plant away immediately. This is a sign of mildew from which the plant will not recover.

Begonia Elatior hybrid

Begonia

Begonia Lorraine hybrid

The countless Lorraine hybrids have been cultivated from *Begonia socotrana*, a native of the Yemeni island Socotra, and the South African species *Begonia dregei*. The rounded plants flower in late season and winter with natural-looking flowers. The buds will not develop into flowers in too warm a spot .

Put Lorraine in a cool place (at least cooler than 20ºC 68ºF)) and give sufficient fresh air and plenty of light, but no direct afternoon sun. To avoid mildew and stem rot it is best to water into a saucer or dish under the pot, or into an outer pot, using water at room temperature. After about an hour make sure the pot is not still standing in water because Lorraine will defenitely not tolerate this. It is better to water too little than too much.

Begonia minor

Begonia minor belongs to the approximately 1000 natural species of begonia which grow in the warmer regions of America, Africa and Asia. *Begonia minor* (also called *Begonia nitida*), which originates in Jamaica, is one of

Page 147: *Aphelandra squarrosa*

Begonia Lorraine hybrid

the few botanical species which are in cultivation. In the house it can grow over the whole of a north or east facing window. The stems are up to 2m (6ft) in height and grow towards the light. Keep the plant away from direct sunlight. A relatively light, cool but not chilly spot is best.

Begonia nitida

See: *Begonia minor*

Below: *Begonia minor*

Begonia sutherlandii

This African tuberous begonia has orange flowers which contrast beautifully with its olive-green foliage. Nowadays it is often sold as a hanging plant for terraces. This is a good choice because *Begonia sutherlandii* likes fresh air and can tolerate low temperatures. It does not need to be brought inside until the first night frosts are expected. It will flower throughout the summer on a windowsill indoors and eventually the pot will be completely hidden by a curtain of flowering stems. Give average amounts of water and put the plant in a very light position, protected from the hottest afternoon sun. Keep it cool and quite dry throughout the winter. In late season you will find little tubers in the leaf axils which you can plant in a pot. If looked after properly they will flower in their second year.

Begonia 'Tamaya'

Foliage and flowers of this newly introduced cultivar hang down from a single short stem which makes 'Tamaya' look like a bonsai. The plant is usually for sale planted in a decorative

Begonia 'Tamaya'

pot which reinforces the bonsai effect. Just like a real bonsai the plant has to be pruned to keep its shape. This is best done after flowering because the pendulous flowers with their conspicuous ovaries are far too beautiful to be snipped off. Put 'Tamaya' in a light position but not in the bright afternoon sun. Give average amounts of water and feed regularly.

Beloperone guttata

Beloperone guttata

SHRIMP PLANT

The flowers of the shrimp plant are protected by greenish to pink overlapping bracts which together look rather like a shrimp. The small flowers are inconspicuous. If looked at closely they are a beautiful white with deep-red flecks. This plant originates in Mexico and can safely be put in direct sunlight which will encourage the flower structure to form better colours. The shrimp plant is a rewarding house plant which can reach a height of about 50cm (20in). Put in a light, cool spot during the winter and keep quite dry. Prune back hard in spring.

Water liberally in summer and feed regularly to encourage flowering. The plant can be propagated in spring from semi-ripe cuttings.

Browallia speciosa

BUSH VIOLET

The purple-blue flowers of *Browallia speciosa* appear month after month. This mini- shrub will keep flowering longer if you pinch out the dead flowers. Put it in a sunny, bright posi-

Browallia speciosa

tion, water regularly, without overwatering, and feed occasionally.

In the wild *Browallia spesiosa* is a native perennial of Colombia. In northern Europe it is usually grown as an annual. Sow from late winter onwards, providing warmth from beneath of as least 18°C (64°F). Pinch out the tips of the seedlings to get compact plants, which will flower about ten weeks after sowing.

Calceolaria

SLIPPER FLOWER, POCKET BOOK PLANT

The sunny slipper flower is an annual pot plant which only grows well in shady places. Put it by a north or east facing window and enjoy the inflated flowers. These plants are all on the market under the name *Calceolaria x herbeohybrida* despite being available in various patterns of colours and spots.

The true lover of this plant, who knows that it likes a position in the shade and that it is averse to the heat and needs quite a lot of water, will be rewarded with an abundance of flowers. As soon as the plant has finished flowering you may as well throw it away because it will not flower again.

Slipper flowers are sown in late season. If you are really keen you can get the seedlings through the winter but it is much easier to buy new plants in spring.

Calceolaria

Campanula isophylla

ITALIAN BELLFLOWER

The blue, star-shaped flowers of the Italian bellflower shine brightly throughout the summer. New flowers keep appearing and give months of enjoyment especially when the plant is given an airy and temperate position. Keep it away from direct sunlight but give it a bright place.

When the Italian bellflower grows in the wild in the mountains of northern Italy it can tolerate frost. This is definitely not the case with the pot-grown plants, which need a minimum temperature of 5°C (41°F) in the winter. The best place is a cool room where the plants need very little water. However, water liberally in summer. The compost needs to be free draining because the roots will rot in stagnant water.

As well as the blue-flowering species the white-flowering *Campanula isophylla* 'Alba' is sold a lot. *Campanula isophylla* 'Mayi' is the most popular blue cultivar. It has larger, purple-blue flowers.

Campanula isophylla 'Alba'

Capsicum annuum

CHILLIES, RED/SWEET PEPPER

Chillies and sweet peppers descend from *Capsicum annuum* which probably used to grow wild in South America. The species is also the parent of countless cultivars which have been bred as decorative plants. From early summer onwards there is a choice of

Capsicum annuum

plants available in plant shops and garden centres. The plants have red, orange-yellow, green or aubergine-coloured fruits which develop from white flowers. They remain on the plants till well into the winter.

Place your decorative pepper in a very light and airy spot, preferably in direct sunlight and give an average amount of water. When the fruits eventually shrivel up you may as well throw the plant away because it will not flower again. You can collect the seeds and sow them in early spring keeping them at a temperature of about 20°C 68°F).

Catharanthus roseus

MADAGASCAR PERIWINKLE

The Madagascar periwinkle is one of the most popular of annual border plants because it flowers profusely for a very long time. This plant from Madagascar also rewards you with flowers throughout the summer if grown on a balcony, a terrace or windowsill.

Catharanthus (until recently better known under its old name *Vinca rosea)* can go outside when all danger of frost has passed. Indoors as well as outdoors it needs a sunny position and plenty of moisture. However if its roots are left to stand in water they will rot away.

Throw the plant away after a season of flowering unless you want to take cuttings. In that case keep the plant in a cool room and water moderately. Stem cuttings taken in spring will root well in water. Propagation from seed is also possible by sowing the seed in March or April under glass.

Catharanthus roseus

Celosia argentea

This plant originates in Indonesia where it grows alongside fields and roads in places where there has been a fire recently. Where I photographed the plant it grew slender and erect with pink plumes at the end of stems of about 50cm (20in) in length. Traces of an earlier fire were still visible.

The plumes of the true species may also be silvery. The plant has such unprecedented beauty that it cannot be improved by breeding in any way. Even so, there are an incredible number of cultivars of *Celosia argentea* in which the species can hardly be recognized. The plants are compact and have thick plumes (these are the so-called *Plumosa* hybrids). The plumes are sometimes cristate (these are the *Cristata* hybrids). All of them come in very artificial, fluorescent yellow, pink, red or orange colours.

They can be grown in the garden as annuals but the plumes will become unsightly in wet summers whereas indoors they remain pretty. Put the plants in a sunny spot but protect them from the hottest effects of the afternoon sun. The cultivars have no special requiremants for care and an average amount of water is fine.

Celosia argentea

Chrysanthemum Indicum-hybrids

FLORISTS' CHRYSANTHEMUM

The most important parent of the florists' chrysanthemum is *Chrysanthemum indicum*, a native of Japan or China. Its origin is not certain because the Chinese have been crossbreeding species since at least 500bc. These ancient ancestors have given rise to all the countless modern cultivars.

Originally the florists' chrysanthemum flowered inlate season; the shorter hours of daylight encouraged the plant to flower. Now, breeders trick chrysanthemums by giving them either more hours of darkness or more hours of light. This way flowering chrysanthemums are kept available throughout the year. Breeders also use growth inhibitors, to keep the plants compact, and a lot of pesticides. Because the cultivation of chrysanthemums is energy-intensive and very polluting it comes in for a lot of criticism. You can help by only buying them in late season.

Keep the root ball of chrysanthemums mildly damp because if the compost dries out the foliage will turn yellow. If you water too much the plant will rot. Make sure the flower buds do not get wet, because they rot easily and do not spray the plant. Put it in a light spot out of direct sunlight. It should be kept quite cool. At

Chrysanthemum Indicum hybride

a temperature of about 16°C (62°F) to 18°C (64°F) the plant will flower for weeks.

The plumes of *Celosia argentea*

Chrysothemis pulchella

Not very long ago it was generally assumed that *Chrysothemis* could not be cultivated in the house because the rooms were too dry. The deep-green foliage of this plant requires a high humidity.

Spray the plant often in the summer during the growing season or raise the humidity surrounding the plant by putting it on a bed of wet gravel.

Fortunately *Chrysothemis* loses its leaves and stems in the winter and spends the cold months as a dormant root tuber.

In spring put the tuber in fertile, mildly moist compost so that the leaves can sprout again. Flowers will follow if you put the plant in a light position but out of direct sunlight and at a temperature of at least 16°C (61°F).

Cineraria

See: *Senecio* Cruentus-hybrids

Chrysothemis pulchella

Clerodendrum paniculatum

PAGODA FLOWER

This plant originates in South-East Asia where it is called the pagoda flower. Some species have medicinal properties. Their effect on patients appears to be rather variable. Specimens of *Clerodendrum paniculatum* such as the cultivar 'Starshine' have only recently been made available for living room cultivation. They require as much humidity as possible, a large pot of fertile compost, plenty of water in the growing season and a sunny position. In the winter they like a cool room

Clerodendrum paniculatum

154

Clerodendrum paniculatum 'Starshine'

(with a maximum temperature of 15°C (59°F)) and little water. Prune the plant lightly after flowering to encourage bushy growth and beautiful flowers in spring.

Clerodendrum thomsoniae

BLEEDING HEART VINE, GLORY BOWER

The bleeding heart vine originates in West Africa and has been in cultivation as a house plant for a long time. Bright red flowers with long stamens appear from white bell-shaped calyces.

This plant is bought as small shrub, kept low with growth inhibitors. As soon as these have lost their efficacy the true character of the plant will become apparent. In its second year *thomsoniae* will start to climb and will have to be pruned hard after flowering to be kept within bounds.

The bleeding heart vine should be grown in a very light spot that is preferably sunny but not too hot. Water moderately in summer and less in winter keeping the temperature at a minimum of 15°C (59°F) during this resting period.

Clerodendrum ugandense

BLUE GLORY BOWER

This gem from Central Africa has only recently become available. It grows like a bush and is sold flowering with elegant purple to light-blue flowers resembling a butterfly, the stamens being the antennae.

Blue glory bower requires a warm and sunny position and high humidity. Put it on a bed of

Clerodendrum thomsoniae

wet gravel and spray as often as possible. Water freely in summer.

Put it in a cool room in winter (minimum temperature 15°C (59°F)) and water little.

Clerodendrum ugandense

Clivia miniata

KAFFIR LILY

This clivia originates in South Africa where it rests during the dry season. If you give it a period of rest it will reward you with an abundance of flowers. In late season put the clivia in a cool (between 8°C (46°F) and 15°C

Clivia miniata

(59°F)) and dry spot. In spring a flower stem will appear in the centre of the plant. Wait till this is at least 10cm (4in) high before bringing the plant into a heated room. Gradually give more water. The plant responds well to plenty of water and feed during flowering but never allow it to stand in water. Clivias do not tolerate direct sunlight but can tolerate quite a lot of shade.

Re-pot as little as possible. In time potable offshoots will develop at the base of the plants. It is possible to propagate from seed but it will take many years to produce a flowering plant this way.

Clivia nobilis

CLIVIA

This clivia is rarely available. It flowers profusely with pendent, orange-red flowers which grow on a relatively slender stalk. The leaves are also slender and have rough edges. Maintenance is the same as for *Clivia miniata*.

Clivia nobilis

Curcuma domestica

See: *Curcuma longa*

Curcuma zedoaria

Curcuma zedoaria is related to turmeric *(Curcuma longa)*, a rare Indian plant for the tropical greenhouse. It belongs to the ginger family (Zingiberaceae) and, like ginger, has knobbly yellow rhizomes. These are used to produce turmeric, the well known Indian cooking spice.

Curcuma zedoaria, which is itself is used to produce a different spice, has, in recent times, become available as a house plant. Long, green and pink flower spikes arise erect from between the beautiful, oblong leaves. The flowers themselves are inconspicuous, half-hidden between the lower, green bracts.

Curcumas are not easy house plants to care for. In summer they require heat and moist air. They like a light position but it must be out of direct sunlight. Water in moderation. Late in the growing season, after the foliage has died off, the pot can be put somewhere dry and cool, 10°C (50°F) to 15°C (59°F). Re-pot in early spring when the root tubers can be divided. Start watering when the buds/growing points begin to sprout.

Curcuma zedoaria

Cyclamen Persicum hybrids

Cyclamen persicum originates in the mountains from Greece to Iran. It is the ancestor of the florists' cyclamen which is sold in every possible colour and form. Although there are forms with large flowers, in bright colours, sometimes with fringed petals, nowadays the cultivars with small flowers are more in demand. This is no surprise because they are more robust and smell lovely.

Cyclamen are often disappointing. The leaves turn yellow, the flower stalks droop or the centre of the plant rots. Sometimes the trouble has already started before the plant is bought as a result of incorrect treatment by the supplier. Never buy a cyclamen which has been sitting outside at a temperature below 10°C (50°F) or one with yellow or limp foliage. Unwrap the cyclamen as soon as you get it home. Put it in a cool, light spot out of direct sunlight: 16°C (61°F) is ideal. In a warmer place it flowers for a much shorter period. Give the plant plenty of fresh air but avoid draughts.

Water with boiled water or rainwater at room temperature. Never water in the centre of the plant because that will cause rot. It is best to fill a dish with water under the plant pot. Do not spray the cyclamen while it is flowering and keep the compost well watered but not soaking wet. Withering leaves and dead flowers can be pulled away from the corm using a twisting movement.

The cyclamen likes fertilizer during and after flowering . Stop watering and feeding as soon as the leaves start to wither. The plant is entering a resting period. Lay the pot on its side in a cool place (about 10°C (50°F)).

Cyclamen persicum

As soon as growth begins again re-pot the corm in a relatively small pot and put it in a warmer place.

Dendrathema indicum

See: *Chrysanthemum indica*

Dianthus

Dianthus is usually grown for the garden but there are also special varieties for indoor cultivation. They are usually the offspring of typical outdoor plants like *Dianthus caryophyllus* (Carnation), which is often double flowered, and *Dianthus chinensis* (Indian pink). But there are also other species which can produce offspring for pot culture.

Put the flowering plants on a windowsill preferably in full sun but do not allow to become too hot.

Keep the compost moderately moist and feed regularly. *Dianthus* can be planted outside after flowering.

Dianthus

Eustoma grandiflorum

PRAIRIE GENTIAN

Eustoma grows in the wild in the dry and sunny border region between Mexico and the United States. The foliage is waxy and adapted to these conditions. Put the plant in a sunny position and do not water too much. It can tolerate dry air very well. *Eustoma* likes fresh air and a constant temperature. Do not put the

Eustoma grandiflorum

pot above a central heating radiator as the compost should not get too warm. As well as the pink strains eustomas are available with white and purple flowers and every shade in between. The centre is usually darker.

Exacum affine

This plant was discovered on the Yemeni island of Socotra where it is extremely dry. *Exacum* grows on the edges of wadis, the dry channels through which water flows after heavy rain storms. These are the places that stay damp the longest.

Water *Exacum* sufficiently but make sure the bottom of the plant does not stay standing in water. The plant reaches a height of several tens of centimetres and grows best in a very light but not too sunny position at room temperature.

Flowering plants are available between March and October depending on when the growers sowed them. They are blue-purple or white, and single or double flowered. Throw *Exacum* away after flowering because, although it can survive the winter, it is better to treat it as an annual.

Exacum affine

Exacum affine

Freesia

Freesias surprise us in the dark months of the year with sweet smelling flowers in all kinds of colours, especially white, yellow and pink to

Exacum affine

blue. The yellow ones are the most fragrant. They are offered as cut-flowers in the winter and spring but can equally well be supplied as flowering pot plants. They originate in South Africa where they form corms which survive the dry season while the foliage dies off completely. This also happens with a pot-grown freesia.

In theory it is possible to keep the corms alive until the following year by starting to grow them outside in late summer when the temperature is lower. The keen amateur can try this but others just throw the plant away after it flowers.

Sometimes flowering pot freesias are available in summer. These are grown from specially treated corms which produce the so-called garden freesias. It is not worth trying to keep these corms alive.

In the dark months freesias may be kept in the sun, in summer in a light place out of the sun. At lower temperatures they flower longer (16°C (61°F) is the best). Water normally.

Fritillaria meleagris

SNAKE'S HEAD FRITILLARY

The snake's head fritillary is one of the most rewarding bulbous plants and is nowadays sold as a flowering pot plant in spring. It has narrow, waxy blue-green foliage and slender stems which carry bell-shaped flowers about the size of an egg. They have a chequered pattern in deep-red to aubergine, or are white. Put the plant in a light, preferably sunny position and always keep the compost moist during growing and flowering. Do not throw the plant away after flowering. Put it outside in the wettest spot in the garden, for example near a pond. As long as the soil stays moist even in summer it will come back year after year and sow itself.

You can also re-pot the bulbs in late season and dig them in, in their pot, outside. Bring them back inside in April when they are flowering.

Flowering can be brought forward by bringing the plants in sooner. Make sure the compost never dries out and do not keep the plant too warm because a hotter plant means shorter flowering period.

Gardenia augusta

See: *Gardenia jasminoides*

Gardenia grandiflora

See: *Gardenia jasminoides*

Left: *Fritillaria meleagris*

Below: *Freesia*

Gardenia jasminoides

COMMON GARDENIA, CAPE JASMINE

The Cape jasmine originates in South-East Asia. Its cream-coloured flowers smell delicious. They appear from early summer until well into the winter on the evergreen shrubs. These can be kept healthy by putting them in a light, warm and humid spot out of direct sunlight. Water only with rainwater or boiled water at room temperature. Gardenia is allergic to chalk which causes its leaves to turn yellow and drop off. The plant does not need to be re-potted often but when this is done use an acid, humus-rich, compost. Give plenty of water during the growing season but little after flowering in late winter and spring when the plant is resting. Keep it cool at 12°C (54°F) to 16°C (61°F). It can be pruned when it grows too big.

Gerbera jamesonii

BARBERTON DAISY

This plant from South Africa has given rise to countless hybrids with flowers in all possible colours, single or double. They are often used

Gerbera jamesonii hybrid

in bouquets, the stems supported by wire. The short stemmed strains are best for pot culture. After choosing a colour, put the flowering plant in a very light spot with some protection against direct sun. Water a little at a time so that the compost never dries out or becomes soaking wet. Gerberas like warmth when they are flowering. They can survive the winter if

Gardenia jasminoides

162

kept cool and drier but they will never flower as abundantly as in their first year.

Gloxinia latifolia

The true gloxinia, *Gloxinia latifolia*, (also called *Seemannia*) is from the tropical Americas. The plant with large bell-shaped flowers which is sold under the name "gloxinia" is described in the entry under its correct name *Sinningia..* The true *Gloxinia* is being dealt with here. It has bladder-shaped red flowers carried on juicy stems with oblong leaves. It can be treated in the same way as *Achimenes*. Put it in a light and sunny position but not in direct sunlight. Keep the root ball evenly moist by watering regularly with luke-warm water and make sure the humidity is as high as possible. Do not spray the flowers. In late season the foliage dies off and the plant enters a resting period. Stop watering and put the pot in a cool place (minimum temperature 10°C (50°F)), if necessary in the dark. Take the rhizomes out of the pot in spring when the first shoots appear, and put them in fresh compost. Gradually increase watering and put the plant back in a lighter and warmer position.

Gloxinia latifolia

Haemanthus coccineus

This brilliant variety is rarely on offer. The plant flowers with cup-shaped red bracts in late season before its foliage appears. The real flowers are within the bracts and only the yellow stamens are visible. Immediately after

flowering the plant produces two or three beautifully marked leaves. For maintenance see *Haemanthus multiflorus*.

Haemanthus coccineus

Haemanthus multiflorus

BLOOD FLOWER

Blood flowers may be found in bloom on the East African island of Zanzibar in the shelter of shrubs, where it is warm and quite dry. This climate is similar to that in a living room and this bulbous plant can flower there profusely with pink-red flowers arranged in large umbels

Haemanthus multiflorus in the wild on Zanzibar

which are 20cm (8in) to 30cm (12in) across. The stamens are most conspicuous: they stick a long way out like the hairs on a paint brush. Plant the bulb with it nose just below soil level or buy the plant in flower in summer or later. The plant thrives in a very light but not too sunny position and requires plenty of water and plant feed during the growing period.

Give the bulb a rest as soon as the foliage turns yellow by keeping it in its pot in a cool place at minimum temperature of 10°C (50°F), and hardly water it at all. Let the bulb remain in its pot as long as possible because it dislikes disturbance to its roots.

Hippeastrum

See: *Amaryllis*

Hydrangea macrophylla

COMMON/FRENCH HYDRANGEA

The common hydrangea has naturalized in the Azores which have ideal conditions for it, a mild sea climate and acid volcanic soil. Living rooms are now too dry for the common

Hydrangea macrophylla

hydrangea. Put it in as cool a place as possible, preferably light and above all humid. In these conditions the rounded blooms will provide enjoyment for a long time.

Give hydrangeas plenty of soft water - rainwater is ideal, boiled water a good second choice.

If the leaves turn yellow but do not droop the soil has become too alkaline. Re-pot the hydrangea in humus-rich, acid compost, preferably very fertile. The leaves will droop if you forget to water the plant. In that case

Impatiens hawkeri 'New Guinea' hybrid

immerse the pot until the compost is saturated. After flowering, the plant can be pruned and put outside, but it is not certain to survive the winter. and it may be kept indoors instead. From late season until the new buds open in spring, keep the plant fairly dry.

As well as the mop-headed cultivars, the hortensias, there are the so-called serrata cultivars, the lacecaps. They have inconspicuous fertile flowers which are surrounded by a ring of larger, more conspicuous, sterile flowers.

Impatiens hawkeri

The countless cultivars of *Impatiens hawkeri* are together called the "New Guinea" hybrids since the species originates there.

These sturdy plants can grow to several tens of centimetres in height. They often have dark foliage and sharply contrasting brightly-coloured flowers. Suppliers usually have a mixed selection of hybrids which they sell under the collective name 'New Guinea'.

Treat them as annuals. Put them in a light but not too sunny spot and they will flower throughout the summer. A lot of moisture evaporates through the leaves and this needs to be replenished through copious watering. Do not let the roots stand in water because this will make them rot. The plants appreciate being sprayed on warm days but keep them dry on dark days otherwise the flowers, as well as the buds, will become mouldy. Take off the affected flowers if this happens. For methods of propagation, see Impatiens walleriana.

Impatiens linearifolia

See: *Impatiens hawkeri*

Impatiens 'New Guinea' hybrids

See: *Impatiens hawkeri*

Impatiens walleriana

BUSY LIZZIE, PATIENT LUCY

The cultivars of this East African *Impatiens* are mainly sold as garden annuals, but they are also very well suited to hanging baskets and flower tubs on terraces and balconies as well as for pots in conservatories and indoor rooms. In places like Madeira which never get any frost, Busy Lizzies grow into shrubs of about 1m (3ft) in height. In colder climates there is not much point in keeping them through the winter. Lack of light in the winter causes lanky growth and leaf drop, and the plants look battered in spring. You could try to keep the healthiest specimens of *walleriana* and *Impatiens* hawkeri and use them for taking cuttings in early spring. These will root very easily in water and can then be potted on. For further maintenance see *Impatiens hawkeri*.

Ixora coccinea

FLAME-OF-THE-WOODS

This plant from India and Sri Lanka used to be cultivated only in tropical greenhouses. However the brilliant corymbs tempted

Impatiens walleriana hybrid

traders to make Ixora available as an indoor plant. The corymbs can be yellow, salmon-pink, pink, orange or brick-red depending on the subspecies or cultivar.

Unfortunately the pleasure is usually short-lived. This evergreen plant only grows well in a warm, humid atmosphere in a light spot protected from direct sunlight. Although the leathery foliage does not suggest it, this Ixora needs plenty of water, preferably luke-warm rainwater. It also benefits from regular low doses of house plant fertilizer. The life-span of this beautiful plant can be prolonged by

Ixora coccinea

position in winter although the temperature should never drop below 15°C (59°F).

Jacobinia carnea

KING'S CROWN

Nowadays this species is officially called *Justicia carnea* but the old name is still in general use in the plant trade. "Carnea" refers to the flesh-coloured flowers which appear from summer until late season. Breeders are able to produce flowering plants for the market from April by propagating the plants very early.

The species originates in South America where it grows into a shrub of about 2m (6ft) in height. In our climate it is best grown in a tropical greenhouse, although you could try it in a light, warm spot in the living room. Make the humidity as high as possible by spraying often and by putting the pot on a bed of wet gravel or on an upside-down saucer in a tray of water. Water and feed liberally in summer. Water little in winter and put the plant in a light place at a minimum temperature of 15°C (59°F).

If it still loses a lot of leaves and becomes permanently bare at its base you can produce

putting it in a large pot of humus-rich, fertile compost. After it has flowered, spray the plant regularly.

The cultivars of coccinea like a light, cool

Ixora coccinea

Jacobinia carnea

new plants by taking semi-hardwood stem cuttings in spring.

Justicia carnea

See: *Jacobinia carnea*

Justicia brandegeana

See: *Beloperone guttata*

Kohleria amabilis

The flowers of the Colombian plant, *Kohleria amabilis*, are about 7cm (3in) long and 3cm (1in) wide. They appear on stalks from the upper leaf axils. The plant grows to about 50 cm ((20in) high. Stems and leaves are covered in downy hairs. This beautiful plant rises from oblong underground rhizomes which keep the plant alive during the winter when the rest of it has died down. There is therefore no reason to be alarmed if *Kohleria* withers in late season. Put the pot in a cool (10°C) (50°F) to 15°C (59°F)), even dark spot. Keep the root ball dry but not bone-dry. In spring you can take the thick roots out of the pot and re-pot them. This also a good time to divide the roots.

Give average amounts of water in the summer. Because this plant grows best in a light place, put it in a greenhouse or conservatory but protect it from the hot afternoon sun.

Lisianthius russellianus

See: *Eustoma grandiflorum*

Medinilla magnifica

ROSE GRAPE

In the Philippines large leaves on square stems can be seen hanging from the trees. These are the leaves of the tropical forest plant *Medinilla magnifica*. When blooming, pink spheres hang down through the foliage and open into 40cm (16in) long panicles of pink flowers. It is quite appropriate to cultivate *Medillina* in a greenhouse or conservatory as these are warm and humid like the tropics. In the house you can only permanently enjoy this plant if you can re-create tropical conditions as closely as possible. Put the plant in a light

Kohleria amabilis

Detail of *Medinilla magnifica*

spot out of direct sunlight and give plenty of water and food during flowering. Less care is needed in winter but never let the temperature drop below 15°C (59°F). High humidity is very important, so spray as often as possible. The pendulous stems of *Medinilla magnifica* easily cause the pot to overbalance and this effect is reinforced because the plant needs to be grown in a very light compost. You could use a bigger, heavier pot, but still use a porous, humus-rich compost.

Narcissus 'Tête-à-tête'

This cultivar of *Narcissus cyclamineus* has become very popular because it is compact and produces several flowers per bulb. They can be bought in a pot in February, March and April. In a cool and light position they can flower at least as long as a bunch of daffodils. Water them occasionally.

The great advantage is that you do not have to throw away the remains after flowering. Knock the bulbs out of the pot and put them somewhere in the garden. They are completely hardy as a garden plant and will flower again in spring. Most other pot-narcissi, like *Narcissus pseudonarcissus*, can be treated in the same way.

Medinilla magnifica

Narcissus 'Tete-à-tete'

Nertera depressa

See: *Nertera granadensis*

Nertera granadensis

BEAD PLANT

The bead plant covers the whole upper surface of its pot with creeping stems and small leaves. When it eventually grows over the edge of the pot it strongly resembles "mind your own business" *(Soleirolia)* but the two are not related.

After flowering with inconspicuous flowers, Nertera becomes covered in shiny orange berries.

This plant occurs in many places of the southern hemisphere. Grow it in a light and airy spot in the home but definitely not in direct sunlight.

Never let the compost dry out. Water by placing the plant in a tray under the pot or in an outer pot but do not leave it standing in water. Watering the compost itself may lead to rot. In winter the bead plant can be put in a very cool but frost free place and will need little water but still quite a lot of light. In the open ground it seems to be able to tolerate a light frost.

Nertera granadensis

Nierembergia hippomanica

Nierembergia develops into a little shrub in the year in which it was sown. It flowers profusely from mid-summer onwards with violet-blue flowers. It may be put in the garden during the summer. Put it in a sheltered spot or else the wind will cause damage. This member of the potato family is better grown in a pot. Sow at room temperature from March to April. Prick out the seedlings into loose, well-draining compost. The shrubs will start to flower in late June. Give average amounts of water and food throughout summer and late season and put them in a sunny place. The leaves of the subspecies *Nierembergia hippomanica violacea* are decidedly longer and the flowers more violet.

Nierembergia hippomanica violacea 'Purple Robe'

Oxalis adenophylla

Oxalis adenophylla is adapted for extreme weather conditions. It flowers on the southern spurs of the Andes where it can be bitterly cold and very windy. To protect itself against these conditions its grey-green foliage opens close to the ground. It grows from a stem tuber in the soil which looks like a brown hairy bulb. The plant survives our climate easily if grown in a spot which is not too wet. It is very suitable for a rock garden as well as for being grown inside in a pot.

In early summer *adenophylla* is for sale as a flowering pot plant with flowers of unparalleled beauty. They are 2 to 3cm (about 1in) across and appear in equally attractive foliage. In bad weather the flowers and foliage close up.

If grown indoors put this pot plant in full sun to enjoy the flowers for a few weeks. Water and feed liberally in that period.

The foliage becomes straggly and limp after a while. Therefore, put it in the garden straight after flowering and enjoy it as a garden plant in the following year.

Oxalis regnellii

See: *Oxalis triangularis*

Oxalis triangularis

Soft-pink clusters of flowers unfold above foliage coloured aubergine to deep-red. *Oxalis* is sold as a flowering pot plant from early summer until late winter. Allow as much light as possible but protect from direct sunlight.

More plants may be easily propagated from the bulbous rhizomes. After about ten weeks they will be in full flower. Put them in a free-draining compost of sand and peat and keep

Oxalis triangularis

them moist but not soaking wet while they are growing.

Occasionally give liquid fertilizer. Stop watering as soon as the foliage starts to die off and put the pot in a cool but frost-free place. Start watering again in spring when the new shoots appear. As well as the species itself, which has dark red leaves and pink flowers, there is the subspecies *papilionacea* which has green leaves and pure white flowers. *Oxalis triangularis* and *Oxalis triangularis papilionacea* are trade names. In professional

Oxalis adenophylla

170

literature the plants are called *Oxalis regnellii.*

Pachystachys coccinea

CARDINAL'S GUARD

The red *Pachystachys coccinea* is the little known sister plant of *Pachystachys* lutea (lollipop-plant) which has been known as a hous eplant for many years. It has erect flower spikes made up of white flowers protruding from yellow bracts. *Pachystachys coccinea* has fiery-red flowers which grow from a spike made up of green bracts. Both species flower in the summer and need plenty of water and food while flowering. They only grow well in a very light position, preferably in direct sun. *Pachystachys coccinea* originates in tropical America. It benefits from the highest possible humidity in the summer. Keep it cooler in winter but not below 15°C (59°F) and water sparingly.

Pachystachys coccinea

Pavonia multiflora

See: *Triplochlamys multiflora*

Pentas lanceolata

(EGYPTIAN) STAR CLUSTER

Pentas lanceolata is a shrub from Yemen and East Africa. Flowers appear when the plants are still young, arranged in corymbs between 5cm (2in) and 10cm (4in) across. The colour varies from white through soft-pink, fleshy-coloured and pink to magenta and light-purple. Give plants a light position away from bright sunlight and average water and food. Normally the shrub form will not reach the size of an adult plant, which is more than 1m (3ft). Usually the plants are thrown away after flowering but it is possible to keep them through the winter by putting them in a cool place (at a minimum of 10°C (50°F)) and watering less. If the plant becomes woody it can be propagated in summer from the soft stems; let them root in a sandy medium giving warmth from beneath.

Pentas lanceolata

Pericallis cruenta

See: *Senecio* Cruentus hybrids

Pericallis x hybrida

See: *Senecio* Cruentus hybrids

Plumbago auriculata

BLUE CAPE PLUMBAGO/LEADWORT

This South African shrub grows into a large plant in southern Europe where it hardly ever gets any frost. Specimens in the flower shops have been kept small and have often been trained around a wire hoop, utilizing their natural climbing tendency. The flowers appear in the summer on stems which have grown the same year. They are carried closely together in spikes at the end of the stems and are delicately light or purple-blue. *Plumbago auriculata* 'Alba' has pure white flowers.

Plumbago auriculata

Give the plant a light and preferably sunny location with some protection from the very hottest sun. Water liberally while the plant is growing and flowering and feed regularly. *Plumbago* is best grown in a large pot because it likes a lot of water and food. It will grow rampantly, but can be pruned as necessary during its winter resting period. Put the plant in a cool room and give very little water so that it will stop growing. In spring it can be warmed up again and gradually given more water.

The plant can be propagated from seed or from cuttings taken in summer from non-flowering young shoots. Put them in a sandy medium and keep them moderately moist.

☼ ◊

Plumbago indica

SCARLET LEADWORT

This variety with red flowers is not often on offer because it likes tropical temperatures. It will grow well in a greenhouse or a heated room in a light, humid position. It is a twining plant and produces red plumes of flowers from late summer onwards. Keep at a minimum temperature of 15°C (59°F) in the winter and water sparingly. Lanky stems can be pruned back in early spring if you have not managed to stop the winter growth.

☼ ◊

Plubago auriculata 'Alba'

Plumbago indica

Polygala myrtifolia

This South African species looks like a member of the pea-family and in temperate climates has to be grown indoors. The best way

Polygala myrtifolia grandiflora

to do this is in a greenhouse or conservatory but it is also possible in the house. Give this half-metre high plant an airy location or put it outside in summer. It likes to grow with its waxy foliage facing the full sun in moist, fertile compost. Keep it cool (minimum temperature 7°C (45°F), light and dry enough in winter to stop growth and prune off any leggy shoots in early spring.

The species itself is hardly ever on offer. The subspecies *Polygala myrtifolia grandiflora* is more often, but still infrequently available. It has larger purple and white flowers.

Primula obconica

Some people are allergic to this primula. The fine hairs on its leaves cause itchiness and a red rash, even if the skin has not been in contact with the plant. Do not grow this species (or *Primula sinensis,* which causes the same symptoms,) if any member of the household is sensitive. Those that are not can enjoy this plant which will flower for months, producing round clusters of large flowers on long stalks. Flowering specimens are available throughout the year as growers sow them in all seasons.

Primula obconica

Primula obconica belongs to the Chinese primulas. This group is particularly sensitive to heat and sun. Put the plant therefore in a cool, shady spot but with as much light as possible.

Grow in humus-rich compost and keep mildly moist with rainwater. After flowering you can collect the very fine seeds. It is best to sow them in late summer under glass where they will germinate at about 15°C (59°F). Help them through the winter at about 5°C (41°F) by keeping them just moist and aired; they will develop into flowering plants early the following spring.

Popular cultivars which are offered as named plants are, 'Aschat' (white changing to dark-pink towards the centre) and 'Appleblossom' (salmon-coloured flowers).

ly the sort conditions which *Rhododendron* does not like.

Try to grow these magnificent pot plants in a cool but light place. They can tolerate the winter sun. Remove them from the heated room immediately after flowering and put them in a cooler spot. Keep watering them moderately because drying-out kills them. Too much water is just as harmful as the roots rot easily if they do not get enough air.

An old growers tip may be helpful: cut some extra holes in the sides of the plastic pot (in which the plant is growing) to give the roots more air.

There are many cultivars of the Indian azalea on the market. They can be single or double flowered in colours that range from pure white through light pink, salmon pink, carmine-red, bright-red to violet.

Rhododendron Simsii hybrid

Primula obconica 'Aschat'

Rhododendron Simsii hybrids

You may have come across homes where the Indian and Japanese azaleas *(Rhododendron* Obtusum hybrids) flower luxuriantly in winter. In other houses the leaves shrivel up and the flower buds do not open. The temperature in those houses is often too high and the humidity consequently too low, exact-

Rosa x *hybrida*

MINIATURE ROSE

The Chinese have cultivated miniature roses for at least 200 years. The name used then, *Rosa chinensis* 'Minima, is still sometimes used now even though the origins of these plants have been diluted by cross-hybridization with many other roses. The important thing is that we are dealing here with roses that can remain small and can grow and flower indoors. They are available in all kinds of colours such as white, yellow, salmon, pink and red and subtle shades in between. They prefer a place on a sunny windowsill. All roses benefit from fresh air as it prevents pests and diseases. Never forget to water these pot roses because the roots should never dry out. Use water at room temperature and water in a tray under the pot but do not leave the pot standing in water. The plants flower in spring and summer after which there is a resting period. Keep the roses frost-free but as cool as possible and give little water. Prune them in early spring to encourage flowering. Start feeding occasionally as soon as the plants are growing well again.

Rosa x *hybrida*

Saintpaulia

AFRICAN VIOLET

About twenty species of African violet grow in the wild in East Africa but the number of cultivars is countless. They have been bred mainly from *Saintpaulia ionantha* and *Saintpaulia confusa*.

Saintpaulia Ionantha hybrid

African violets are rewarding as flowering house plants. They can tolerate heat and dry air very well and can flower for months on end. Nowadays miniature forms are for sale that require the same care as the large forms. Keep them in a warm living room in summer and winter (at a minimum temperature of 18°C (64°F)) in a light spot but out of direct sunlight. In the dark winter months they will benefit from artificially increasing the length of the day with lamp light. Never spray them and water only when the compost has nearly dried out. Put them in permeable compost as stagnant water causes the roots to rot. Feed the plants during flowering but only with a fertilizer rich in potassium. Nitrogen encourages leaf growth but not flowers.

Scadoxus multiflorus

See: *Haemanthus multiflorus*

Scutellaria costaricana

The native *Scutellaria* is a rewarding garden plant but the species *Scutellaria costaricana* definitely needs to be kept indoors in winter. It originates in Central America and does not tolerate any frost. Indoors it will flower profusely in the summer if given a light posi-

Scutellaria costaricana

tion, out of direct sunlight, and at a temperature of 16°C (61°F) or more. Give an average amount of water, preferably using rainwater or boiled tap water otherwise the compost will become too alkaline. Renew the compost or take cuttings as soon as the plant starts to look less healthy or take cuttings. They will root readily if kept at 20°C (68°F)or more. Pot-on in humus-rich, compost which contains some clay. Put *Scutellaria* in a cool (minimum temperature 10°C (50°F)), light room in winter and water less.

Seemannia

See: *Gloxinia latifolia*

Senecio Cruentus hybrids

CINERARIA

Cinerarias are usually thrown away as soon as they have finished flowering so that aphids do not have a chance to attack them. Cruentus hybrids are available in bloom throughout the year and can add colour to the windowsill in

Left: *Sinningia speciosa*
Below: *Senecio* Cruentus hybrid

winter and spring. Keep them as cool as possible to prolong flowering and give an average amount of water.

Senecio Cruentus hybrids originate in Tenerife. They cannot tolerate drying out but dislike soaked compost even more: if left standing in water the plant will soon collapse. If treated normally and kept in a light spot without direct sunlight you will be able to enjoy this 'bouquet of flowers with roots' for a long time.

Sinningia speciosa

GLOXINIA

Gloxinias originate in Brazil. They have large, cup-shaped flowers. *Gloxinia speciosa*, in its natural habitat, has white, red or purple flowers.

Breeders have extended the range of colours enormously and plenty of multicoloured forms are also available.

Put the flowering plant in a heated living room in a light spot but definitely out of the sun - 18°C (64°F) is ideal. Water with luke-warm water on a tray or in an outer pot so that the water can be absorbed from the bottom and never touches the leaves. Do not leave the plant standing in water or spray it because the leaves need to be kept dry.

Gradually water less after flowering. The foliage will die down. A tuber remains which can be put away in its pot in a cool rather dry place. Plant the tuber or cut off pieces of it if you want to propagate the plant) in spring in standard compost about 2cm (1in) under the soil surface. Gradually water more during the growing period and keep as warm as possible. The plant will probably flower again the following summer.

Solanum pseudocapsicum

JERUSALEM CHERRY

Jerusalem cherry looks very ordinary in summer. Its foliage is dark green and the white flowers look like the flowers of tomato or potato plants - they are all members of the same family. If the flowers are pollinated (which can be encouraged by putting the plant outside in summer) they will produce at the end of the season green berries which change colour via yellow to bright orange. They give

Solanum pseudocapsicum

dry and as cool as possible (but frost-free) through the winter.

Sprekelia formosissima

JACOBEAN/AZTEC LILY

This large bulb from Mexico produces a 30cm (12in) long flower stalk in spring. In early summer the flower unfolds, 12cm (5in) wide and long and strikingly red and it appears among the foliage which is only just starting to develop.

Put this bulbous plant in a sunny spot and water freely until late summer when the foliage dies. Keep the bulb in a cool place in winter between 5°C (41°F) and 10°C (50°F)) and put in fresh compost in very early spring. At this time offsets can be taken from the main bulb and used to propagate the plant.

Stephanotis floribunda

MADAGASCAR JASMINE

The lovely smell of the Madagascar jasmine does not appeal to everyone. This evergreen, twining plant requires a resting period in the winter otherwise it will hardly flower, if at all. In the dark months it needs to be kept nearly dry, in a light spot in a cool room. It can be pruned in early spring. The flowers appear on the new shoots. Put this plant from Madagascar in a warm and light place in spring but not in direct sunlight. Increase the watering gradually. Do not alter the position of the plant once the flower buds have started to appear. Give average to large amounts of

colour to a windowsill inlate season. *Solanum* is often supplied with berries earlier in the season.

Put the plant in a cool place to get the maximum enjoyment from it. .

Solanum originates in Madeira and will tolerate the full sun. Never let it dry out completely but only water when the compost feels quite dry.

The life of the poisonous berries is prolonged by spraying. After the berries have dropped off *Solanum* will benefit from being kept rather

The flowers of *Solanum pseudocapsicum*

Stephanotis floribunda

water in the summer but do not let the pot stand in water.

If the plant is not treated well it will always stop flowering and be attacked by pests. The plant is particularly prone to red spider mite and scale insects when grown in a dry and sunny position. If these pests occur, put the plant outside in summer in a warm and sheltered spot in semi-shade and rub the scales off leathery leaves not forgetting the stalks.

Streptocarpus

CAPE PRIMROSE

Streptocarpus is undoubtedly one of the most rewarding of flowering plants. It flowers from spring until late season, all the time producing new flower stalks which uncurl from the centre of the plant. Only cultivars are on sale which have been bred from quite a few different wild species from southern Africa. They have a rosette of oblong leaves which are usually slightly hairy and ribbed. The plants have a shallow root system and rarely stand firmly in their pot. They can be grown in

Streptocarpus

shallow pots, ideally in permeable compost with some sharp sand and clay added. Keep *Streptocarpus* in a warm living room (at a minimum of 18°C (64°F)) in summer, in a light spot out of direct sunlight. Move it to a light spot in a cool room (at a minimum of 10° (50°F)) in winter and keep it almost dry. Bring the plant back into the living room round about March or April when it starts to come back to life.

Never spray the foliage. Water on a tray (under the plant pot) preferably with rainwater or luke-warm soft water and only water when the compost is nearly dry. Stagnant moisture causes root rot. Only feed with fertilizer that is high in potassium; nitrogen promotes leaf growth at the expense of flower production.

Propagate by cutting the leaf lengthways right through the mid-rib. Push the two halves wounds downwards into moderately moist sandy compost, cover with transparent plastic and put in a warm spot. Eventually a row of young plants will develop along the mid-rib.

Torenia fournieri

WISHBONE FLOWER

Torenia fournieri is an annual from Asia. Its flowers vary in colour but always have a characteristic shape and a yellow spot on the lower lip. The petals are usually pink with violet or purple. If they have a white throat with purple around it they are called 'Alba'.

The plants can be bought in bloom from late spring. As long as they are always kept moist and put in a light, even sunny, place they will flower until the end of the growing season. After flowering they can be thrown on the compost heap because they are annuals.

Triplochlamys multiflora

Until recently this Brazilian plant could be found only in tropical greenhouses where it benefited from high humidity and heat. Nowadays the characteristically twisted flowers of this member of the *Malvadeae* family are very tempting when seen in the garden centre. Indoors it can grow in a light to semi-shady spot but must be protected from the very hot sun. The provision of enough air humidity in winter can be a problem. Water less in winter and put the plant somewhere

cool, but never colder than 16°C (61°F) so that the evergreen foliage suffers as little as possible from the central heating.

Prune the plant back hard in spring and get it growing again in a warm place. Always keep moist during flowering and feed occasionally. The flowers appear from the young leaf axils.

Vinca rosea

See: *Catharanthus roseus*

Zantedeschia

CALLAS, ARUM LILIES

Zantedeschias are natives of southern Africa. The six known species have given rise to many hybrids. These are usually on offer unspecified but often have *Zantedeschia aethiopica* (see the chapter on container plants), *Zantedeschia rehmannii* (pink) or *Zantedeschia elliotiana* (yellow) as one of their ancestors. The spathes surrounding the spadices of the cultivars come in all shades from white through lemon-yellow, golden-yellow, orange, peach, pink to carmine.

Arum lilies are easy to grow. They need a light position and can tolerate sun. Their compost should be light and airy and always moist.

Water evaporates quickly from the foliage so, in a sunny spot, the plant will have to be watered regularly to stop the compost from drying out.

However, avoid stagnant water which is even more harmful since it causes the rhizomes to rot. If the rhizomes dry out the leaves wither. But this does not mean that the plant needs to be written off. *Zantedeschias* have a resting period in their natural environment. Keep the compost nearly dry for a while and give gradually more water when new foliage appears. Put the plant in a cool room during the winter (at a minimum of 12° C (54°F)). The plant can be put in the garden during the resting period in the summer.

The plant is poisonous. Do not let the sap come into contact with the skin or the eyes and consult a doctor if someone swallows any. The best first aid is to drink a lot of water.

Left: *Triplochlamys multiflora*

Below: *Torenia fournieri* 'Alba'

11. Bromeliads

Nearly all members of the pineapple family (Bromeliaceae) grow in the tropical and subtropical forests of America. They attach themselves to trees and their roots never reach the soil. Dead leaves and the droppings of birds and monkeys collect in tree hollows and between tree roots. The channel-shaped leaves catch rainwater and convey it to the centre of the plant which is cup-shaped to hold the water.

The bromeliad-type plants grow in acid soil. They should only be watered and sprayed with de-calcified water or rainwater and they like high humidity. It takes years for a young plant to flower; only then does it come on to the market. The leaf rosette from which the flower stalk rises will certainly die after flowering and it therefore does not require special care. These very demanding plants can flower for months on end in the living room. After flowering the young plants, which develop at the base of the old plant, can be grown on but even with the best care it will be years before they flower and all that time they require very special care which cannot be provided in the house.

Most members of the pineapple family are therefore eventually thrown away. It is quite a challenge for an amateur to get any of the 2000 beautiful species to flower.

Left: *Vriesea psittacina*

Aechmea fasciata

SILVER VASE, URN PLANT

The large, blunt leaves of *Aechmea fasciata* are green, but make up a funnel which looks grey because the leaves are covered with a dense white haze formed from minuscule scales. These disappear when touched, when the plant is sprayed or if the plant does not get enough light. The plant is always sold in flower. The funnel of leaves is about 50cm (20in) high. The pink flower spike, which rises up from the funnel, goes beautifully with the chalky-grey leaves. The flowers themselves are violet and are sometimes visible between the pink bracts. This *Aechmea* flowers in the summer but nurserymen provide flowering plants throughout the year. Of the *Bromeliaceae Aechmea fasciata* is one of the easiest to keep. It can tolerate relatively dry indoor air, and the sun, but will also grow in semi-shade. It likes room temperature. After flowering the leaf funnel dies. Young leaf funnels usually develop at the base of the old one which should be allowed to root properly before they can be potted separately. Grow them in a light and warm place (never less than 18°C (64°F), out of bright sunlight, and give an average amount of water. You can leave the strongest looking young plant in the old pot.

Ananas comosus

PINEAPPLE

The pineapple is a native of South America but is cultivated in every tropical and subtropical country nowadays because of its juicy fruit. In the Azores in 1890 it was accidentally discovered that the smoke of a wood fire promotes bud formation. Later it was discovered that the plants respond to acetylene. Nowadays this gas is used to promote early flowering in this plant and many other *Bromeliaceae*. Do not expect a rich harvest of pineapples in the house although pot plants can produce small fruits. Put the plants in a warm and sunny position but protect them from the worst of the summer sun. Water liberally in summer. Put in a cooler spot in winter (at a minimum of 15°C) and water sparingly. The plant is difficult to handle

because of the spines on the leaf edges. If you brush against it and get stuck turn away from the centre of the plant in the direction of the spines. If you want to propagate this plant use the young plants which form at the base of the dying rosette after it has flowered. You can also use the leaf rosette of a pineapple bought from the greengrocers'. Cut this off with a slice of the pineapple attached. Let it dry out for a few hours, then put it on sandy compost, cover with plastic and put in a light spot.

The two cultivars of the common pineapple which you are likely to buy as decorative plants are *Ananas comosus* 'Porteanus', which has a yellow stripe in the centre of the leaf, and *Ananas comosus* 'Variegatus', which has yellow stripes, chiefly along the leaf margin and sometimes suffused with pink.

Ananas comosus

Ananas nanus

See: *Ananas comosus*

Ananas sativa

See: *Ananas comosus*

Left: *Aechmea fasciata*

Billbergia x *windii*

This cross between *Billbergia decora* and *Billbergia nutans* is one of the easiest of indoor plants. It is grown in a hanging basket or against a stick. The long leaves form rosettes from which flower stems arch down. The flower spikes atop these stalks consist of green flowers which stick out from pink bracts. Unfortunately they do not last long.

Hang *Billbergia* in a light or semi-shady place, out of the bright sun. If watered normally, with normal room temperature and normal air humidity, it will greatly increase in size by forming more and more new rosettes. These can be detached from the plant when they are well rooted and be potted separately in well aerated, humus-rich compost.

Cryptanthus

EARTH STARS

These plants, although totally different from each other, are usually sold under the name *Cryptanthus* without any further indication as to which species or cultivar they are. The colour of their leaves is very variable but they tend to be on offer as one of a mixed batch. They are usually sold as young plants in a very small pot. Eventually they will grow to about two to four times their original size.

Choose the leaf colour you like and remember that the greener the foliage is the less light the plants need to grow well. The whitish-red and very dark forms like a sunny spot where the marking of the foliage will show better. For further maintenance see *Cryptanthus* zonatus.

Cryptanthus zonatus

The leaves of *Cryptanthus zonatus* are about 15cm (6in) in length. Their ground colour is olive-green to chocolate-brown, adorned with contrasting bands made up of a pattern of very small scales. They are particularly striking in the cultivar 'Zebrinus' where they resemble the stripes of a zebra. *Cryptanthus Zonatus* originates in the dry regions of Brazil and tolerates dry air well although it benefits from being sprayed occasionally. Grow the plant in well aerated soil or in peat moss which is tied to a branch. Make sure that water can drain away easily as too much water is about the

only thing that will kill this very tough plant. It can survive without water for a very long time and will even tolerate full sun although some protection is better. It can keep going in the shade although the colour of the foliage will not be as good.

The white flowers in the centre of the plant are so small that they have hardly any decorative value. Use some of the numerous sideshoots to propagate the plant.

Guzmania

When you buy a flowering *Guzmania* you will be able to enjoy its flower-spike for a long time. The flowers are not very conspicuous but the bracts are usually a lively red. Since the funnel of leaves from which the flower stalk arises will eventually die, the plant needs hardly any care while it is flowering. Give average amounts of water and keep *Guzmania* away from direct sunlight.

If you want to grow on the young rosettes at the base of the old plant, bear in mind the climate of the countries where this plant is native. In Central and South America guzmanias grow on the forest floors or, more

Cryptanthus zonatus 'Zebrinus'

often, on trees in a warm and humid atmosphere. These conditions will have to be imitated at home. The plants do not like temperatures below 18°C (64°F) and they also require air humidity of about 80%, which can only be achieved in a living room if the plants are grown in a herbarium. The compost should be very well aerated and free-draining or the roots will rot. Water with rainwater or de-calcified water. The plant needs a lot of extra light in the winter to be able to produce flowers in later life. It is probably more sensible for the average plant lover to throw away *Guzmania* after it has flowered.

Left: *Billbergia* x *windii*

Below: *Cryptanthus*

There are many species and cultivars of *Guzmania* on the market. You can make an informed choice because they are always flowering when offered for sale. The cultivars from *Guzmania minor* are particularly popular because of their bright-red flower spikes.

Guzmania lingulata var. *minor*

See: *Guzmania minor*

Neoregelia

The purple-blue flowers of *Neoregelia* are not very conspicuous and do not attract the creatures needed to pollinate them. Instead animals are attracted by the red leaves at the centre of the plant. This red colour suggests that the flowers are pollinated by butterflies and probably also by miniature birds since both are attracted to it.
Neoregalias hang in the trees of South America where it is warm and humid. The plants can flower for 4 to 6 months in the living room after which the main rosette dies off. If you want to propagate the young offsets, see *Guzmania* for details.

Neoregelia 'Flandria'

Normal room temperature is ideal during flowering. Give average amounts of water, preferably rainwater, and do not leave water standing in the pot. Make sure there is always some rainwater in the heart of the plant.

Left: *Guzmania* Minor hybrid

Below: *Guzmania zahnii*

Tillandsia usneoides

The colour of the foliage only stays bright if the plant is given a very light, preferably sunny position. It only needs protection from direct summer sun. There are various cultivars on offer which usually have *Neoregelia carolinae* as a significant parent plant: 'Meyendorf' (leaf rosette green with carmine-red centre), 'Flandria' (creamy-white to pale-yellow stripes along the leaf edges) 'Tricolor' (closely resembles 'Flandria') and 'Tricolor Perfecta' (leaves with abundant yellow stripes, especially along the main vein).

Tillandsia

In tropical and subtropical America tillandsias grow on rocks, on tree trunks and even on electricity cables where there is, of course, no soil at all. And tillandsia does not need soil. There are about 400 species of tillandsia and they occur in such a variety of shapes and flowers that some enthusiastic home growers specialize in just this group of plants. Their maintenance depends to a great extent on their appearance. If the plant is green, has a rosette and is in a pot (like *Tillandsia cyanea* and the related species *Tillandsia lindenii*) it needs to be kept out of direct sunlight and can be treated as a flowering Guzmania. If the leaves are chalky-white from microscopically small scales, like the so-called Spanish moss *(Tillandsia usneoides)*, it needs a sunny, or at least very light location. These varieties absorb water and food directly through the leaves. They need to be sprayed daily with rainwater to which has been added special foliar feed or some other strongly diluted low-nitrogen fertilizer.

Vriesea

The flower-spikes of most cultivated species of *Vriesea* rise some tens of centimetres above

Vriesea x *poelmannii* 'White Line'

190

Tillandsia xerographica

Care is simple as soon as the plant flowers. Give it a warm position at a minimum of 17°C (60°F) with plenty of light and protect it against the hottest sun in the summer. Regularly fill the leaf funnels with rainwater and keep the compost moderately moist, preferably with rainwater or de-calcified water. The roots should definitely not remain standing in water and spraying is beneficial. The flowering leaf rosette dies after a few months. If you want to grow on the young shoots which grow at the base of the old plant, see *Guzmania* for details.

Some species and numerous hybrid cultivars are on offer. Vriesea splendens, also called "flaming sword", is the best known and has a lanceolate, red flower-spike of about 40cm (16in) in length. Cultivars of *Vriesea psittacina* "painted feather" have multi-coloured flower-spikes. The lower bracts are red, towards the tip they change to yellow and eventually to greenish-yellow. *Vriesea x poelmannii* is a brilliant hybrid which is raised from two other hybrids: *Vriesea x gloriosa* and *Vriesea x vangeertii*. The bracts on the branched flower spike are red. The cultivar 'White Line' has wide, creamy-white bands along the main vein.

the leaf rosette. The actual flowers are often yellow and green and appear between the overlapping bracts which themselves are lively red or yellow.

☼ ◑

Detail of the flower structure of *Vriesea*

12. Orchids

Orchids form the largest family of plants on earth, comprising about 25,000 species. New ones are discovered each month. They grow in the most divergent climates from the tundra to the tropical forest. Only in the driest deserts and on the polar ice do they not occur.

One would therefore expect the choice of house orchids to be enormous, but it is in fact disappointing. Until recently it was very difficult to grow them on the windowsill. The species from temperate regions are mostly terrestrial orchids whose roots need certain fungi in the soil if they are to absorb nutrients properly. Tropical orchids often grow in trees where they profit from high air humidity and feed on humus that collects between their roots or in tree hollows.

It is the tropical orchids which can be brought into flower in the living room as long as the air humidity is kept sufficiently high. Fortunately, there are more and more hybrids on offer nowadays which can better tolerate the climate in a dry living room.

Cattleya

Cattleya has driven plant collectors to distraction. The first species was brought to flower in Europe in 1824 and its curiously shaped flowers caused plant lovers to turn their heads and take note. Nowadays beautiful hybrids are available which can be grown in the living room.

The cultivars often strongly resemble Cattleya

Left: a colourful orchid exhibition

Below: Cattleya 'Cinnabar'

intermedia, a species from southern Brazil, Uruguay and Paraguay. After flowering they need a period of rest during which they should be given just sufficient water to prevent drying out. If the pseudobulbs from which the leaf pairs arise start to shrivel the plant needs to be given more water to swell them until they are tight again. If the period of rest occurs in winter, put the *Cattleya* hybrids in a cool room in a very light spot.

When they are actively growing they also like the lightest possible place, preferably in the sun but protected from the bright afternoon sun. It is safe to submerge the pots in luke-warm water when the plants are actively growing, but let them drain very well afterwards and do not water again until they are completely dry. When choosing a *Cattleya* use your nose (as well as your eyes) because some species are deliciously fragrant.

Coelogyne lawrenceana

The majority of orchid species are not available from retailers. If you want to enjoy them at home you will have to get in touch with an orchid society. However more and

more species are commercially grown and available to the public.

Coelogyne is one of them. Several of the approximately 200 species of *Coelogyne* can flower and grow in the living room. Originally it was thought that plants from the Himalayas such as *Coelogyne cristata* would be the most suitable. However it has turned out that the species from the warmer regions of South-East Asia grow better in living rooms. For example, *Coelogyne massangeana* from the *Malaysian peninsular* and *Coelogyne lawrenceana* from many places between Malaysia and Vietnam.

These species can be grown throughout the year in a light not too sunny position in the living room. They like fresh air and benefit greatly from being sprayed regularly with rainwater or de-calcified water.

Cymbidium hybrids

Cymbidiums were the first orchids to be sold as house plants. This trade was a by-product of the cultivation of *Cymbidiums* as cut flowers which had been going on for some time. The plants that were available used to be very large in size. Nowadays more and more

Below: *Cattleya*-hybrid

Right: *Coelogyne lawrenceana*

smaller cultivars (the so-called "mini" and "midi" *Cymbidiums)* are available which feel perfectly at home in the living room. They flower for about two to three months.

Cymbidiums are easy house plants and are fairly insensitive to being badly treated. If you want to enjoy the flowers for a long time put the plant in a light, sunny place out of the hottest summer sun. Give it some fresh air but avoid draughts and cold. Water liberally, preferably with rainwater or de-calcified tap water at room temperature, but never leave the pot standing in water. Regularly spray the leaves but avoid wetting the flowers.

Flowering usually occurs in late season and winter after which the plant needs a resting period. Put it in a cool place and keep it drier. This is the right time to divide the plant but only do this when the plant has outgrown its pot. In summer it is best to put the plant outside in a sheltered position. Keep it constantly moist and give special orchid fertilizer or a strongly diluted solution of house plant fertilizer. The difference in day and night temperature promotes bud development. Bring the plant inside as soon as the night temperature drops below about 8°C (46°F). Put it in a warmer place when the buds have appeared.

Left: *Cymbidium*
Below: *Cymbidium* hybrid

Cymbidium eburneum

The first *Cymbidium* hybrid flowered at the British nursery, Veitch, in 1889. This hybrid was a cross between *Cymbidium eburneum* and *Cymbidium lowianum*, two species from eastern Asia. The flowers of the first hybrid are creamy-white with a yellow lip. They are so perfect compared with the sickly sweet colours of the cultivars which you get nowadays, that the firm of Veitch might just as well have not bothered to "improve" these plants. For maintenance see *Cymbidium* hybrids.

Cymbidium eburneum

Dendrobium

There are about 200 species of *Dendrobium* which grow wild in the enormous triangle formed by the Himalayas, southern Japan and new Zealand. Those from the cooler regions flower readily in the living room. The plants which are on offer are usually cultivars of *Dendrobium nobile*, a native or the mountainous regions of South-East Asia. The cultivars have white or pink flowers, nearly always with a large, dark patch on the wide lip. The flowers rise from a segmented pseudobulb which forms a little stem but is so flexible that it often needs to be supported.

Keep the plant in a light and airy place when it is flowering, away from direct sunlight and preferably at a temperature of about 18°C (64°F) or slightly less. The roots are very sensitive to stagnant water. Some people never water the plant but spray daily which allows some moisture to get through to the roots.

In the summer after flowering the plant can be put outside in a place where it will not get soaked by the rain. It is now in its growing period and needs orchid fertilizer regularly. At the end of the summer keep the plant outside in a dry place. Give it a period of rest of about 6 to 8 weeks by not feeding it and hardly watering it. It can tolerate temperatures down to 0°C (32°F). Only when the buds appear should the plant be kept warmer and be given more water. Put it back in the living room to start it flowering again.

Miltonia

PANSY ORCHIDS

These South American orchids have only recently become offered for sale in house-plant outlets. These modern hybrids appear to be better able to tolerate the climate of a

Miltonia

windowsill than the original species which grow mainly in the higher regions of Paraguay, Brazil and Central America where it is relatively light and the air is cool and fresh.

Cultivated Miltonias are mainly of Brazilian origin but hybridized with *Oncidium* and *Odontoglossum*. Commercial growers keep the temperature of the greenhouse at between 18°C and 24°C (64°F and 75°F) during the day and at between 12°C and 15°C (54°F and 59°F) during the night. This corresponds more or less with the climate of a living room.

Below: *Dendrobium* 'Seigyoku Queen'   Right: *Oncidium*

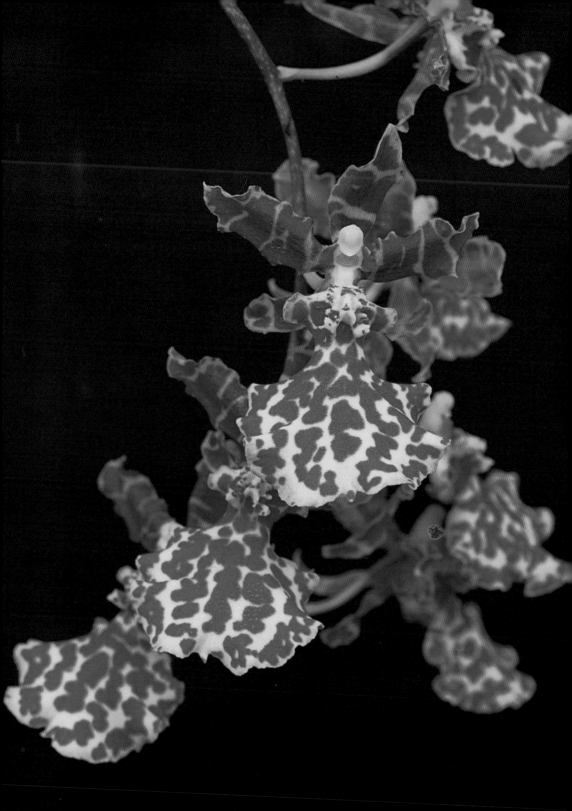

Put *Miltonia* in as light a place as possible preferably in sunlight but not in the early afternoon sun of spring and summer: light shade is better during those few hours. Submerge the pot weekly and give special orchid fertilizer every month (or give house plant fertilizer at one tenth of the normal dose). A centrally heated room is really too dry for *Miltonia*. Spray often but avoid getting the flowers wet, or put the plant on wet gravel, but make sure the roots do not stand in water. It is most important to provide as much fresh air as possible - they like similar conditions to people! Take some time to find the nicest hybrid. There is great variation although you will usually find cultivars that will produce white flowers with a centre of yellow and carmine. There are also velvety-red and deep-red forms which all have brilliant patterns of spots in contrasting colours.

Oncidium

In the forests of South America the flowers of *Oncidium* appear to be floating. At the slightest puff of wind they rock backwards and forwards on their long stalks. Researchers were surprised to see *Centris* bees flying into these flowers with deliberation and force. These bees defend their territories in the forest against members of the same species and apparently they think that the *Oncidium* flower is one of them. When a bee collides with a flower the latter becomes pollinated and this is probably precisely why the flower resembles the *Centris* bee so closely. This is only one of the many amazing ways in which orchids ensure that they become pollinated. *Oncidium* has done this very successfully. There are about 800 species which grow throughout a vast area: from Florida through Central America and the Amazonian region to Argentina. They grow in tropical lowland forests as well as high in the mountains. The actual mountain species and the plants from the tropical forests cannot be grown in the living room but fortunately, there are also species and cultivars that are able to grow in such a temperate climate. The popular *Oncidium* 'Susie Kaufman' (yellow with velvety-red spots) is one of them as is the vigorous 'Cherry Baby' (red-white).

Growers usually supply multi-hybrids (crosses between hybrids) with a large palette of colours that differ on each plant. *Oncidium* requires a bit more care than other windowsill orchids. It should definitely be kept out of

Miltonia

direct sunlight. It is better to put by an east or north-west facing window or to screen it in sunny weather. The growing medium in the pot should not dry out completely but it should not stay wet either. Submerge the plant in its pot in de-calcified, luke-warm water just before the contents of the pot are bone-dry. It is best to do this in the morning so that the leaves are dry before the evening. Add some fertilizer to this water once a month. This should be orchid fertilizer or house plant fertilizer at one tenth of the normal strength. Only feed during flowering and active growth. After flowering a resting period follows. Put *Oncidium* in a cool room at about 15°C (59°F) and water just enough to prevent the pseudobulbs (from which the leaves rise) from wrinkling. Try to give this orchid a high humidity throughout the year and as much fresh air as possible.

Oncidium

Paphiopedilum

SLIPPER ORCHIDS

There are about sixty species of slipper orchid and they are all natives of South-East Asia. Many cultivars have been raised because the flowers capture the imagination . One of the

parent species is *Paphiopedilum callosum* which is often for sale in its true form.

The temperature requirement of the plants is indicated by their leaves and flowers. The plants will nearly always tolerate the cold badly if the leaves are mottled whereas the varieties with more than one flower per stalk also like the warmth.

Slippers orchids should only be put in the winter sun. In summer they prefer a north-facing window. The warmth-loving varieties grow well at room temperature and in higher than average humidity. Put slipper orchids closely together on a bed of wet gravel or on a upside-down saucer in a tray of water. If you spray them make sure that the plants, especially their centres, are completely dry again by evening. Keep the soil always moderately moist.

Re-pot yearly in fresh, acidic, loose compost, for example, a mixture of fern root, sphagnum moss and coarse peat. These plants also require some lime. Submerge the plants a few times per year in water to which marl or ground limestone has been added.

Phalaenopsis

There are about forty species of *Phalaenopsis* which grow on trees in South-East Asia where it is warm and humid. Despite this, *Phalaenopsis* species are among the toughest species for the living room and can flower profusely and for a long time indoors. In particular, the *Phalaenopsis* hybrids, which are crosses between wild species, are very resilient and can flower for nine months on the trot.

When you buy the plant it will have a flower stalk with a few flowers. Handles with care this stalk will grow longer and continue to produce new flowers while the old ones remain attractive for at least a month before they shrivel and drop off.

The period just after buying is critical for *Phalaenopsis*. Sometimes the largest flower buds drop off after a few days. There are two reasons for this. The plant may have been too cold. Do not buy orchids from street traders if the temperature is below 15°C (59°F) and protect the plants against the cold when taking them home by leaving them in their plastic wrapping. The second reason could be that the plant has been placed near ripe fruit or vegetables. These produce ethylene gas which causes bud-drop.

Phalaenopsis 'Christmas Tree'

Phalaenopsis 'Temple Cloud'

Phalaenopsis is easy to look after. Put the plant in a light position but not in direct sunlight. Submerge the plant in its pot in luke-warm and preferably boiled water. Only submerge it again when the bark, which is the medium in which the plant is usually grown, has dried out completely. Drain the pot very carefully after it has been submerged and before it is put back in its outer pot because the roots should never be allowed to remain in standing water. High air humidity is beneficial but not absolutely necessary. The plant does not need feeding in the first season.

Left: *Paphiopedilum*

Below: *Pleione tolima*

After flowering the flower stalk turns yellow or produces a shoot about halfway up the stem. The yellow part can be cut off. If a new flower stalk appears you can submerge the plant just once in water to which house plant fertilizer has been added, but never use more than one tenth of the recommended dose.

Pleione

Some *Pleione* species, such as *Pleione formosana* and *Pleione limprichtii,* can be successfully cultivated in the garden throughout the year. Although most of the other species need more warmth they definitely do not like heated rooms during the months when the heating is on. During flowering, which usually occurs in spring, they prefer an east or north facing window. Never allow the plant to dry out or stand in water.

In summer it is best to put *Pleione* outside in its pot, in a shady or semi-shady place. Always keep the compost evenly moist with rainwater until the foliage starts to die down. Gradually decrease watering and bring the plant inside as winter approaches. During the winter keep the pseudobulbs in their pot in a cool spot (at a minimum temperature of 5°C (41°F)) and water just enough to prevent the pseudobulbs from drying out.

Re-pot in spring in a light, humus-rich mixture of, for instance, bark, tree fern and coarse turf

Vanda x rothschildiana

with some well-rotted cow manure added. Gradually bring the plants into flower by tending them at room temperature and giving them more water.

Vanda x *rothschildiana*

Vandas with their leaves carried on long stalks, their clusters of aerial roots and their beautiful flowers really capture the imagination. *Vanda coerulea,* particularly popular because of its blue colour, has been used for cross breeding. *Vanda x rothschildiana* is a cross between coerulea and *Vanda sanderiana.*

Unfortunately these plants are not suitable for the ordinary living room. They need a great deal of warmth and high humidity to produce flowers. Many species will drop their buds if the temperature is not well over 20°C (68°F). Grow Vandas therefore under glass, preferably by an east or west facing window where the plants will get sufficient sun but not the hottest summer sun. The roots should grow in a well aerated medium: preferably coarse bark and fern root. The aerial roots are very important for healthy growth and should be sprayed regularly with de-calcified water or preferably rainwater.

x *Vuylstekeara*

A cross between three different species of orchid, *Cochloidea, Miltonia* and *Odontoglossum,* lies hidden behind this impossible name. x Vuylstekeara is also referred to by the name *Cambria* hybrid. The cultivar best known to the trade is x *Vuylstekeara* Cambria 'Plush'. The plant has butterfly-like flowers, each carried on a long stalk. The petals are velvety-red with beautiful white patterns on the lip and the flower has a yellow botch in the centre.

The flowers usually appear in winter and spring and remain in good condition for a long time if kept in a light spot out of the sun. Give the plant an airy position at normal room temperature and always give enough water so the compost never dries out.

Right: x *Vuylstekeara Cambria* 'Plush'

13. Cacti

There are hundreds of species of cactus and they are all native to the Americas, from the southern United States as far as chilly Tierra del Fuego, and from the hot Carribean Islands to high in the Andes mountains. Nearly all species have thorns. These arm the plants against being eaten by animals, protect them from bright ultra-violet radiation and temper the drying wind. As well as this, the thorns of some species absorb water in the form of dew which condenses on the thorns and is absorbed directly by the plant. Cacti are popular house plants because of their bizarre shapes and their decorative thorns and flowers. They only flower if they are allowed a strict period of rest in the winter during which growth stops completely. This can be achieved by putting them in a very cool place and keeping them completely dry.

As desert plants, cacti benefit from standing in the full sun. During the growing period most species are able use more water than is often thought. In mildly moist compost they will grow more quickly and flower more profusely.

The latest nomenclature for cacti is being used in this chapter because this has become the fashion with amateurs. In shops the plants are usually on offer unspecified. If you look for a plant under its old name the index will direct you to the correct page.

Left: *Parodia rutilans*

Below: *Cactus seedlings*

Astrophytum myriostigma

BISHOP'S CAP CACTUS

This spineless cactus is shaped like a bishop's cap. The whole body of the plant is covered in small spots each having minuscule hairs which protect the plant against the bright Mexican sun. With proper care, yellow flowers will appear regularly from the top of the plant in summer. The roots of all *Astrophytum* species are very sensitive to moisture, therefore water sparingly. It needs porous compost which should contain hardly any organic material, although some marl is beneficial. The plant will only flower if it grows well during the summer. Keep *Astrophytums* completely dry in the winter in a cool, frost-free and light place. As well as the species dealt with above, *Astrophytum ornatum* is regularly offered for sale. It has fewer, but larger woolly spots and long, sharp spines that are usually golden-yellow. The species cross-fertilize easily and give rise to hybrids which are identified by the initial letters of the name of the species. For example, *Astrophytum* ORMY stands for a cross between *ornatum and myriostigma*.

Astrophytum hybrid ORMY

Aylostera

See: *Rebutia*

Astrophytum myriostigma

208

Bartschella

See: *Mammillaria*

Brasilicactus

See: *Parodia*

Brasilparodia

See: *Parodia*

Cereus uruguayanus 'Monstruosus'

In South America *Cereus uruguayanus* grows into a column of more than 5m (16ft) in height. In the wild, the top of the column may become mis-shapen as is also the case with other columnar cacti, such as *Cereus jamacura* and *Cereus peruvianus*. Normally the column has one growing point. Some plants produce a cancer-like growth by developing new growing points all the time known as a "monstrosity"; cuttings from these growths are sold as *Cereus uruguayanus* 'Monstruosus'.

Cereus varieties are very easy cacti to maintain. They like a sunny and warm position. Their root system is not very vulnerable and does not rot easily; they can therefore be given a little more water in summer than the average cactus. Keep the plant completely dry in winter at a temperature of between 10°C and 15°C (50°F and 59°F). You can also keep it at room temperature, in which case it occasionally needs some water to prevent shrivelling.

Chamaecereus

See: *Echinopsis chamaecereus*

Digitorebutia

See: *Rebutia*

Dolichothele

See: *Mammillaria*

Echinocactus grusonii

GOLDEN BARREL, GOLDEN BALL

Echinocactus grusonii originates in Mexico, but has become extinct there partly through over-collecting. It is one of the most common cacti in cultivation and is grown on a large scale in America, North Africa and the Canary

Echinocactus grusonii

Cereus uruguayanus 'Monstruosus'

209

Islands. They are sometimes sold as globular young plants with spines growing from small humps. When the plants get older the humps grow together to form ribs which have very sharp, golden-yellow spines. Put the plant by a sunny window and give average amounts of water in summer. It can also be grown in a sheltered and sunny spot outside in the summer. It is best to put it in a cool place in winter (at a minimum of 5°C (41°F)), in as light a position as possible, keeping it completely dry. If it is kept in the living room it will need to be watered a little. Growth should be avoided at this time, because growth in the low light levels of winter would produce a permanently mis-shaped plant.

Echinocereus

Most of the *Echinocereus* cacti grow in the southern United States and northern Mexico. They form short columns. To produce flowers they need a lot of sun and a cool and completely dry period during the winter. They are very partial to fresh air which means that they are best grown in a greenhouse or conservatory.

Echinocereus

Keep them dry for longer than other cacti. Shrivelling in the rest period does not do any harm. If the weather is fine the plant may be watered from mid-April onwards. Use a very porous compost with a lot of grit, sand or other well-draining material to help the

Echinocereus reichenbachii var. *baileyi*

Echinocereus rigidissimus

compost dry out quickly after it has been watered. The densely spined species needs most light. Some species are:

Echinocereus adustus which develops in summer light pink flowers (5cm (2in) wide) which grow on top of a short column with flat clusters of spines.

Echinocereus poselgeri was, until recently, called *Wilcoxia poselgeri* because of its different shape. Its flowers are up to 8cm (3in) wide and unfold on very slender stems. It is a plant for very keen plant-lovers and is only

Echinocereus subinermis

suitable for growing in a greenhouse.

Echinocereus reichenbachii can tolerate frost as long as it is in a dry place. Its short columnar shape is hidden behind spreading spines. The subspecies *baileyi* is less densely spined and also produces shiny red flowers which are about 9cm (3.5in) wide.

Echinocereus rigidissemus is closely related to *Echinocereus pectinatus*. Both species have spreading spines which protect the plant against bright sunshine. The flowers are pink with a lighter centre and are up to 10 cm (4in)

wide. The spines of *rigidissimus* are arranged in distinct bands of separate colour which have given this cactus the name rainbow cactus. It requires a lot of sun and very careful watering and is really only suitable for the keen cactus grower.

Echinocereus subinermis is globular and has few spines so that its round, green body shows clearly. It needs protection from bright sunlight in early spring. This species, which can have flowers that are more than 10cm (4in) wide, is often available as a house plant. It needs less light than the others, but it still needs the lightest spot on a windowsill. It needs porous compost which should be left to dry out completely after each watering.

Echinocereus poselgeri

Echinofossulocactus

See: *Stenocactus*

Echinopsis

SEA URCHIN CACTUS

Until recently only globular cacti with long, white flowers were classified as *Echinopsis*. Nowadays most species of *Trichocereus*, *Lobivia* and *Pseudolobivia* are also grouped under this name. The original *Echinopsis* is one of the most frequently found living room cacti. Its dark green body is about as big as an orange but eventually becomes columnar in shape with sharply edged ribs and sharp spines. Some plants develop many off-shoots which can be removed and put in separate pots. These young plants will also produce off-shoots but they will hardly ever flower. If you

Echinopsis backebergii

Echinopsis

want flowers you will have to buy or sow new plants. Keep *Echinopsis* as cool as possible but frost-free in a light place in winter and keep it completely dry. It will then produce its marvellous flowers in early summer. These are nearly 20cm (8in) long and white. In South America they attract night insects with their delicious smell. The *Echinopsis* species that used to be called *Lobivia* have shorter flowers which are at least as wide and often bright-yellow, orange, red or carmine. To produce flowers these plants need a lot of sun, fresh air

and cold during the winter. This makes them suitable for greenhouses. They can tolerate a few degrees of frost as long as they are kept completely dry in winter. Some species are:
Echinopsis backebergii (previously *Lobivia winteriana*) which has a globular body and flowers, up to 9cm (3.5in) in width, which are carmine-red to violet with a lighter centre.
Echinopsis chamaecereus (previously *Chamaecereus silvestrii*) is called the peanut cactus. The segments are peanut-shaped and hang over the edge of the pot. It will bloom

Echinopsis chamaecereus hybrid

with orange-red flowers in early summer, but only after a dry and very cold winter resting period in which it can tolerate temperatures down to minus 10°C (14°F). This species cross-fertilizes easily with other Echinopsis species and has given rise to countless hybrids with fatter "peanuts" and larger flowers in different colours.

Echinopsis haematantha (previously *Lobivia rebutioides*) is small, bulbous to barrel-shaped. The body is covered in flat clusters of spines. It produces 4cm (2in) wide flowers which are red to orange with a white or greenish throat.

Echinopsis haematantha

Echinopsis pentlandii (previously *Lobivia boliviensis*) produces numerous offsets. These are shiny-green, barrel-shaped stems with very sharp spines. Its flowers are about 3cm (1in) wide and are pink to red.

Echinopsis tiegeliana (previously *Lobivia tiegeliana*) has carmine-red flowers on a shiny, irregularly ribbed body.

All *Echinopsis* species prefer to be outside during the summer, in a sunny spot and protected from the rain. In the growing season they need as much water as the average house plant.

Eriocactus

See: *Parodia*

Ferocactus

Ferocacti can grow very old. In the wild they eventually become barrel-shaped and grow to a height of more than 1m (3ft). The small plants which are bought in the shops do not show a natural growing habit; in cultivation they rarely get enough sun and nutrients to grow large.

In the Canary Islands ferocacti develop in a few years into plants of several tens of centimetres across.

They also flower there, something which hardly ever happens in more temperate climates.

Try to imitate favourable conditions as much as possible by putting ferocactus in the full sun in summer giving it an average amount of water. Keep it completely dry in winter but with as much sun as possible. Use porous but fertile compost preferably containing some clay.

Some species are:

Ferocactus cylindraceus is columnar and has pinkish-red spines.

Ferocactus glaucescens remains more or less bulbous and is easily confused with *Echinocactus grusonii*. The ribs of the latter are more densely covered in spines.

Ferocactus histrix is often offered as a young plant. The small humps eventually form ribs. The yellow spines are brown to pink at the base.

Ferocactus peninsulae has a curved, fleshy-coloured central spine and orange and yellow flowers.

Ferocactus schwarzii looks very much like

Ferocactus histrix

Frailea phaeodisca

glaucescens but it gives yellow flowers when the young plant is about 10cm (4in) wide.

Frailea

Frailea species remain very small with bodies of a few centimetres across at the most. They are rarely to be found, which is a shame because they are easy to cultivate. The large,

brown, triangular seeds germinate readily and grow, within a year, into a plant that can bear flowers. Grow fraileas in aerated but nutritious compost and keep them moderately moist in spring. Put them in a very light place

Ferocactus glaucescens

but protect them from the hottest afternoon sun. Keep them nearly dry and in the sun in winter at a minimum temperature of 5°C (41°F). New flowers are produced throughout the summer. They are yellow, sometimes with a little red. In gloomy weather they do not open but self-fertilize and produce seed with good germinating capacity. Do not wait too long before sowing them because the germinating capacity decreases rapidly. Some species are: *Frailea colombiana* (yellow flowers 2 to 3cm 1 to 1.5in) wide; *Frailea pygmaea* (body 2cm (1in) wide, completely smooth, flat clusters of spines and flowers yellow from a woolly bud); *Frailea phaeodisca* (looks like *Frailea pygmea* but the areoles from which the spines grow are browner).

Gymnocalycium

These cacti from the southern half of South America are often bulbous and depressed at the top and are rarely densely spined. In summer spineless buds develop in the centre of the plant and open into fleshy flowers. The plants need to grow well in early summer to flower at their best. The roots are less vulnerable to rot than those of many other

Gymnocalycium mihanovichii 'Japan'

cacti and can therefore be watered more liberally during the growing season. Keep the plant dry during the winter at 5°C (41°F) to 10°C (50°F) or, if kept in the living room, water it occasionally on its tray. *Gymnoca-*

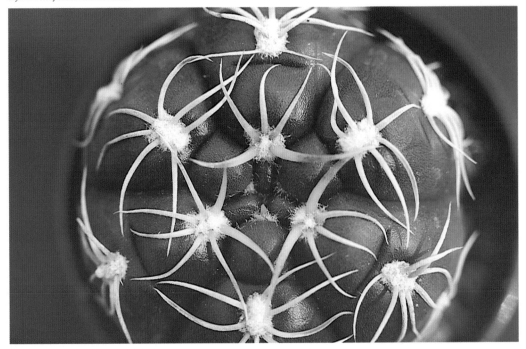

Gymnocalycium denudatum

cycium will only flower if their growth has stopped during the winter. Protect from bright sunlight in spring.

Some species are:

Gymnocalycium bruchii off-shoots profusely forming clumps of green stems with white spines. In spring, light-pink flowers appear on the tops of the stems. The species originates in Argentina and can tolerate frost in dry conditions.

Gymnocalycium denudatum originates in the south of Brazil and northern Argentina. It occurs in the form of a flattened bulb, about 8cm (3in) wide. It is dark green and shiny and has flat clusters of straw-yellow spines. Its flowers are slender and white.

Gymnocalycium mihanovichii. The true species has olive-green and red-brown bands over its stem and is seldom available. The so-called "Japanese cultivars" are common. Because they have no chlorophyll they cannot grow on their own. They are therefore grafted onto *Hylocereus*, which can be recognized by its triangular shape. On top of the hylocereus stem a cluster of orange-red , pink or yellow globules grows. The red forms have names like 'Hibotan' or 'Japan'. Others are red and green or red and yellow. Always keep these plants in the living room at a minimum temperature of 10°C (50°F) because the stock does not tolerate the cold. If the stock produces side-

shoots they need to be cut off immediately, otherwise the grafted *Gymnocalycium* will eventually shrivel up.

Hamatocactus setispinus

See: *Thelocactus setispinus*

Hatiora cylindrica

See: *Hatiora salicornioides*

Hatiora salicornioides

DANCING BONES (USA), DRUNKARD'S DREAM (USA), SPICE CACTUS (USA)

This freely branching shrub is not easily recognizable as a cactus, partly because it does not have spines. It grows in south-east Brazil where it is relatively humid, so *Hatiora* requires totally different care from most other cacti. Do not put it in the bright sun in summer and give an average amount of water. Spray the plant as often as possible. Decrease watering at the end of the growing season and put the plant in a slightly cooler place at about 15°C (59°F). Buds will appear and open into orange-yellow flowers in as winter approaches. After

Gymnocalycium bruchii

flowering, the plant has a period of rest until late spring when it comes back to life. Use the normal, slightly acid compost when re-potting.

Hatiora salicornioides

Horridocactus

See: *Neoporteria*

Islaya

See: *Neoporteria*

Krainzia

See: *Mamillaria*

Lobivia

See: *Echinopsis*

Lobivia famatimensis

See: *Rebutia famatimensis*

Lophophora williamsii

DUMPLING CACTUS, PEYOTE, MESCAL BUTTON

Indians of Central America regularly travel to the natural habitats of the so-called "peyote" in Mexico. They cut and eat parts of the plants and use it to induce a trance during religious celebrations. Peyotes contain mescaline, a drug which is deadly if taken in large doses. Peyotes are totally spineless and use the poison to stop animals eating them. The smooth, green round stems are decorated by little tufts of hair. They have a thick tap-root and this pulls the plant into the ground in times of drought. Put peyote, therefore, in a deep pot of well-drained compost which contains clay, and water moderately in summer. Keep the plant sunny, cool (at a minimum of 5°C (41°F)) and completely dry in winter. The plant then becomes soft and shrinks. Put it in a sunny and warmer place from April and give more water in warm weather. During the summer light-pink flowers develop in the centre of the plant, followed by berries. *Lophophora williamsii* rarely produces off-shoots unlike the subspecies caespitosa.

Lophophora williamsii

Mammillaria

TEPELCACTUS

The spines of *Mammillaria* grow on tubercles (teat-shaped prominences). The flowers open between these tubercles. There are hundreds of species, most of which originate in Central America. Some of them are very sensitive to moisture and are only worth trying to grow if you are very keen (these have been marked with*). Some of them, however, are very robust house plants and they usually bloom with flowers in a circle round the top of the stem, followed by oblong, usually orange-red berries. The enthusiasts' plants marked with * need full sun in summer as well as winter in a greenhouse or conservatory.

Mammillaria boolii

Mammillaria senilis

218

Mammillaria deherdtiana

Mammillaria elongata

219

Mammillaria longiflora

Mammillaria perbella

They need very porous compost and water only in hot weather. They need to be kept completely dry in winter at temperatures between 5 and 10°C (41 and 59°F). The other mammmillarias can tolerate more water in summer but otherwise need the same treatment as the ones marked with*, although they can tolerate less light. They can be kept in the windowsill during the winter but will hardly, or not at all, flower if kept at these higher temperatures. Some species are: *Mammillaria bombycina:* beautiful spination, small pink flowers.
Mammillaria boolii:* light green, white

spines and large pink flowers.
Mammillaria deherdtiana:* a compact globe-like plant with large, deep-red flowers.
Mammillaria elongata (lace cactus): stems about as wide as a gherkin, clumps of short cylindrical shoots with golden-yellow spines. This cactus is widely available. It has small, white flowers.
Mammillaria formosa (Mammillaria microthele): forms clusters of short and wide columns which are covered with white spines. Flowers are pale-pink.
Mammillaria guelzowiana (Krainzia guelzowiana):* covered in white hairs. Large, bright-

Mammillaria matudae

Mammillaria zeilmanniana

Mammillaria sphaerica

red flowers appear in summer. *Mammillaria haageana*: stem globular, up to 12cm (5in) across covered with short white and brown spines. Small, deep-pink flowers.

Mammillaria longiflora (Kranzia longiflora): large and long pink flowers grow from a densely spined stem.

Mammillaria matudae: long columnar stems which eventually grow horizontally. Densely covered with honey-yellow spines. Small deep-red flowers.

Mammillara microhelia: short and columnar. Spines spread out like the rays of the sun. Small pale-pink to light yellow flowers.

Mammillaria perbella: globular at first, growing into a column later. Stem completely covered with white spines and white woolly hair. Deep-red flowers.

Mammillaria pettersonii (Mammillaria heeseana): stem broadly columnar, dark with a lot of white wool, which appears like snow between the spines. Small pink flowers.

Mammillaria rhodantha: stem globular to broadly columnar with very variable spination and deep-pink flowers. A best selling species. The variety crassispina has honey-yellow spines. *Mammillaria schumannii (Bartschella schumannii)*: very small, grey-green globular stems with brown and white thorns

Mammillaria schumannii

and relatively large, violet-pink flowers. *Mammillaria senilis (Mammillopsis senilis)**: stem the shape of a flattened globe, densely covered with spines, completely white with yellow hooked spines. Flowers bright-red, large with a strikingly long flower tube.
Mammillaria sphaerica (Dolichothele sphaerica)*: short, broad plants with long tubercles and spreading straw-yellow spines. Large yellow flowers.
Mammillaria supertexta (Mammillaria lanata): stem globular to columnar, completely covered in white wool. Small pinkish-red flowers.
Mammillaria zeilmanniana: one of the most sold cacti. Red-brown and white spines, the central ones hooked. Stems shortly columnar carrying a crown of pink flowers.

Mamillopsis

See: *Mammillaria*

Mediolobivia

See: *Rebutia*

Melocactus

On reaching maturity melocacti develop a "bonnet". Young plants are globular with ribs and spines. When they mature they develop a terminal cephalium, the "bonnet",a dense cluster of growing points with wool, small spines and flowers between. The flowers are followed by conspicuous berries. The plant grows larger by extending its cephalium which eventually grows into a column of many tens of centimetres high.
In temperate climates it takes many years for a seedling to form a cephalium. In warmer regions, such as the Canary Islands, it only takes a few years. Nowadays plants are cultivated in the Canary Islands and sold with the cephalium just beginning to develop. Plants are also still taken out of their natural habitat. Buying one of the latter is a mistake as plants which already have a cephalium do not easily re-grow roots which have been damaged. Plants that have been taken from the wild and imported therefore usually die after a few months. You can check the condition of the roots by pushing the plant sideways. If there is little or no give the roots should be fine.
To make sure that you are not buying a plant that has been taken from its natural habitat - and in doing so contributing to the extinction of the species - you should ask the supplier of

Melocactus

your plant about its origin. *Melocacti* prefer a sunny and warm spot with some protection against the hottest sun in spring. They need an average amount of water in the summer. In winter they can be put in a light position in a cool room at a minimum of 10°C (50°F). Species from the Caribbean need a minimum temperature of 15°C (59°F). Only water when the plant starts to shrivel. Some species:
Melocactus azureas from Brazil has a striking, chalky-blue skin which is an effective protection from the bright sun.
Melocactus neryi grows in the North Brazilian interior and can tolerate lower temperatures reasonably well (down to 5°C (41°F)).

Neochilenia

See: *Neoporteria*

Neoporteria

There are about sixty recorded species of *Neoporteria*. Most of these are very spiny and flower in summer with tufts of white, yellow, pink or red flowers on the crown. They grow in the Andes regions of Chile, Argentina and Peru where ultraviolet radiation is high. They

Neoporteria nidus

Neoporteria islayensis

can therefore tolerate full sun. Water very sparingly and pot the plants in very porous compost which should be about half mineral particles (such as sand and gravel) because the roots are vulnerable to rot. The ideal place to grow these plants is in a greenhouse or conservatory. A sunny, airy windowsill is second best. The plants need to be kept light, cool, but just frost-free, and completely dry in winter. Some species:
Neoporteria clavata (Neoporteria nigrihorrida) is heavily armed with sharp, black spines. It has fluorescent pink flowers.
Neoporteria horrida (previously *Horridocactus tuberisulcatus*) is large for a Neoporteria. Its globular stems grow to more than 10cm (4in) across. They are green and have strong spines. The colour of the flowers may be white, soft-yellow, pink or red-brown.
Neoporteria islayensis (Islaya islayensis) is grey-green and woolly-white on top. The shiny black spines eventually turn grey; the flowers are yellow.
Neoporteria nidus (Neoporteria multicolor) is hidden by very long curved spines, notprickly, which are wrapped round the whole of the stem. Pink flowers manage to work their way through these spines in spring and early summer.
Neoporteria paucicostata (previously *Neochilenia paucicostata*) is available as a small flowering plant. The skin of the stem is brownish-red, the flowers are creamy coloured with

Neoporteria clavata

pink hues. The variety that used to be called *Neochilenia carneoflora* has fleshy-coloured flowers. This very variable genus now also comprises the species which used to be called *Neochilenia deherdtiana* and *Neochilenia pygmaea*.

Left: *Neoporteria horrida*
Below: *Neoporteria paucicostata*

Notocactus

See: *Parodia*

Opuntia

PRICKLY PEARS

Prickly pears are usually sold in flower. The red, orange or yellow flowers grow out of the edge of the pads. When you buy an *Opuntia* you buy a pad which has fairly recently been broken off a parent plant and rooted, which it does easily. After flowering new, young pads start to grow on the plant. It is best to put the plant outside in a sunny place in the summer. Give it an average amount of water and fertilizer to enable the young pads to develop fully. If they are also given a cool, dry and frost-free spell during the winter they may flower but usually fail to do so.

Opuntia is therefore a very unrewarding

Opuntia

Opuntia cylindrica

Oreocereus celsianus

plant, although it is widely sold. Moreover the pads have not only have very vicious spines but also glochids, very thin, short spines with hooks. When touched the glochids hook into the skin and can cause terrible itchiness. They can be removed by sticking clear celluloid tape onto the affected area of skin then pulling it off with a sharp tug.

The only species that can be recommended for the living room are: *Opuntia microdasys* (Bunny ears), a plant with small pads without spines but with closely set golden-yellow glochids. It can produce yellow flowers but they rarely appear under room cultivation.

Opuntia microdasys 'Albispina' has white glochids. Those of *Opuntia rufida* are red-brown.

Oreocereus

All white columnar cacti work on the imagination. Young plants of the following species are often available:

Cephalocereus senilis (old man cactus) takes the form of short colums when young with horizontal, white hairs. The plant needs a sunny position which never gets colder than 10°C (50°F). Keep completely dry in a cool room in winter. Water very sparingly because the base of the plant rots easily.

Cleistocactus forms columns a few tens of centimetres in height, which are quite slender with closely set white spines. They often

Opuntia

produce clusters of off-shoots. Only after a strict period of rest during the winter (at about 10°C (50°F) without water and very light) will they produce flowers in the summer. These are red, orange or yellow, tubular growing out of the sides of the stems.

Espotoa lanata looks like candyfloss. Young plants have the shape of a short cigar and are wrapped in white densely clustered hairs through which poke sharp thorns that are usually golden-yellow in colour. The treatment is the same as for *Cephalocereus senilis*.

Oreocereus is usually sold as a slightly larger column. Three closely related species are normally available: *Oriocereus celsianus*, which grows to a height of 3m (10ft), *Oreocereus trollii*, which grows to a height of 1m (3ft) at the most and *Oriocereus pseudofossulatus*, which has slender columns that can grow up to 4m (13ft) in height in Bolivia. These three plants can all tolerate winter temperatures down to zero and they are stronger than other "white columns" in every respect.

Oreocereus fossulatus

See: *Oreocereus pseudofossulatus*

Parodia alacriportana

Parodia

These cacti are striking because of the colour of their flowers which are pure red, orange or yellow. They form a fine spectacle being relatively large and arranged together on the crown of the plant. They occur naturally in a large area in the southern half of South America, east of the Andes, and they can tolerate more water than many aother species of cacti. They benefit greatly from spraying with a fine mist.

Give them a very sunny position but do not let them get too hot even in summer. Keep them

Parodia ayopayana

Parodia penicillata

Parodia lanii

dry in winter and put them in a cool, just frost-free, place. Occasionally give them some water on a tray under the pot if they shrivel noticeably. Some species:

Parodia alacriportana (previously *Brasilparodia alacriportana*) comes as a flattened globe, densely covered with spines and yellow flowers;

Parodia ayopayana has conspicuous white areoles (this is where the spines appear from) and orange flowers.

Parodia gracilis is bulbous with orange to yellow flowers.

Parodia haselbergii (Brasilicactus haselberg-

ii) is a popular house plant. It is covered with straight, white spines and has a lot of red flowers from the crown of the plant. Keep this species slightly warmer in winter (at about

Parodia haselbergii

Parodia rutilans

Parodia weberiana

10°C (50°F)) and water occasionally on the tray. *Parodia lauii* is a variable species, globular with large white areoles and red to orange flowers.

Parodia microsperma (synonymous with *Parodia sanguiniflora*). The new name refers to the small seeds, the old one to the bright red flowers of this species. It is often in flower when on sale but it is also very decorative without flowers. *Parodia penicillata* is armoured with glassy, white thorns and has large orange to deep-red flowers. *Parodia rutilans (Notocactus rutilans)* forms small stems with very beautiful spination and large light-pink or yellow flowers.

Parodia weberiana looks a lot like *Parodia microsperma*. The plant is hidden from sight by large orange flowers.

Pyrrhocactus

See: *Neoporteria*

Rebutia

These small bulbous cacti grow on plateaux in the Andes (in Bolivia and northern Argentina

Rebutia

and Chile) often at heights of 2000 to over 3000 m (nearly 2 miles). Therefore it comes as no surprise that they like fresh air, sun and not too hot a location. They are very suitable for placing outside in the summer, with shelter from the rain.

Since the classification of cactus species has been revised, whole genera have been abandoned and included in the genus *Rebutia*, all the species of *Aylostera*, *Mediolobivia*, *Sulcorebutia* and *Weingartia* and some of *Lobivia* being among them. The latter three are plants for enthusiast and are best kept in a sunny and airy greenhouse.

Rebutia heliosa

Rebutia

Rebutia

Rebutia famatimensis

Rebutia pulchra

Aylostera, Mediolobivia and the original rebutias can be grown indoors. In winter they like a light position as cool as possible but frost-free. Moisten the small globular stems with a fine mist of de-calcified water on sunny days in February and March. During the flowering period of April, May and June you can enjoy their presence in the living room. Put them in light spot but not in the hot afternoon sun. An east facing window is best. Keep spraying with a fine mist to help prevent red spider mite. The plants can be put outside in the fresh air after flowering; keep the soil averagely moist in the growing season and spray the plants regularly in warm weather.

They can grow in standard compost. Bring them inside as soon as there is a frost. In summer fruits will form after the flowers. These fruits tear open when they are ripe releasing many seeds which germinate easily but do not keep for long. Sow the seeds the next spring in sandy compost. The first young cacti could flower the year after with yellow, orange, red to violet flowers. Some species:
Rebutia cajacensis (previously *Aylostera*): red-orange flowers.
Rebutia heliosa (Aylostera): orange flowers. Only suitable for the advanced amateur.
Rebutia kupperiana (Aylostera): orange-red flowers.

Rebutia kupperiana

Rebutia frankiana (Sulcorebutia): shiny pink-red flowers.
Rebutia famatimensis (Lobivia): large red flowers.
Rebutia marsoneri (Rebutia): flowers profusely with yellow flowers.
Rebutia pulchra (Sulcoributia rauschii): purply-green plant with pinkish-red flowers.
Rebutia riograndensis (Weingartia): very spiny stem with yellow flowers.
Rebutia ritterii (Mediolobivia): dark, cylindrical stems with orange flowers.

Stenocactus

Stenocactus

There are about ten species of *Stenocactus* and they are all natives to Mexico. They grow in shrubby patches in dry areas and are difficult to distinguish from each other. There are numerous intermediate forms among the species. Most of them have many ribs which are as thin as leaves and have long, prickly, and often flattened spines. These sheet-like ribs and flattened spines probably create a micro-climate so ensuring that moisture evaporates less quickly from around the plant. *Stenocactus multicostatus* grows to about 10cm (4in) in width and has up to 120 very thin ribs. Give stenocacti as sunny a spot as possible and water moderately in summer. Keep dry and cool from late season to the spring (minimum 5°C (41°F)). The round stem will shrink and this will bring the ribs even more closely together. Gradually water more from spring onwards. *Stenocactus* will flower only if it gets a lot of light in summer and winter and a strict resting period in winter. The flowers are usually striped, white and pink to red and purple.

Sulcorebutia

See: *Rebutia*

Rebutia marsoneri var. spathulata

Thelocactus

Thelocacti grow in the hot border region between Mexico and the United States. They are popular with cactus lovers because of their large, brilliantly coloured flowers. *Thelocactus bicolor* (Glory of Texas) is the most often cultivated. It is a very variable species in which *Thelocactus wagnerianus* and *Thelocactus flavidispinus* are included nowadays. They require heat and sun in the summer. The compost should be porous and, even then, they have to be watered carefully. Keep light, cool and completely dry in winter.

Thelocactus setispinus (Strawberry cactus) is the easiest species. It is better known under its old name *Hamatocactus setispinus* and it is quite different from most other thelocacti. Its ribs are sharp, sometimes wavy, and the flowers yellow with a red centre. These are followed by orange-red berries. This species is often on the market because it is easily raised from seed and it tolerates moisture better than the other species. Keep it dry, cold (minimum 5°C (41°F)) and light in winter. Water in small amounts on a dish under the pot if the plant shrivels up too much. Protect shrivelled plants from the bright sun in spring.

Thelocactus flavidispinus

See: *Thelocactus bicolor*

Thelocactus wagnerianus

See: *Thelocactus bicolor*

Thelocephala

See: *Neoporteria*

Trichocereus

See: *Echinopsis*

Weingartia

See: *Rebutia*

Wigginsia

See: *Parodia*

Thelocactus setispinus

Right: *Thelocactus bicolor*

14. Euphorbias

There are about 5000 species in the Euphorbia family, the Euphorbiaceae. They grow throughout the world, especially in warm regions. Most species ooze white latex when damaged. It is poisonous but fortunately tastes too disgusting to be swallowed. There is no problem as long as you make sure that you do not to get the latex on your skin or in your eyes. Wash with lots of water straight away if this does happen.

Euphorbias are popular house plants because of the colourful bracts round their flowers and their resemblance to cacti. Species with spines are often, incorrectly, called cacti. The succulent species in particular are very long-lived and tolerate the warm, dry air of the living room so well that they eventually become tree-like in shape.

In the dry parts of Africa and Asia they grow like trees in among the dry grasses, their thick branches looking like the arms of a candelabra. The branches act as a moisture reserve and help the plant to survive the dry season.

Jatropha podagrica

TARTOGO, GOUT PLANT

The gout plant lives in Central America and has special characteristics to cope with the seasons. In the rainy season it has leaves and flowers. In the dry season it loses its leaves and lives on the moisture retained in its tuberous main stem - this can grow to a height of several tens of centimetres.

The gout plant likes a very light, preferably sunny position in a heated living room, summer and winter. It tolerates dry air well. Give average amounts of water when the plant

Left: *Euphorbia milii*, crown of thorns

is in leaf, but do not let the roots remain standing in water.

In late season the leaves yellow and drop off. The plant needs hardly any water until new growth shows in the spring. Clusters of orange-red flowers very often appear before the fig-like leaves of the plant.

Jatropha podagrica

Euphorbia ammak

Euphorbia ammak is a typical representative of the large, tree-like euphorbias from the dry regions of Asia and Africa. It is shown in the picture in its natural habitat in Yemen, but as a house plant it is only grown by enthusiasts. A similar African species, *Euphorbia candelabrum*, can grow in the wild up to a height of 20m (65ft). *Euphorbia ingens* is available and suitable for the modern interior. In southern and eastern Africa the plant grows into a tree of more than 10m (33ft) in height. Indoors it can reach the ceiling. Its stems have four wing-like angles.

The stems can be cut off with a strong, sharp knife if the plant becomes too big (be careful

237

with the latex). Taper the cuttings, wash them water and let them dry out for a few days. They can then be put to root moist, warm compost supported by four sticks, one between each pair of wings. The stumps on the main plant will sprout and branch after this treatment.

For maintenance of the above-mentioned species see *Euphorbia canariensis*.

Euphorbia canariensis

Groups of erect stems grow on the south-facing slopes of the Canary Islands. They are each about 8cm (3in) across and can grow more than 10m (33ft) in height.

Grown in the living room the stems are initially nearly square, with four wings, and are much thinner than those in the wild. *Euphorbia canariensis spiralis* is the subspecies which is often on sale. Its stems are slightly spiralled and they are reddish rather than green.

If the plant becomes very red, this is a sign that the roots have not developed properly. Give this tree-euphorbia a sunny position but protect it from the hottest sun. Water sparingly during active growth. No water should ever be

Euphorbia ammak in its natural setting in Yemen

allowed to stand around the roots. Give the plant an airy growing medium which mainly consists of non-organic material such as clay, sand and grit, and only a little peat or leaf-mould.

Euphorbia canariensis photographed on Tenerife

Give hardly any water during the winter rest. The plant should not grow at all in this period because it would produce soft, lanky growth which would disfigure it permanently. To stop growth put the euphorbia in a very light but cool place in winter (at a minimum of 10°C (50°F)).

Euphorbia grandicornis

COW'S HORN

This euphorbia from South Africa is characterized by tall, irregular stems with twisted wings and impressive spines. This plant which grows up to 2m (6ft) in height is not cultivated for its flowers but for the outlandish shapes of its shoots with three wing-like angles which are of high decorative value in a modern interior.
For maintenance see *Euphorbia canariensis*. For propagation see *Euphorbia ammak*.

Euphorbia grandicornis

Euphorbia milii

CROWN OF THORNS

The crown of thorns is a spiny shrub from Madagascar. It can thrive in a sunny window in a heated room. The stems are irregular in shape, densely spiny and branch freely. They carry spatula-shaped leaves and produce flowers on stalks from their tips. The flowers are inconspicuous but the orange to red bracts are very showy. They can be enjoyed almost all the year round. The plant only stops flowering and drops its leaves during its winter resting period.
This euphorbia likes a compost with humus. Give average amounts of preferably luke-warm water during active growth, less during the resting period. Keep the plant in the living room in summer and winter because it cannot tolerate cold and draughts.
The species *Euphorbia milii* is rarely available, but the subspecies *splendens* is often to be found. The latter is generally larger and has richly red flowers. There are also numerous hybrids such as 'Olympus' (pink-red), 'Pyramid Eyes' (with triangular yellow patches on the pinkish-red bracts) and x keysii (a compact plant with large leaves and red bracts).

Euphorbia milii 'Pyramide Eyes'

Euphorbia pulcherrima

POINSETTIA

Plant outlets are full of poinsettias towards Christmas. This euphorbia is a native of Mexico and has very inconspicuous flowers. The leaves at the top of the plant give it its decorative value. Depending on the cultivar they can be red, pink, salmon or creamy-white and are sometimes bi-coloured. Poinsettias can be enjoyed for many weeks if they are given a light spot and an average amount of water and are fertilized regularly. The water should be at room temperature. This species is particularly sensitive to cold and draughts. Never buy a plant from an outdoor stall in cold weather. Keep any plant you buy wrapped up during the journey home. Give poinsettias as humid a place as possible, for instance on wet gravel, to stop the leaves and flowers buds dropping off. Do not spray the leaves because that can cause fungus infection.

Poinsettias can be kept after flowering. Prune off at least half of the stems after the leaves have dropped and keep the plants cooler and dry for a while. However they will never grow into the same compact plants as before because growers keep the plants short with growth inhibitors.

Euphorbia resinifera

Euphorbia resinifera was the first euphorbia to be described. It was discovered by king Juba II from Mauritania in the first century AD and was named for the Greek natural philosopher

Euphorbos. He used the latex for medicinal purposes.

The species grew originally in North Africa where it covered large areas with short, columnar stems.

Grown in the living room the fleshy, blue-green stems can also branch into a dense group. The flowers are inconspicuous.

Grow this easy *Euphorbia* in a wide, shallow pot or dish in clay compost with sand and grit

Euphorbia resinifera

Euphorbia pulcherrima

mixed in. For further care see *Euphorbia canariensis.*

Euphorbia schimperi

This species originates in Arabia. The stems are spine-less and cylindrical and rather like erect pencils (hence the Dutch common name "pencil euphorbia"). Clusters of greeny-yellow flowers shining with nectar occur at the end of the stems if the plant is well looked after. Most plants that are sold under this name are in fact Euphorbia nubica, a related species from eastern Africa.
For maintenance see *Euphorbia tirucalli.*

Euphorbia schimperi

Euphorbia splendens

See: *Euphorbia milii*

Euphorbia tirucalli

RUBBER SPURGE, FINGER TREE, MILK BUSH
This freely branching tree euphorbia forms dense scrub in its native East Africa, India and Indonesia. The soft, cylindrical stems carry minuscule leaves in the rainy season. Finger euphorbias do not tolerate the cold. They need higher temperatures, not dropping below 15°C (59°F) than other succulent euphorbias which can easily get through the winter at 10°C (50°F).
Give this plant a light and preferably sunny position in summer and winter. Water hardly at all in winter, moderately in summer. Let the soil dry out before watering again preferably with luke-warm tap water.

Euphorbia tirucalli

Euphorbia trigona

The stems of *Euphorbia trigona* have three wing-like angles and they carry short, sharp spines as well as leaves. Its flowers are very inconspicuous. Eventually the plant grows into a freely-branching giant of 2m (6ft) or more; it is then usually thrown away. Try to propagate it instead by cutting off young shoots at their base (make sure the latex does not come into contact with mouth, eyes or skin).
Wash the latex off the cuttings, let them dry for a few days and put them in mildly moist, warm compost.
Euphorbia trigona likes full sun, moderate amounts of water in the summer and little water in the winter. The leaves die off in winter but this is a natural process. The plant will produce new ones in spring. Make sure the spines do not pierce the stems when you

move the plant or latex will ooze out and disfigure it, especially as fungi will grow on the latex.

Euphorbia viguieri

Euphorbia viguieri is increasingly available from garden centres. It grows into a bush of more than 1m (3ft) in height in south west Madagascar, where it is dry. *Euphorbia leuconeura*, which is also a native of Madagascar, is very similar to viguieri and better known. It grows in a way similar to "crown of thorns" (*Euphorbia milii*), regularly producing new flower stalks from the growing point of the plant. The leaves also grow from the growing point. They soon drop off and leaving moon-shaped scars behind on the stems. Antler-shaped spines grow on the edges of the scars.

See for maintenance *Euphorbia milii*.

Pedilanthus tithymaloides

REDBIRD CACTUS, SLIPPER CACTUS

The stems of *Pedilanthus* form a zig-zag pattern by making a sharp kink at every leaf

Left: *Euphorbia trigona*
Below: *Euphorbia viguieri*

node. It is called "devils backbone" in Holland because of this characteristic. However, the plant is actually very well-behaved and the only "devilish" thing about it could be its poisonous latex. The plant tolerates dry air very well and is therefore eminently suitable for keeping in a sunny window in the living room, summer and winter.

The cultivar 'Variegatus' needs the most light. Water moderately in summer, even less in winter but enough to prevent the falling of the leaves.

Cut the stems off a few centimetres above soil level if they become bare at the base with age. New shoots will sprout from the buds. The cuttings can be put in sandy compost to propagate the plant. Make sure the white latex does not get into the eyes, nose or mouth. Wash the latex off the cuttings before putting them in the compost, or dip them in ash or powdered charcoal. Do not cover with plastic.

Poinsettia

See: *Euphorbia pulcherrima*

Pedilanthus tithymaloides 'Variegatus'

15. Succulents

Succulents grow in regions with well defined rainy and dry seasons. In the wet months they absorb moisture and store it in their leaves, stems or trunk. In the dry season they live on these stored reserves. Cacti and many euphorbias are also succulents and have the same rhythm of growth and rest. Looking after succulents is an art which requires giving them enough light, water and nutrients during the growing period and stopping this at the right moment so that they can enter their resting period.

Many species grow and flower in the summer. But some species from the southern hemisphere stick to their internal clock and come to life inlate season in northern Europe, the time when it is spring in their native environments. They do not get enough natural light in our winters and need extra light to flower.

Adenium obesum

DESERT ROSE

Shrubs with beautiful pink flowers bloom against the dry slopes of Arabia and in the hot African Sahel. On closer inspection an enormous tuber-like main stem is visible under the succulent, cylindrical branches. On the Arabian peninsula it is usually irregular and often more than 2m (6ft) across with a large part of it lying underground. On the island of Socotra it is bottle-shaped and up to 5m (16ft) in height. *Adenium obesum* has only recently become available as a house plant. It is usually bought as a rooted cutting which can flower while quite young. The flowers show that the plant is a member of the *apocynaceae* family. They have five petals and are light pink in the centre with a darker edge. If cared for well *Adenium* can flower a number of times in the summer, at short intervals. Water only when the soil is nearly dried out, using luke-warm water. If the plant is kept dry in winter, it will lose its leaves. You can also keep *Adenium* growing by carrying on watering regularly. Put it in full sun in a warm place (never below 10ºC (50ºF)). A combination of wet compost and cold leads inevitably to rot.

It is easy to propagate the plant from shoots. Make sure not to touch the poisonous latex. Cut off a shoot and wash it under the tap. Let it dry for a few days and put in a warm spot in moderately moist, sandy compost.

Adenium obesum in its natural setting

Left: *Agave bovicornuta*

Aeonium

The well-known *Aeonium arboreum* is discussed in the chapter on container plants. The two species that are dealt with here need more attention and can be grown indoors on a sunny windowsill or outdoors in summer.

Aeonium decorum originates on Gomera, one of the Canary Islands.. It produces small, fleshy-leafed rosettes. The bottom leaves drop off and because of this the rosettes eventually stand on a bare stalk. These stalks can grow up to 50cm (20in) in length on Gomera. The rosettes flower in late summer and then die. Grow the plants in a mineral-rich compost (clay, sand, gravel) and a little humus. In summer water as soon as the compost is dry. Keep dry and cool (minimum 5°C (41°F)) in winter but always sunny.

Aeonium tabuliforme forms a completely flat rosette of fringed leaves which overlap each other spirally. The species originates in Tenerife. The leaves are quite thin and need water in winter. Give an average amount of water in the summer and slightly less in the winter and keep at a minimum temperature of 15°C (59°F). The rosettes can flower in late season producing flower structures which are about 25cm (10in) long and wide, and have pale-yellow flowers. The rosettes die off after flowering so you will have to collect seed to keep the plant.

Aeonium tabuliforme

very decorative they have been planted in other warm countries and have naturalized there. On the arid west coast of Costa Rica the leaves remain green even in the dry season

Aeonium decorum

Agave

CENTURY PLANTS

Agave species are natives of tropical America. They produce sturdy rosettes. Because their leaves and enormous flower structures are

Agave americana 'Medio-picta'

while the trees drop their leaves. As house plants, agaves are just about indestructible. Most species eventually grow too large for a living room but they can then be kept as container plants and grown outside in the summer. In winter they are put in a light, cool position and hardly watered at all. If kept indoors they can be watered in summer and winter but the roots should not be left standing in water. They grow best in clayey soil.

Agave americana is the best-known species. In the wild the leaves can reach a length of nearly 2m (6ft). It remains considerably smaller when grown in a pot or a container. The variegated forms of this species are the ones usually available.

Agave americana 'Marginata' (with wide, yellow leaf edges).

Agave americana 'Variegata' (with creamy-white leaf edges).

Agave americana 'Medio-picta' (with a wide, creamy-white band through the centre of the leaf).

Agave bovicornuta originates, like *Agave americana*, in Mexico but remains about half the size of the latter. The leaves are light green and waxy with a narrow red-yellow spiny margin and a red terminal spine. This terminal spine is very decorative but it is perhaps best to snip it off if their are small children in the house.

Agave in its natural setting

Agave parryi remains smaller still but will eventually reach a width of about 50cm (20in). The flower stalk can grow to a height of 5m (16ft) but not in a cool climate. With this

Agave parryi

variety you can appreciate the leaves which are covered in a blue-grey haze and show their clear impression on other leaves left behind after they have unfolded. The spines are chocolate-brown. This species is native to the scorching hot south-western United States and neighbouring Mexico and a position in full sun is particularly important to maintain the haze on its leaves.

Alluaudia

The lively green leaves of *Alluaudia* form a bright contrast with its silvery stems. They grow into poles several metres high in Madagascar where they are part of the thorny forests of dry regions. Until recently *Alluaudia* was a plant for the very keen amateur. Nowadays it is often available from well-stocked garden centres. Give it the sunniest place available. Water little in spring and summer and only when the compost is dry. Keep the plant completely dry in winter and put it in a cooler place at a minimum temperature of 12°C (54°F). The leaves will drop off. Put the plant back into the living room when new leaves appear and gradually give more water. Repot in very airy compost which contains hardly any humus and do not give any fertilizer.

Alluaudia

Aloe

Aloes are popular garden plants in places which never get any frost. The plant has rosettes of thick, fleshy leaves from which long stems rise carrying dense rows of oblong flowers. The flowers are red, orange, yellow (often with some green) or any hue in between. Aloes are natives of Africa.

In northern Europe the plants need to be brought inside in winter, although most of them can tolerate some cold or even a few degrees of frost. It is best to put them outside in summer in full sun. Indoors they need to be protected from the hottest sun otherwise the leaves will turn reddish. Their maintenance is very simple. Water liberally but let the potting soil dry out completely before watering again. The compost should be loose and preferably contain a lot of minerals such as sand, stone and clay. Never leave any water standing in the outer pot. Feeding is hardly necessary if you re-pot the plant every two or three years.

Aloe vera (medicine plant, burn plant) contains oils which are in high demand in the cosmetics industry. The plant is often depicted on cream and shampoo containers. Although the species originates in the Cape Verde islands, it has been cultivated in many places and has thereby become naturalixed so that it can now be found on the Canary islands, around the Mediterranean and in South and

Aloe vera

Central America. The succulent leaves grow in a compact rosette from which flower stems with yellow flowers arise in summer.

Aloe striatula grows outside in summer and winter on the Scilly Isles off the south-west coast of Cornwall, England. There is hardly ever any frost on these islands and the aloes that have been freely planted outside can tolerate the cold. If grown in a pot aloe needs to be kept out of the frost. You will be able to enjoy the orange and yellow flowers if the plant grows well. If it does not produce flowers try growing it outside on a balcony or a terrace for a summer.

Aloe barbadensis

See: *Aloe vera*

Beaucarnea recurvata

PONY TAIL, ELEPHANT FOOT

This species is often for sale under the name *Nolina recurvata*. Young plants of the species have a rosette of strap-shaped leaves which grow out of a round tuberous stem. They are often sold three to a pot. When the plant matures the stem first swells up and then becomes bottle-shaped. The plant reaches tree size in its native environment in Central America and in the southern United States. It will not reach that size in the living room because it grows steadily but not very quickly. Sometimes older plants are on the market which have a bottle-shaped stem and several tufts of leaves. These are imported stem tubers. *Beaucarnea recurvata* is easy to look after and can tolerate dry air and full sun well. Keep it in the light as much as possible and give an

Beaucarnea recurvata

Aloe striatula

average amount of water. Put it in a cool spot in winter (minimum 5°C (41°F)) and water little. It can also remain in the living room. *Beaucarnea stricta* is very similar to *recurvata* but the leaf edges are rougher. Maintenance is the same for both.

Ceropegia

STRING OF HEARTS

The flowers of *Ceropegia* are among the most complicated flowers on earth. As happens with some orchids, insects are held captive in the flower for a short while until they have pollinated it. When pollination has taken place they are allowed to leave. The best known species is *Ceropegia woodii* (string of hearts, rosary vine). The shoots from a tuber in the soil are thin and thread-like and hang down over the edge of the pot. They produce small, green and silver marbled leaves and eventually also the characteristically shaped flowers. These are pink with aubergine-coloured hairy lobes joined together at the tips to form a cage. Hang the plant in a very light place and only protect it from the hottest summer sun. Only water when the soil has dried out completely. Eventually the tubers

Ceropegia radicans

expand to fill the pot. This is the time to re-pot using a mixture of clay, sand and humus. Aerial tubers which develop on the stems root easily in compost. Some species of *Ceropegia*, which are really plants for the keen amateur, are generally available nowadays. *Ceropegia radicans*, a species from Cape Province, South Africa, is one of them. It does not grow tubers on its stems which are cylindrical, green and succulent. On the nodes, rudimen-

Ceropegia woodii subs. *woodii*, string of hearts

tary roots develop which grow down to the soil. This makes the plant very easy to propagate. It produces flowers which are about 5cm (2in) long and they appear mainly in late season. You will be able to enjoy the characteristic shape and modest colours of this plant if you hang it in a light place. Hang it in a cool place in winter but not below about 10°C (50°F), and water hardly at all.

Ceropegia linearis woodii

See: *Ceropegia woodii*

Conophytum

To obtain these beautifully flowered succulents you will need to go to specialist nurseries where you will find different species with white, yellow, orange, salmon, pink, carmine or violet flowers. *Conophytums* grow in South Africa and they look like "living stones". They are very inconspicuous amongst the quartz gravel and are therefore well-protected from being grazed by animals. In this respect they are similar to *Lithops* species which are the true "living stones". In South Africa *Conophy-*

tum grows and flowers in spring (September, October) and it stubbornly sticks to this rhythm in the northern hemisphere. Put the plant in as sunny a spot as possible during these months and water when the compost has nearly dried out. Water about once a week when you grow them in a loose compost mixture in a shallow dish (which is what they like). Extra light during flowering and growing period which follows is beneficial. Stop active growth during the rest of the winter by putting the plant in a cool (minimum 5°C (41°F)) spot as light as possible and by keeping it dry. Water hardly at all during spring and summer until buds appear again from the centres of the "stones".

Crassula ovata

There are about 300 species of *Crassula* which mostly grow in southern Africa. They have fat, very fleshy leaves which can completely hide the stems. *Crassula ovata* is one of the easiest of house plants. It can tolerate dry air, bad compost, full sun, but also semi-shade and irregular watering. The only thing it cannot tolerate is a foot bath! Its growth is unstoppable: the round stems

A collection of *Conophytum* in Leiden (The Netherlands)

branch abundantly so that the plant forms a shrub several tens of centimetres high.

When it flowers it produces whitish starry flowers which grow together in small clusters. But this seldom happens in a living room. It is easy to rejuvenate the plant if it becomes too big: break some older leaves from the stem, put them in the soil at the base of the old plant and young plants will develop spontaneously.

Crassula ovata

Crassula portulacea

See: *Crassula ovata*

Crassula schmidtii

This *Crassula* has soft stems and moisture filled leaves. It forms a loose mat which can flower for months on end with deep-pink flowers. Water when the soil is nearly dried out and put the plant in a sunny position.

Echeveria

The rosettes of fleshy leaves of this plant have a blue-green appearance caused by a waxy layer which protects the plants from the hot

Echeveria

sunshine in Central America. Put echeverias therefore in as sunny a spot as possible. In summer they prefer a place outside in full sun. Water regularly but let the compost dry out between waterings.

The rosettes often flower with yellow, orange or red flowers in late season.

After flowering, echeverias like a light but cool position and need very little watering. In time the lower leaves drop off and bare stems are formed with the rosettes on top. The rosettes can be cut off, dried for a few days and put in sandy compost.

The stumps will usually sprout again. It is the

Crassula schmidtii

cultivars of *Echeveria* which are usually on sale.

Frithia pulchra

In South Africa *Frithia* grows almost totally underground. Only the tips of the leaves show at the surface. The tips are flattened and transparent so that light can shine through them into the leaves!
There are two other "window" plants which grow according to the same principle: *Fenestraria aurantiaca* and *Fenestraria rhopalopylla*. The latter two species have yellow and white flowers in late summer and winter respectively. *Frithia pulchra* is easier to maintain then the two species of *Fenestraria* because it flowers in summer, producing pink flowers often with a white centre. Until recently this was a species for advanced amateurs only. Nowadays it is for sale as a house plant.

In temperate regions it needs every ray of light it can get. It should not be buried and the long leaves should be kept above ground. Put this succulent in the sunniest possible place and only water in spring and summer if the weather is warm. The compost should be porous so that any left-over water can drain away easily.
Keep it completely dry in winter in a cool room (minimum 5°C (41°F)).

Fouquieria splendens

In Mexico the spiny stems of this shrub grow to a height of nearly 10m (33ft). They are used as impenetrable dividing screens. *Fouquieria* grows at a moderate rate in the living room and should be watered moderately, only in summer. From August the plant should be given less and less water.
The leaves will drop, as they do in the wild, during dry spells. Keep it completely dry in winter and put it in a cool, frost-free place. Start watering again in spring and reddish cluster of flowers may develop. However this plant deserves the name "splendens" (brilliant) even without flowers.

Frithia pulchra

253

Fouquieria splendens

leaves and flowers. In summer you can enjoy the sweet smell of the pendent flower umbels. The flowers are waxy white with a deep-pink crown in the centre.

The miniature wax plant can be grown as a shrub or a hanging plant. Put the plant in as humid a spot as possible and very light but protect the leaves from bright summer sun to avoid pale-brown patches caused by burning. Water liberally but only when the compost has nearly dried out. The compost should be humus-rich with some clay and gravel added to aerate it.

Keep the miniature wax plant drier in winter and put in a cool, light spot but never below 15° (59°F).

Hoya carnosa

WAX PLANT

The wax plant is more robust than *Hoya bella*. The foliage of carnosa is thicker and better protected against drying out. This plant can tolerate a living room climate better and can endure lower temperatures in winter. Hardly water at all in winter and keep at a minimum temperature of 10°C (50°F).

Hoya bella

MINIATURE WAX PLANT

The miniature wax plant has cylindrical stems which hang down under the weight of its

Below: *Hoya bella*

Right: *Hoya carnosa* 'Compact'

Water normally in summer but do not let the soil remain soaking wet after watering. If grown in a very light spot, rounded umbels will develop which are very fragrant.

Hoya carnosa 'Compact' is a widely sold cultivar which has pendent stems and wavy, often variegated leaves.

Hoya lanceolata bella

See: *Hoya bella*

Hoya multiflora

The name means literally "multi-flowered" wax plant. Each umbel produces tens of sweetly smelling flowers.

They are more or less arrow-shaped, white and light yellow and are often partly covered by the large tough leaves which are about 10cm (4in) in length.

The "multi-flowered" wax plant originates in South-East Asia where it grows as a small climber.

The stems are quite sturdy but need support to be able to carry the heavy weight of the foliage and flowers. For further maintenance see *Hoya bella*.

Hoya multiflora

Kalanchoe blossfeldiana

FLAMING KATY

There are numerous cultivars of this species. They have glossy green leaves and white,

yellow, orange, red or pink flowers. They are available covered in flowers throughout the year. If you manage to get them to bloom again you will find that naturally they flower in late season.

Most people do not manage to get *Kalanchoe blossfeldiana* to flower again. If the plants are kept in a heated living room and are watered regularly they will grow well but they will not flower. To bring them into flower they need to be kept cool in winter (minimum 10°C (50°F) and watered very little. Re-pot in spring in loose, fertile compost (standard potting soil with some clay and gravel) and gradually water more. They will flower in late season if put in a sunny position.

Kalanchoe blossfeldiana

Kalanchoe manginii 'Tessa'

See: *Kalanchoe* 'Tessa'

Kalanchoe 'Tessa'

This popular hanging plant, for use in sunny spots, was bred from, among others, *Kalanchoe* manginii. The latter is a creeping plant from Madagascar and produces bell-shaped flowers as well as ready-made young plantlets on its stems.

'Tessa' is easy to maintain. Hang the pot in the sun or in a light place and water liberally in the summer. A resting period is beneficial after 'Tessa' has flowered in late summer, winter or spring. Hardly water at all and put the plant in a cool and light place. Start it growing again

Kalanchoe 'Tessa'

Kalanchoe tomentosa

after a few months by giving it more water and higher temperatures.

Kalanchoe tomentosa

PUSSY EARS, PANDA PLANT

This *Kalanchoe* is not grown for its flowers but for its felt-like foliage. The leaves are covered in white wool and have red-brown spots at the tips. It is a low-growing plant which should be put in as sunny a spot as possible to produce a denser cover of hairs and larger red-brown spots. Water moderately. The panda plant originates in the mountains of Madagascar. It likes a very light position in winter as well as summer but preferably cooler (minimum 10°C (50°F)). Water little to stop growth. If it becomes etiolated and bare from growth during the winter it can be propagated by cutting off stem sections or by breaking off mature leaves. Let them dry for a day and then root them in sandy soil.

Lithops

LIVING STONES

In 1811 the English plant expert Burchell tried to lift up a stone from the South-African plain but found that it refused to move and was in fact a plant. It consists of two leaves each of which is completely underground except for the surface. The surfaces are almost identical to the natural stones of the region. In regions with different coloured stones the colour of the plants is adapted to give perfect camouflage.

There are more than 30 species of living stones and they are good house plants even though they originate in the driest regions of South Africa. They start to grow in about May and flower after the summer. The flowers emerge from between the two leaves. They are usually yellow or white and wider than the two leaves. Only water in sunny weather during growth and flowering and not until the compost has dried out again. Keep the plants completely dry in winter preferably in a cool room (minimum 5°C (41°F)). Always keep living stones in the full sun. They have a thread-like root system which only grows well in very loose compost (preferably with some stone-dust mixed in) and do not tolerate the cold. *Lithops* is best grown in a shallow tray which

should not be put on a cold windowsill but on a piece of polystyrene.

Lithops

Myrmecodia echinata

Myrmecodia has a tuberous root which makes it looks like a succulent. This tuber is not meant to store moisture though, but ants. Inside it is a network of chambers intended to give a home to ants which protect the plant against the voracity of aphids and other insects in exchange for this hospitality. They even eat through the intrusive stems of other plants. *Myrmecodia* moreover benefits from the excretions which the ants leave behind in the chambers.

Myrmecodia

Numerous "ant plants" exist, each from totally different families. The best known one is *Dischidia pectenoides* which has on its branches oval, green bladders in which ants can live. *Dischidia* grows best in a light, but not too sunny place. Maintenance is otherwise the same as for *Myrmecodia*.

Myrmecodia is new as a house plant. In South-East Asia it grows on trees and therefore needs a very airy, humus-rich and acidic soil mixture.

Water with rainwater or boiled tap water and make sure that the roots never remain wet. This ant plant likes a very light location, preferably in the sun. The temperature should never drop below about 12°C (54°F).

Nolina recurvata

See: *Beaucarnea recurvata*

Pachypodium

Pachypodium lamerei is a well known house plant with long, dark green leaves which grow from a very spiny, thick stem. Eventually it will grow as high as a person and is then often thrown away. *Pachypodium* is very robust and can tolerate the climate in a dry living room very well. The plant likes warm and sunny locations and is not very sensitive to incorrect watering. Water liberally with lukewarm water and do not let the roots remain standing in water.

The plant does not need a resting period but does not mind if it is given one by being watered less in the winter. Most of the leaves will drop in that case and new leaves will grow only at the top.

Pachypodium geayi looks nearly the same as *lamerei*. The difference is in the flowers which hardly ever form in the living room, and in the hairs which adorn the top and the young leaves of *geayi*. Give this species slightly less water. Otherwise maintenance is the same as for *lamerei*.

Pachypodium lealii saundersii originates in southern Africa. Its stem has a silvery-grey bark to protect it against the relentless sun. The contrast between its bark and the glossy-green leaves is a pleasure to behold. This species can produce large, white flowers but usually the buds drop off through lack of light as they develop in late season. It is possible to rescue them by giving them extra light in good

time. Apart from that, maintenance is simple. Give an average amount of water in summer but stop watering as soon as the leaves turn yellow and drop off. Water again when the plant produces new growth. The plant grows best in a very sunny position in a heated living room (minimum 10°C (50°F)) and is easy to propagate from seed. Be careful with the sap of this plant - the local inhabitants use it to make arrows poisonous!

Pachypodium lealii saundersii

Pachypodium saundersii

See: *Pachypodium lealii saundersii*

Saxifraga

SAXIFRAGES

Most saxifrages grow wild in mountainous areas and are cultivated for the rock garden. Generally they remain small and flower abundantly mostly in May and June. During the growing season in the summer they like a lot of water but their roots do not tolerate stagnant moisture and will rot easily, especially in winter. If kept dry they can tolerate severe frosts.

Keen amateurs keep succulent saxifrages under glass but very cool in winter. A cold greenhouse is ideal. Failing that, the plants

can also be kept indoors by the window of an unheated room. Air the plant as often as possible. In spring put the plants in their pots outside in a sunny position.

Sedum rubrotinctum

STONECROP

There are about 300 species of stonecrop. Most of them creep along the ground with their leafy stems. The foliage is nearly always succulent and full of moisture.

Sedum rubrotinctum originates in Mexico. In our climate it is an easy house plant which can tolerate dry air very well, does not have very onerous soil requirements and likes as much sun as possible. In the shade the red colour on the leaves disappears and the stems become etiolated and bare.

Water normally in summer. Keep the plant dry in the dark months and put it in a cool room (minimum 5°C (41°F)) in as light a spot as possible.

Other popular species are: *Sedum pachyphyllum* (with large, milky-green leaves with a red tip), *Sedum morganianum* (see the chapter

on climbing and hanging plants) and *Sedum sieboldii* (with round foliage, flattened at the top, on cylindrical stems). The cultivar *Sedum sieboldii* 'Media-Variegatum' has grey-green leaves with a cream-coloured marking in the centre.

Saxifraga

Left: *Sedum rubrotinctum*

Below: *Saxifraga species in a nursery*

261

16. Carnivorous plants

Not all plants act like vegetables!. Some n ove about to catch small creatures. Insects land on the sticky tentacles of sundew and cannot get away. The tentacles bend down to the surface of the leaf where the insect is digested.

Carnivorous plants need to eat insects to flourish. They grow in acid, peaty swamps where nutrients are few and those available are not easily be absorbed by the roots. The plants h ive therefore developed incredibly ingenious methods to trap flies and other insects. It is fascinating to watch the plants do this.

Unfortunately it is not easy to keep carnivorous plants alive for very long. They need rainwater and the high humidity of a swamp. However it is possible to grow and admire carnivorous plants in the living room by creating special conditions for them.

Drosera aliciae

SUNDEW

The leaves of *Drosera aliciae,* a South African species, form perfect rosettes which are pressed against the soil. The rosettes are about 5cm (2in) across and covered with red tentacles, each having a sticky terminal globule. Small creatures stick to the globules. They are then pushed towards the leaf surface by the tentacles and digested.

If looked after properly *Drosera aliciae* blooms with red flowers which are wider than

Left: *Nepenthes truncata*

1cm (0.5in) and are carried on a stem which can reach about 50cm (20in) in length.

Grow this species in the full sun. The compost should be acid. Sphagnum moss is ideal but a mixture of plenty of peat and some sand is also fine. Put the plant pot in a wide dish of water in summer to raise the humidity around the plant.

Only water into the dish, always using rainwater. Growing the plant in an almost closed glass tank or aquarium is ideal. Do not leave any water in the dish in winter but keep the compost moist. Put the plant in an unheated room in winter, at the lowest possible temperature but frost free.

☼ ◊

Drosera aliciae

Nepenthes

Nepenthes species are natives of the tropical forests between Madagascar and Australia. They are often called "pitcher plants", the pitchers being modified leaves. These pitchers only develop if the plant gets enough light and all other conditions are ideal.

There is nectar on the lid above the pitcher. Insects that find this nectar crawl into the pitcher looking for more. They find some on the rim of the pitcher but just underneath this is a slippery, waxy area and many insects slide down this into the pitcher.

Their struggling activates glands in the pitcher which excrete a strong acid which can digest a house fly in two days leaving only the husk.

263

The ordinary windowsill is not suitable for *Nepenthes* species which can only survive if given high air humidity.

Grow them in a tropical greenhouse or indoors under glass (for instance in a large fish tank which is almost entirely closed with sheets of glass). To grow well the plants need tropical temperatures in summer and an average amount of light away from direct sunlight. Water with luke-warm rainwater. Keep the compost constantly moist but make sure that the water can drain away freely.

Nepenthes x *chelsonii*

Use loose, permeable compost made up of fern root, fir bark, coarse peat dust and/or sphagnum moss.

Pitcher plants from higher regions are able tolerate lower temperatures (minimum 10°C (50°F)) in winter but it is better to keep them warm all winter.

Nepenthes alata and *Nepenthes ventricosa* grow in mountainous forests and can be kept relatively cool.

Nepenthes gracilis is a species from low regions as are *Nepenthes rafflesiana* and *Nepenthes truncata* and the hybrid *Nepenthes x chelsonii*. They like extra warm conditions.

Numerous hybrids have been cultivated since the last century. *Nepenthes* 'Mizuho Kondo' has conspicuous wavy edged flanges on its stem.

Pinguicula

BUTTERWORTS

Pinguicula (Butterwort) is a native plant in large areas of Europe but is rarely found. It grows in peat bogs in the wild and can be grown outside in the garden if you can imitate a peat bog.

It is difficult to keep butterwort in a living room, but varieties from Central America, for example, *Pinguicula moranensis* from Mexico, come into their own in such conditions. This plant needs a lot of rainwater in the summer and it should be given on a wide dish under the plant pot. The water evaporates and provides a high level of humidity. Unlike most other carnivorous plants this butterwort likes some clay in its compost which should otherwise consist mostly of peat dust and some sharp sand.

Put the plant in a dish of water or a terrarium in a sunny windowsill and protect from the hot summer sun. The plant will then produce long stalks with pink flowers which look like pansies.

Keep the plant moderately moist in late season and during the winter. The summer leaves, which have numerous minuscule tentacles with globules of fluid, die off and are replaced by winter leaves. These are about half the size

Right: *Nepenthes* 'Mizuho Kondo'
Below: *Pinguicula moranensis*

of the summer leaves and lack the sticky substance which in summer catches small flies and crawling creatures and digests them on the leaf surface.

Sundew and butterwort belong to the group of carnivorous plants that can actively move. The edges of the leaves of butterwort gradually curl up when a larger prey creature lands on them. The leaves of the cultivar *Pinguicula* 'Weser' are curled upwards even if there is nothing to prey on.

Pinguicula 'Weser'

Pinguicula caudata

See: *Pinguicula moranensis*

Pinguicula mexicana

See: *Pinguicula moranensis*

Sarracenia flava

YELLOW PITCHER PLANT, HUNTSMAN'S HORN

The slender funnels-shaped flowers of the yellow pitcher plant can fulfil their role in the house. They attract flies into the pitchers and digest them. The plant is a very effective fly-catcher and is often bought for that reason.

In spring it produces strangely shaped flowers which can reach 10cm (4in) across. They look a bit like a narcissus with a bulging trumpet closed at the front. Its colour is chiefly greenish yellow.

This pitcher plant from the southern United States is relatively easy to grow. It can be kept in a window in the full sun although some protection when the sun is at its hottest is recommended.

Water with rainwater on a wide tray under the pot. Leave some water in the tray to increase the humidity around the plant. Water in the same way in winter but put the plant in a light but cool place (minimum 5°C (41°F)). The compost should ideally consist of chiefly of sphagnum moss and peat with some sharp sand added.

Sarracenia purpurea

COMMON PITCHER PLANT

This species grows in the wild from the United States to northern Canada. The northern plants are called *Sarracenia purpurea* sub-species *purpurea* (northern pitcher plant).

Sarracenia flava

They are quite slender and completely hardy. Plant outlets usually sell the so-called "southern pitcher plant" *Sarracenia purpurea* subspecies *venosa*. For maintenance of the latter species see *Sarracenia flava*. The northern pitcher plant is more easily grown outside throughout the year than in a living room.

Utricularia sandersonii

Utricularia sandersonii from South Africa has very small leaves and foliage. The leaves are only a few millimetres (less than 0.25in) long, the flowers just over 1cm (0.5in) wide. *Utricularis vulgare* is a water plant whereas *Utricularis sandersonii* grows in soil.

Its compost should consist of a mixture of peat and some sand. Put the pot in a wide tray of rainwater in a windowsill and protect from direct sunlight. The plant likes a moist atmosphere in winter as well, but a cooler position (never below 5°C (41°F)).

Sarracenia purpurea

Utricularia sandersonii

17. Container plants

A home is not limited by its threshold. There is space for plants in pots and containers around the house, in a conservatory or greenhouse, on a terrace or balcony. Although ordinary garden plants can be grown like this, this chapter deals with species that cannot remain outside during the winter because they are not hardy, but prefer fresh air in summer. Here they are called "container plants", but they are also called orangery plants, or Cape plants if they are natives of South Africa. Most of them like to stand in the sun when outside. They like a lot of water and fertilizer. From about halfway through the year, more often from late summer onwards, they produce flowers of tropical splendour. This is followed by a resting period during the winter in which the evergreen species need a light, cool location, but the deciduous ones can tolerate a dark location. In spring, after the last frosts, they can be put back outside to add a tropical touch to a balcony or terrace.

Acidanthera bicolor

See: *Gladiolus callianthus*

Aeonium arboreum

Aeonium has large, green rosettes. As the plant matures branched stems some tens of centimetres long develop below the rosettes.

The cultivars which are usually on offer have dark leaves, for example, 'Atropurpureum' (dark red) or 'Zwartkop' (deep-aubergine).

Left: *Bougainvillea glabra* 'Sanderiana'

Variegated forms like 'Variegatum' (creamy-white and green) are also very popular. The plant originates in Morocco. In summer place it in a large pot outside in a sunny spot. Any compost will do although *Aeonium* prefers mineral rich soil with clay and sand.

It likes a moderate amount of water in the summer and needs protection from too much rain.
Keep *Aeonium arboreum* almost dry in winter, in a light and cool, but frost-free room.

Aeonium arboreum 'Zwartkop'

Agapanthus

AFRICAN LILY

Agapanthus is hardy in south-west England. The round umbels of blue flowers bloom among bent-grass on the Scilly Isles. In the cooler regions of Europe it is better to grow it as a container plant. From June it can go outside in a large pot or tub and should be put in a warm, sunny and sheltered position. Water liberally and feed regularly. Later in the summer long, cylindrical stems grow up between the strap-shaped leaves. The plant flowers profusely for a few weeks in July and August. Gradually water less after flowering. Leave the plant outside until the first frosts and then put it in a cool, frost-free place keeping it almost dry.

The tight root clump can be divided in spring. Put the root sections in fertile, moisture-retentive soil, preferably containing some clay, and bring them into growth in a light and warm place. Agapanthus species cross-fertilize very easily. For this reason some plant experts include all ten known species in one species. The plants in cultivation are nearly all hybrids with blue, purple or white flowers.

from the Pacific Ocean region its decorative value. Water and feed liberally in summer and provide the highest possible humidity. Alpinia likes a lot of light but it does not like direct sun. The plant does not need much water in the winter but it likes a light and warm (minimum 15°C (59°F)) position. *Alpinia purpurata* forms plantlets between the bracts. These can be potted separately and will start to grow readily if kept at a temperature of at least 20°C (68°F).

Agapanthus praecox orientalis

Alpinia purpurata

RED GINGER

Alpinia has only recently been introduced to the market and then only in small numbers because it is a plant only for the keen amateur. It only thrives in a warm greenhouse or conservatory and there it can easily reach a height of 2m (6ft). In summer it produces white flowers which grow between conspicuous red bracts. These bracts give this plant

Alpinia purpurata

Alyogyne huegeli

Alyogyne is a native of Australia and a member of the same family as hibiscus. It has only recently be seen flowering in our conservatories and outside on our terraces. The plant is shrubby and grows to a height of about 1.5m (5ft). In summer it produces deep pink flowers which look very beautiful between the soft, deeply lobed leaves.

Water liberally during flowering and feed occasionally. Bring the plant indoors in late summer as soon as the night temperature drops below 10°C (50°F). This is the minimum temperature for this plant in winter. Water little during this period. Water moderately if the plant is kept at temperatures above 15°C (59°F). It will keep growing in the latter case and will need to be cut back hard in spring.

Anisodontea capensis

This shrub from South Africa will flower throughout the summer. From June onwards it will keep producing flowers as long as it receives moderate amounts of water and fertilizer. *Anisodontea* needs to be brought in at the first frosts at which time it is usually still flowering.

Anisodontea capensis

Alyogyne huegeli 'Trumpet Serenade'

The plant should not actively grow in winter. Gradually water less and put the plant in a cool room (minimum 5°C (41°F)). Cut back hard in spring and growth will start again followed by another long summer replete with flowers.

Argyranthemum frutescens

See: *Chrysanthemum frutescens*

Anisodontea capensis

Azalea

See: *Rhododendron*

Bougainvillea

BOUGAINVILLE

Around the Mediterranean, high climbing *Bougainvillaeas* grow against the houses. They flower so profusely that holiday makers are tempted to try and grow them at home. This often turns out to be disappointing because this South American species needs more sun and heat than it can get in northern Europe. The shrub needs a rest in winter and it takes a long time to get going again afterwards. It usually does not flower until late in the growing season or slightly sooner in a conservatory or greenhouse or on a light windowsill. Water and feed liberally in the summer. The plant is encouraged to produce flowers by decreasing watering and feeding in July. The purple, pink, red, orange or white bracts are the striking parts and these remain on the plant much longer than the pale, tubular flowers. Put the plant in a light and airy place in winter and give hardly any water. Most of the leaves will drop off and this is normal. Bougainvillaea likes a cool place in winter at a minimum temperature of 10°C (50°F). Encourage the plant to grow again from March onwards, in a greenhouse or conservatory or on a sunny windowsill. Cut back as much as you like: flowers are produced on new growth. *Bougainvillaea glabra* (paper flower) has given rise to the best known culti-

Left: *Bougainvillea spectabilis* hybrid
Below: *Bougainvillea* 'Aswan'

vars. They can be recognized by their large, creamy-white tubular flowers with flanged edges. The real flowers of *Bougainvillaea spectabilis* are slightly less conspicuous. There are many hybrids between the two species and also between *Bougainvillaea glabra* and *Bougainvillaea peruviana*. The latter hybrids may be found under the name *Bougainvillaea x buttiana*.

Bougainvillea Glabra hybrid

Bougainvillea sanderiana

See: *Bougainvillea glabra* 'Sanderiana'

Brugmansia

The first thing to do after buying Brugmansia should be to throw away the label because this plant is usually sold under an incorrect name. The five original species from the Andes cross-fertilize easily and have thus given rise to numerous hybrids which in turn readily cross-fertilize among themselves.

Maintenance is the same for all of them with the exception of *Brugmansia sanguinea*. This red-flowered species is late coming into bloom, usually not until after it has been brought inside for the winter. It needs to be given a lot of light, warmth and water in late season if the flowers are to be enjoyed.
The other species and hybrids like a warm, sunny or lightly shaded location outside in summer, or a place in a greenhouse or conservatory.

Brugmansia

Close up of the flower of *Brugmansia*

Water liberally and feed regularly to give the plants the strength to flower in late summer. It is best to buy the plants when they are flowering so that you can choose the colour (white, yellow, pink, orange or reddish-orange), shape and smell that you prefer.

Bring them in before the first frosts and keep them almost completely dry in a cool room (minimum 5°C (41°F)). Light is not strictly necessary because the leaves will drop off but the stems remain green and are grateful for any small amount of light.

Re-pot every spring in fertile compost preferably containing some clay and prune the plants in winter. Young plants can be pruned back to about 20cm (8in) above ground level.

All parts of *Brugmansia* and especially the flowers and seeds are extremely poisonous.

Callistemon citrinus

LEMON BOTTLE BRUSH

The flowers of lemon bottle brush consist entirely of stamens. Those of *Callistemon citrinus* are red and stick out in all directions and so look rather like a bottle brush.

It is though that these plants do not produce petals because they originate in the dry parts of Australia where evaporation from the petals would cause unnecessary water loss. The coloured stamens have taken over the func-tion of attracting insects. The lemon bottle brush grows well in houses that have large windows and central heating. It likes a sunny position and a lot of fresh air. If you cannot offer these conditions, enjoy it outside in summer on a sunny terrace. And because it can withstand the wind it is suitable for the breezy conditions of an exposed balcony.

In spring and summer give *Callistemon* average amounts of water. In winter it can be the last container plant to be brought inside because it can stand a few degrees of frost. In winter put it in a light cool place that gets some fresh air. A temperature of between 5°C (41°F) and 10°C (50°F) is ideal. Water hardly at all. Start watering again in spring and the bottle brush will grow into a bushy plant - a gem in a room or conservatory or on a terrace or balcony.

Propagate the plant in August by tearing of side shoots. These have a small amount of material torn from the stem. With this "heel" attached the cutting will root easily in a sandy soil mixture with a heat applied from beneath at a temperature of about 20°C (68°F).

Camellia

Most people drink at least one cup of *Camellia sinensis*, the tea plant, each day. Its low shrubs are cultivated in cool mountainous

Callistemon citrinus

Camellia

regions, and the foliage is dried and cut to produce tea.

The true tea plant is difficult to keep in our climate but numerous other species provide beautiful, decorative, evergreen shrubs. There are cultivars nowadays which can endure eighteen degrees of frost. These plants can remain outside in the open ground if planted in a sheltered and shady spot in acid soil. More sensitive species and hybrids cannot tolerate heated rooms but they are very suitable as container plants. They can stay in an unheated greenhouse in winter or in a cool room. Provide as much light and fresh air as possible because these shrubs keep their leaves. They flower in late winter and early spring with rose-like flowers in all kinds of colours but mainly red, pink and white.

You will be able to enjoy these showy plants to the full if you plant them in acid compost, rich in humus, and water them liberally in summer and moderately in winter.

$\bigcirc - \mathbb{O} \ \bigcirc$

Carissa grandiflora

See: *Carissa macrocarpa*

Carissa macrocarpa

NATAL PLUM

This evergreen container plant is rarely available although it produces lovely smelling, white, starry flowers, which are followed by red fruits. The fruits look like miniature tomatoes which, in the tropics, are eaten. It might be better not to risk this because the plant is very poisonous except for the ripe

Carissa macrocarpa

Flowers and buds of *Cassia corymbosa*

276

fruits. *Carissa* likes to be outside in summer. It will grow well in semi-shade but better in the full sun where it will produce more flowers. It will never flower abundantly though and is a plant for the connoisseur.

Give an average amount in summer and feed occasionally. Make sure the soil does not get soaked by rain. In winter Carissa prefers to be kept nearly dry in a cool (minimum 10°C (50°F)) and light place.

Cassia corymbosa

This American shrub flowers from June until October with golden-yellow flowers which have a characteristically bent pistil and stamens. The flowers unfold between compound leaves. The plant can reach a height of several metres when grown in a pot and can be pruned into a "lollipop" shape. In summer, when *Cassia* is outside, it prefers a sunny location and soil which contains some clay and sand and is always moist. In winter, it should be kept almost dry in a cool (minimum 5°C (41°F)) and light place. You can keep the plant growing and even flowering for some time during the winter by giving it higher

Cassia corymbosa in the castle gardens of Arcen (NL)

temperatures and a very light position. Prune back hard after flowering to encourage *Cassia* to branch freely in the new growing season.

Cassia didymobotrya

The flowers of this cassia are arranged along a stem which grows longer as flowering continues. The leaves consists of numerous leaflets in pairs along the central rib. In Africa and India the shrub grows to a height of about 5m (16ft); in northern Europe to about 2m (6ft). This species can go outside in summer in a large pot or container. Bring it inside as soon as night temperatures drop below 10°C (50°F). For further maintenance see *Cassia corymbosa*.

Cassia didymobotrya

Chrysanthemum frutescens

MARGUERITE

Small marguerites are sold in May as border plants and the larger ones are sold in pots. They flower throughout the summer and carry on flowering in winter if kept in a very light, moderately warm location.

Chrysanthemum frutescens is a native of the Canary Islands and likes warmth, sun and

Chrysanthemum frutescens

The fruit of *Citrus limon*

plenty of fresh air. It is a shrub of rounded habit, several tens of centimetre tall and wide covered with flowers and grey-green leaves. Put it in the garden in a warm position in sun or semi-shade. Water very regularly because a lot of water evaporates from the leaves and the plant should never be allowed to dry out. Occasionally give some liquid fertilizer.

The plant should be brought inside before the first frost. In a living room it will keep on flowering for a little while, but the air will soon be too dry. If kept in a very light spot in a cooler room you will be able to enjoy it for much longer. Keep the plant in a cool place (minimum 5°C (41°F)) in winter, prune back hard in spring and it will form a compact plant when new growth starts. Re-pot in nutritious, moisture-retentive soil.

It is possible to take tip cuttings in late summer. Put them in a cool place to root and keep them cool and quite dry through the winter.

Citrus limon

LEMON

It is very easy to grow this robust container plant. Sow some lemon pips in a pot in the living room. They will germinate into seedlings with glossy green leaves which are beautiful from the start. Orange pips can be sown in the same way to produce orange trees *(Citrus sinensis)* which can tolerate the cold better than lemon plants.

Put the plants outside in late May in sun or semi-shade and make sure the soil does not dry out or become soaking wet. The larger the pot the more quickly they will grow.

Put the lemon tree inside as soon as night temperatures drop below 10°C (50°F). Do not keep it in a warm, dry living room but in a light place in a cool room. Water just enough

for the compost not to dry out completely. Plants that are kept in this way can quite quickly grow into 2m (6ft) high shrubs. They can be kept smaller by pruning. Eventually they will produce very fragrant white flowers in summer followed by lemons. Plants which have been grown from pips take a long time to bear fruit.

It is better to buy a different citrus species if you particularly want the fruit. These species often remain smaller. Citrus limon 'Meyer' (compact with large fruits), *Citrus limon* 'Ponderosa' (compact with very large fruits), *Citrus reticulata* (mandarin, satsuma, tangerine), *x Citrofotunella microcarpa* (sold as "orange tree" or "dwarf orange" in plant outlets - compact shrubs with small oranges which remain on the plant for a long time).

Citrus limon

Citrus mitis

See: x *Citrofortunella microcarpa*

Datura

See: *Brugmansia*

Datura

Daturas used to include annual and perennial species. The perennial plants, which are shrubby with pendulous flowers, are dealt with under the section on *Brugmansia*. Only the annual species with upright flowers are now called *Daturas*. One of them is *Datura stramonium* which has naturalized throughout Europe. It grows particularly well on rubbish tips and similar fertile places.

In plant outlets you will find *Datura metel* which has downy foliage and pendulous fruits. It is a decorative annual pot plant suitable for a sunny terrace, or one with light shade, where it can flower from June until September. Water liberally making sure that any surplus water can drain away freely, and apply fertilizer often. The flowers are usually white to ivory-white but cultivars may have different colours: *Datura metel* 'Alba' (pure white), *Datura*

Datura

metel 'Aurea' (light yellow), *Datura metel* 'Caerulea' (watery blue), Datura metel 'Flore Pleno' (double flowered with colours ranging from white through pink to purple). *Daturas* are very poisonous.

Euonymus japonicus

The many cultivars of *Euonymus japonicus* are grown because of their decorative foliage. They are usually sold as garden plants because they can tolerate fifteen degrees of frost. However pot culture is safer. Keep them in an unheated greenhouse or conservatory or in a light spot in an unheated room. A heated living room is totally unsuitable.

When the danger of frost has passed they can go outside in their pots. In standard compost and with regular watering they will grow slowly but surely, in sun or shade.

The popular cultivars are variegated. *Euonymus japonicus* 'Argentea Variegata' ('Argenteo Variegatum') (white leaf margin), *Euonymus japonicus* 'Aureo-marginatus' (yellow-green leaves with golden margins), *Euonymus japonicus* 'Microphyllus' (leaves small and slender with different patterns of variegation), *Euonymus japonicus* 'Luna'

Euonymus japonicus 'Argentea Variegata'

Euonymus japonicus 'Luna'

(leaves buttery yellow with a green margin), *Euonymus japonicus* 'Marieke' (green or grey-green leaves with a pale yellow margin).

Euonymus japonicus 'Marieke'

Felicia

Despite originating in South Africa, *Felicia* species can tolerate light frost. They are very suitable for cultivation in pots and containers. They are often treated as annuals and flower from mid-summer until winter begins. *Felicia amelloides* (blue marguerite) is the best known species and has blue flowers with yellow centres. It can be put outside in summer in a light position in sun or semi-shade. Avoid a really hot location and do not allow the compost to dry out. *Felicias* are evergreen shrubs and can be kept through the winter in a light spot in a cool room. Give almost no water and, in spring, prune back any spindly growth.

Felicia amelloides

Fremontodendron californicum

After a halting start as a container plant, *Fremontodendron* has now made a general breakthrough. It is ideal for conservatories where it will quickly grow into a large bush

Fremontodendron californicum

with beautifully lobed, felt-like leaves and large yellow flowers which shine like buttercups.

The long branches need to be pruned back regularly to maintain a compact plant. The plant is full of buds during a large part of the year and, because of this, people who like the plant find it very difficult to prune. It often flowers when it is resting in winter.

Keep the plant in compost which preferably contains some clay and water freely in summer. Put *Fremontodendron* outside in a warm, sunny position or keep in a greenhouse or conservatory. It can tolerate a few degrees of frost but it is best to bring it inside before the first frosts keeping it light, cool and quite dry. Leaf-drop is not a problem. The leaves will grow again in spring on new shoots as well as on the old stems.

Gladiolus callianthus

Gladiolus callianthus is a gem even to those people who do not like gladioli. It has very natural looking flowers which appear for weeks on end at from late summer onwards. They are white with a deep-red centre and look very elegant above the metre-tall, sword-shaped leaves. The corms can be planted outside in the border in May but *Gladiolus callianthus* looks better in a pot or container. Make sure any surplus water can always drain away freely. To bring the plant into flower the foliage needs very fertile, moisture-retentive compost. Keep the container in the sun or half-shade and never let the compost dry out.

Steadily decrease watering after flowering and the foliage will die down. Bring the plants in before the first frosts, take the corms out of the pot and keep them cool and dry until the next spring. You will find many off-shoots around the old corm which can be used to propagate the plants. A few years will pass before these are big enough to flower.

Hebe

Hebes are vulnerable to frost especially if they grow in wet soil or are exposed to freezing winds. The variegated species in particular are better cultivated as container plants and kept in an unheated greenhouse or conservatory, or in a cool room. They are evergreen and therefore need a light position.

In the summer the shrubs like a position outside in the fresh air, in sun or semi-shade. Water liberally and make sure the soil never dries out. In fertile compost they will flower

Gladiolus callianthus

Hebe x *andersonii*

Hebe 'Inspiration'

for several weeks from early summer (although some cultivars flower from late summer). They produce short, fat panicles of flowers which are usually purple or blue, but sometimes white.

Hebe x andersonii is a cross between *Hebe salicifolia* and *Hebe Speciosa*. It eventually grows to a height and width of more than a metre (3ft). The cultivar 'Variegata' grows even larger and has green and grey-green leaves with ivory-white margins.

Hebe 'Inspiration' is another variegated cultivar with green and grey-green leaves and very wide, yellow leaf margins.

Hedychium

Hedychium is well suited to being grown in a container. In spring it grows quickly producing wide strap-shaped leaves on cylindrical stems. The flowers of *Hedychium* appear from late summer onwards when many other plants are past their best. The flowers grow in spikes 30cm (12in) long and 10cm (4in) wide and are breathtakingly beautiful and very fragrant.

The plant has thick rhizomes which look like large pieces of root ginger, showing that it is a member of the ginger family.

The species of *Hedychium*, which grow mainly in the Himalayas, are robust and their above-ground parts die off in the winter. The same happens in temperate climates. This makes it possible to keep the plant in a dark place during the winter but the rhizomes need to be kept completely dry. Re-pot them in early spring in a wide pot or container in fertile soil (a narrow pot would easily be blown over because the plant produces a lot of foliage). Put the pot outside when all danger

Below: *Hedychium forrestii*

Right: *Hedychium gardnerianum*

The root of *Hedychium ellipticum*

of frost has passed. Water and feed liberally during the summer.
Hedychium coccinium is the Red/Scarlet ginger lily.
It requires more heat and is best grown in a greenhouse or conservatory. The subspecies *carnea* has fleshy-coloured flowers.
Hedychium ellipticum has elegant white flowers which bend where they join the stem
Hedychium flavum has yellow flowers and is very similar to *Hedychium gardnerianum*.

Hedychium forrestii has very elegant, white flowers.
Hedychium gardnerianum (Kahili ginger) is the best-known species. It is naturalized in some subtropical regions. In late summer it carries large, golden-yellow flower spikes on stalks up to 2m (6ft) tall. This is the only variety which specialist nurseries have made available. So far the other varieties, despite being beautiful and easy to grow, are hardly cultivated because there is insufficient demand for them.

Heliconia

LOBSTER CLAWS

Heliconia is a member of the banana family and grows best in a tropical or temperate greenhouse. It may, in the summer, produce beautiful flowers if grown outside in a large pot or container in a sheltered, light spot (in sun or partial shade). Make sure it gets plenty of water and fertilizer. Keep the plant quite dry in winter in a light position at a minimum temperature of 15°C (59°F).
Heliconia psittacorum produces large leaves up to 2m (6ft) tall, like those of the banana plant (musa). In summer it develops elegant

Below: *Hedychium ellipticum*   Right: *Heliconia rostrata*

flowers in all kinds of colours, although orange is the most common. More than 1000 cultivars have been described.

Heliconia rostrata grows even larger with even larger, musa-like foliage. If grown in warm conditions it eventually develops a long, pendulous inflorescence with conspicuous red and yellow bracts from the pseudo-stem. Heliconias are not yet widely available and, for the time being, remain plants for the keen amateur.

○ – ◑ ○

Hibiscus rosa-sinensis

ROSE OF CHINA

The rose of china is a flower for home-loving people. *Hibiscus rosa-sinensis* will only grow well if cared for constantly and consistently. The root-ball should always be moist but should never stand in water and the plant grows best in humid air at a even temperature of about 20°C (68°F). If this glossy green shrub also gets a monthly dose of house plant fertilizer it will flower continuously. Every day new flowers about 12cm (5in) across will unfold which are fiery-red and velvety. The stigma and stamens grow together as a stem protruding from the flower.

The flower of *Hibiscus rosa-sinensis*

Rosa-sinensis has given rise to numerous cultivars with salmon, white, yellow, orange or creamy-coloured flowers. There are also multi-coloured, double and crested cultivars. It is doubtful whether any of these are an

Hibiscus rosa-sinensis

improvement on the true species. In China, hibiscus grows into a shrub about 2m (6ft) in height. Those specimens for sale as house plants have been kept compact by chemical treatment. Eventually these substances disappear and hibiscus grows more quickly. It can be pruned after its winter rest (during which hibiscus can stay in the living room). You can also allow hibiscus to grow into a shrub and use it as an evergreen container plant on a terrace. Bring the shrub indoors when the night temperature drops below 10°C (50°F).

Cold causes the flower buds to drop. This also happens if the air is too dry or if the plant is turned in relation to the light.

Lantana camara

YELLOW SAGE

Lantana originates in South America and grows like weeds in the tropics. It has been spread all over the world because of its free-flowering habit and in warm climates has become quite rampant. In cooler climates it is well behaved when grown in pots and containers. Give the plants fertile and well-draining compost. *Lantana* likes an average amount of water in the summer but dislikes soggy compost. It prefers a sunny location. New flower heads appear at the end of the branches from early summer onwards. The orange flowers eventually change to dark red creating bi-coloured flower heads. There are numerous so-called *'camara'* hybrids with very different flower colours ranging from white through yellow and orange to salmon, pink and deep red.

Lantana likes to be kept almost dry in winter in a cool (minimum 10°C 50°F)) and light position. The plant will branch out nicely if pruned in spring.

Leonotis leonurus

This perennial from South Africa grows up to 2m (6ft) tall and produces beautiful rings of orange flowers in summer and later. The plant can be put outside in a sunny and sheltered position when all danger of frost has passed. It likes constantly moist, fertile compost so water and feed regularly. New rings of flowers develop from the bottom of the plant from August onwards. The plant is likely to be still

Lantana camara

Leonotis leonurus

in full bloom when it has to be brought in when the first night frost threatens.

Keep the plant cool and the compost almost dry. A light position is not strictly necessary because much of the foliage will drop off. Prune back hard in spring and re-pot in fresh compost.

Leptospermum

TEA TREES

Tea trees grow as wide shrubs or low trees in the dry western region of Australia. In cooler climates some species can tolerate a certain degree of frost. As they are able to tolerate salty wind, they are used as wind screens in coastal regions. If grown in a pot they like loose, acid compost, ericaceous soil being ideal. Do not water too much but do not let the plant dry out either. It grows best in the full sun but another light position will do.

After the first frost the containerized plant should be moved indoors in a light, cool room. A conservatory or unheated greenhouse is ideal. The most widely cultivated species *Leptospermum scoparium* (Manuka, New Zealand tea tree) can easily tolerate ten

degrees of frost if kept dry. Water very little water until early spring when the plant can be put outside again to provide another season of pink to white flowers.

Leptospermum citratum is slightly more vulnerable to the cold. Its foliage smells strongly of lemons. This species also has pale-pink flowers.

Leptospermum petersonii

See: *Leptospermum citratum*

Lobelia tupa

This is one of the many new species of container plant. In late summer its deep-red flowers contrast beautifully with its grey-green foliage. The plant originates in Chile and will do best in the sunniest and warmest spot in the garden. Grow it in a pot or container of standard compost and give an average amount of water. It can tolerate up to about ten degrees of frost. This gem of a plant will have to be brought inside to spend the winter in a light, cool and airy room.

Leptospermum scoparium

A greenhouse or conservatory is ideal. Water just enough for the root ball not to dry out completely.

Lobelia tupa

Lycianthes rantonnetii

See: *Solanum rantonnetii*

Lysimachia congestiflora

Lysimachia congestiflora

Most species of *Lysimachia* are perennial garden plants. *Lysimachia congestiflora* is an exception, not well known so far, which grows and flowers best in hanging baskets outside. Hang in sun or semi-shade in summer and always give sufficient water for the compost not to dry out. From mid-summer clusters of waxy yellow flowers, with some red in their centres, adorn the ends of the branches.
Keep almost dry in winter in a light, cool and airy place.

Malphigia coccigera

MINIATURE HOLLY

The glossy-green leaves of *Malphigia coccigera* are slightly spiny, hence the common name miniature holly. It is a compact shrub, up to 1m (3ft) in height which can easily be pruned. During the summer it regularly produces light pink flowers with unusual fringed petals.
The shrub is a native to the Caribbean and likes a warm place which is as humid as possible. It can only be put outside, in sun or

semi-shade, in the warmest months of the year. Give an average amount of water and make sure the roots do not remain standing in water.

In winter *Malphigia* prefers a light but no too cool position (minimum 15°C (59°F)). It will need to be watered occasionally so that the evergreen foliage does not dry out

Malva capensis

See: *Anisodontea capansis*

Malvastrum capense

See: *Anisodontea capensis*

Nandina domestica

HEAVENLY BAMBOO, SACRED BAMBOO

When the nights grow colder the leaves of *Nandina* change to beautiful autumn colours. Surprisingly they do not drop off but turn green again when brought inside for the winter.

In spring, plumes of white flowers appear between the leaves, followed by berries which are white at first and later turn red. The long thin stems look like bamboo but Nandina does not belong to the bamboo family.

Nandina can be grown in open ground in areas which never get more than ten degrees of frost. Elsewhere it is an ideal container plant.

It sets fruit well if the pot or container is kept in a sheltered spot in sun or semi-shade during the summer.

The plant can pollinate itself but it will produce more fruit if it is grown next to another *Nandina*.

The plant grows best in ordinary, well-drained compost. Water freely in summer and keep dry, light and frost-free in winter.

There are numerous cultivars for example 'Alba' (with matt-white berries), 'Compacta' (low growing, about 70cm (28in) tall), 'Firepower' (low growing, with bright autumn colours) and 'Nana Purpurea' (low growing, with dark purple foliage).

Nandina domestica

Nandina domestica leucocarpa

See: *Nandina domestica* 'Alba'

Malphigia coccigera

Nerium oleander

OLEANDER, ROSE-BAY

In Arabia, oleanders grow in scorching hot places, devoid of any other greenery. They grow only at the edge of "wadi's", the dry river beds through which the water of occasional downpours gushes. The roots of oleander are water-seeking. Give water and food liberally in summer and put the plant in as sunny a place as possible. Keep it in a greenhouse or conservatory, if available, because there the buds will certainly develop into full and rich flower clusters. If the plant is kept outside it will flower very late or not at all. The flowers are usually pink but sometimes white, salmon or red.

Prune the stems which have flowered back hard to retain a compact plant. Do not prune the newly formed shoots because by late season they already carry the buds which will flower next season. Oleander prefers to spend the winter in a cool (minimum 5°C (41°F)), light place in almost dry soil.

Propagation can only be done successfully in summer using semi-hardwood cuttings or heel cuttings which are side shoots which have been torn off the main stem leaving a small piece of the bark of the main stem attached to the shoot. Put the cuttings in water or moist compost. The whole plant is very poisonous.

Petunia

n summer petunias can cheer up garden. But the flowers, especially of the large-flowered cultivars, cannot tolerate prolonged exposure to wind or rain. The advantage of growing them in a container is that they can be brought into a conservatory, a greenhouse or placed on a light windowsill in such conditions.

The annual *Petunia x hybrida* is available in all the common flower colours, from purple, red and pink to yellow, creamy-white and white. There are also multi-coloured petunias and picotee forms (each petal has an edge of a contrasting colour). Hanging petunias are called "Surfinia" and are dealt with in the chapter on climbing and hanging plants.

Petunias can be sown in February-March at room temperature or they can be bought as flowering plants from May onwards. They are sometimes sold in bloom in late season. Such plants can flower for a long time in the living room during the colder months.

Give an average amount of water in standard potting compost which does not need to be very nutritious. A sheltered, sunny but airy location is ideal for petunias.

Petunia

Nerium oleander

Punica granatum

POMEGRANATE

In the Middle East and Asia Minor the pomegranate grows into a large shrub or small tree. The flowers which appear in summer are followed months later by rounded fruits, each about the size of a large orange. Inside the leathery skin of the fruit are many small, bright red, juicy sections. The pleasantly tasting juice can be served as a part of desserts.

The specimens which are offered as container plants are usually dwarf cultivars like 'Nana' with orange flowers smaller than the species. These plants are not sold for their fruits. Cultivars are sometimes on offer as grafted plants and they are sold for the high decorative value of their summer flowers and their fine, green foliage which changes colour in late season before the leaves fall. Keep the container in a sunny and warm spot in summer and water liberally. The pomegranate is not fussy as regards its compost which should be well-draining and contain some clay. Keep it in a cool place in winter minimum 5°C (41°F)) and give hardly any water. Prune back hard and flowers will appear on the new wood the following summer.

Rhododendron x obtusum

Various different species and hybrids of rhododendron are sold under the name azalea

Punica granatum 'Nana'

or Japanese azalea. They are often one of the numerous cultivars of *Rhododendron x obtusum*, a plant which has been bred in Japan for many centuries. The countless hybrids have given rise to numerous cultivars with flowers of all possible colours.

Rhododendron

Rhododendron

shades are poisonous, although the fruits and tubers not always, for example, tomatoes and potatoes. *Solanum rantonnetii* (its official new name is *Lycianthes rantonnetii*) can be grown as decorative plant with long, loose stems and green foliage in a large pot or container. It will grow about as tall as a person. If the plant is given plenty of water and fertilizer during the growing period clusters of blue to violet flowers with strongly contrasting yellow centres and stamens will appear in late summer. In summer *Solanum rantonnetii* likes a warm spot in sun or semi-shade outside, or in a greenhouse or conservatory. This nightshade is a native of Argentina and Paraguay. Bring it inside before the first frosts and keep it almost completely dry in a cool room (minimum 5°C (41°F)) which may be dark. This treatment will cause the plant to lose all its leaves but they will grow again in spring. The lanky shoots can be pruned as much as necessary at any time outside the summer months.

Japanese azaleas can be planted in a sheltered spot in the garden. The leaves will only drop off after a severe frost. The plants suffer a great deal if this occurs late in the season and it takes them a long time to recover.

It is better to grow them in containers except in regions with a mild climate such as Ireland, the west of England and southern countries. Put the plant in a large pot or container in slightly acid compost. The root ball should never dry out completely. Japanese azaleas like a fresh, semi-shade, outside. Even in winter the soil should never dry out completely and the plant should be kept in a frost-free, airy place, giving as much light as possible.

Solanum rantonnetii

Senna corymbosa

See: *Cassia corymbosa*

Senna didymobotrya

See: *Cassia didymobotrya*

Solanum rantonnetii

BLUE POTATO BUSH

Solanum rantonnetii is one of the nightshades. The foliage and flowers of most night-

Strelitzia reginae

BIRD OF PARADISE FLOWER

In South Africa the bird of paradise flower is pollinated by birds. The orange and deep-blue flowers stick up from a horizontal bract on which the birds find it easy to land. In northern European climates *Strelitzia* is especially suitable for a winter garden because it requires a light position even in winter. The foliage does not die down. The plant needs a minimum temperature of 10°C (50°F) in winter. It can be kept warmer but needs more water in that case. In a cool room it only needs enough water to prevent the roots from drying out. From early summer onwards the bird of paradise flower can be kept in a warm, sheltered spot in the garden. Protect it from the hottest sun, and water and feed plentifully making sure the roots do not remain standing in water. The bird of paradise flower should be grown in a large pot and it will then only need to be re-potted every few years. The plant should be given a new top layer of nutritious compost every year.

Tibouchina semidecandra

See: *Tibouchina urvilleana*

Tibouchina urvilleana

GLORY BUSH

This shrub grows in light locations on wooded slopes in the mountainous regions of South America. The leaves are covered with downy hairs and grow on long, square, hairy stems.

Tibouchina urvilleana

In cultivation *Tibouchina* can flower during a large part of the year, even in winter, if kept in a light and warm place. After flowering put the

Strelitzia reginae

294

plant in a cool (minimum 8°C (47°F)), light room and water little to stop active growth. Prune back hard in early spring and give fresh and fertile compost. Gradually move the plant to a warmer location where it will then start to grow again. Keep it outside in a sheltered, warm spot and protect it from only the hottest sun. From about midsummer onwards purple-blue flowers, several centimetres wide, will appear. If watered liberally and fed regularly during flowering, this beautiful plant will bloom until well into late summer and even longer.

Trachelospermum jasminoides

The white flowers of this evergreen Chinese plant are very fragrant, like jasmine. In the wild *Trachelospermum jasminoides* is a climber. If grown in a large pot it will remain for a long time as a moderate shrub with lanky stems. It is very easy to cultivate. *Trachelospermum jasminoides* likes sun or semi-shade and will grow in ordinary compost. A moderate degree of moisture is ideal for this plant but it can tolerate a lot of water in summer and will not be harmed if a watering is occasionally forgotten. After the summer months it can remain outside for a long time because it can easily tolerate five degrees of frost (*Trachelospermum asiaticum* which looks very similar, can even survive fifteen degrees of frost). When kept inside in winter the thick, leathery leaves need a lot of light, otherwise many will drop off. In spring the long stems can be pruned as necessary. The whole plant is poisonous.

Trachelospermum jasminoides

Tulbaghia violacea

Tulbaghia looks like a small form of *Agapanthus*. Like the latter it is a native of South Africa and has lilac flowers. *Agapanthus* flowers for a few weeks in late summer whereas *Tulbaghia* starts flowering in early summer and carries on, at short intervals, for several months. The flower umbels grow at the end of stems which are up to about 50cm (20in) long. The strap-shaped leaves are not longer than about 30cm (12in).

Tulbaghia violacea is a problem-free container plant, which can stay outside the whole summer until winter threatens: it can tolerate a few degrees of frost. Keep it in a cool, airy and light place in winter and water just enough to prevent the root ball from drying out completely.

Water and feed liberally in spring until you can see the flower stalk. After that an average amount of water is better. Give the plant a warm and sunny location. Propagate by division or seed.

Verbena

These perennials from America are usually treated as annuals in temperate climates. In spring countless cultivars of *Verbena x hybrida* are on sale. They can be used as annual bedding plants. The hanging forms show to good advantage in window boxes and hanging baskets while the spreading and erect cultivars are very suitable for containers.

They like full sun but can be grown in semi-shade. Give them fertile, moisture-retentive compost and water liberally during the grow-

Verbena 'Sissinghurst-Pink'

Verbena 'Silver Anne'

ing season. The flower stems will branch if you cut out the dead flowers and they will keep producing blooms from early summer onwards.

Verbena varieties can be sown indoors under glass in early spring or in a greenhouse or conservatory in late summer. Keep them moderately moist and in a light place in winter at a temperature of at least 8°C (47°F). Cuttings can be taken easily in late summer. Give them heat from beneath to help them root and treat them in winter as seedlings.

Verbena x *hybrida* 'Peaches and Cream'

Viola x *wittrockiana*

GARDEN PANSY

Even 400 years or so before Christ pansies were on sale in the markets of Greece. Since then wild species have been hybridized to such an extent that knowledge of the origin of pansies has been lost.

Most of the cultivars which are on offer are *wittrockiana* hybrids which are not fragrant.

Choose plants for their colour and scent if there is any. They are for sale in spring and can be used for borders, boxes and pots. They flower throughout the summer as long as the humus-rich compost is kept moist at all times and the pots are not kept in too sunny a position.

In late season, winter pansies are on offer. They can tolerate a few degrees of frost but are better kept in a cool place indoors where they will continue flowering until spring.

Viola x *wittrockiana*

Zantedeschia aethiopica

ARUM LILY

The arum lily from South Africa has spread through all earth's tropical and, especially, subtropical regions. They are usually grown in pots or containers. The white spathe and cream-coloured spadix are used as funeral flowers in many countries. The species has also naturalized in temperate regions, such as Madeira and the Azores, where it occurs in the wild, particularly in moist places.

This tells us a lot about how to cultivate the plant in temperate regions. When grown outside *Zantedeschia aethiopica* can tolerate the cold very well, even up to ten degrees of frost. If the rhizomes are grown in a pot it is best not to take any risks and to bring the plant inside at the first frost. Plants which have been kept inside during the summer are best kept at a minimum of 10°C (50°F) during winter.

Around Cape Town the arum lily grows in swamps.

It can be grown as an aquarium or pond plant up to 50cm (20in) under water where the rhizomes cannot freeze.

This type of cultivation shows that *aethiopica* can tolerate a lot of moisture although if grown in a pot, moderately moist compost is sufficient.

The plant can be kept in the full sun or semi-shade. In early summer the flower structures appear on stems about 1m (3ft) in length.

The plant is poisonous: make sure that the sap does not get onto the skin or in the eyes and consult a doctor if it is swallowed. Give lots of water to drink by way of first aid.

Zantedeschia aethiopica

Pansies, grape hyacinths and lavender in pots (*Viola* x *wittrockiana*)

18. Fuchsias and Geraniums

It is little wonder that fuchsias and geraniums are very popular. They are no problem to grow and flower for months on end with beautifully coloured blooms.

Fuchsias are chiefly natives of the mountain forests of Latin America where trees offer them protection against wind and against the bright tropical sun, and where the air is fresh and humid.

Nearly all Geraniums, officially called Pelargonium, are native of southern Africa. They pass through a dry period during which the leaves drop off easily, followed by a period in which they grow and flower exuberantly. Geraniums are the best choice for a sunny window, terrace or balcony. Fuchsias are better suited to a shady balcony, terrace or a moderately sunny courtyard.

Fuchsia

Fuchsias create a tropical atmosphere. But there are more than one hundred different species which grow in widely different places and conditions, from the heat of Mexico to the bitter climate of del Fuego, the southerly point of South America. The species that grow in the latter regions, such as *Fuchsia magellanica* (the garden fuchsia), are also hardy in temperate climates.

In the greater part of Latin America, fuchsias tend to grow in the cool mountainous regions rather than in hot lowlands. In some parts of the Andes, fuchsias are of vital importance to humming-birds. These miniature birds hover under the flowers and drink nectar from them. By flowering for such a long time the fuchsias enable the humming-birds to survive even in the higher regions. The fuchsias in turn profit from the humming-birds who pollinate their flowers.

This mutual co-operation between bird and plant is responsible for the beautiful shapes and colours of the flowers. Birds, as opposed to insects, can see red. The outside of many fuchsias, consisting of a tube and sepals, is conspicuously red or pink. These parts of the plant can attract birds over long distances. The petals, hanging under the tube and sepals like a skirt, have contrasting colours which lead the birds to the entrance of the flower. The stamens and pistil extend a long way

Fuchsia boliviana 'Alba'

Left: *Fuchsia* 'Walz Jubelteen'
Below: A fuchsia garden

below the petals and pollen is brushed off them onto the head-feathers of the humming-bird. This pollen is later wiped on to the stigma of another flower.

Over 8000 registered cultivars have arisen from the one hundred or so wild species which grow in New Zealand and Tahiti, as well as in Latin America. About 2000 of these are in cultivation. The most vigorous ones are available to the plant trade. They can be grown indoors on a not too sunny windowsill as long as the air is fresh and not too dry. In stale air the grey mould, *botrytis,* may attack. If the air is too dry many buds drop off.

Water moderately in spring, liberally in summer and feed the plant regularly. It does not need a winter resting period if grown in the living room and can keep on flowering until well into the winter. It then needs to be cut back hard in spring to re-grow into a compact plant.

Fuchsias can also be grown outside. There are about twenty hardy species and cultivars and they can remain in the open ground throughout the year. They die off in winter but sprout again in spring.

All the other cultivars are particularly suited to being grown as container plants, in a conservatory or greenhouse, on a terrace, in window boxes or as hanging plants. They are grouped below according to the treatment they need during the winter.

Fuchsias for 10°C (50°F) to 15°C (59°F)

These are fuchsias which originate in warm regions, such as *Fuchsia triphylla* from Haiti and the Dominican Republic, and its cultivars (the so-called Triphylla hybrids). They cannot be clamped (see the section on "clamping" later in this chapter) and they need a minimum temperature of 10°C (50°F) during the winter.

Fuchsia boliviana is a strong-growing shrub with woody stems, large, velvety foliage and clusters of up to 30cm (12in) long, pink to red tubular flowers. 'Alba' has a white tube.

Fuchsia 'Fuji San' is a beautiful recent addition with a carmine-pink tube, sepals with a light-green tip and an orange corolla.

Fuchsia 'Nell Gwyn' grows best in a sunny spot. It has a waxy, bright-pink tube with lighter sepals and an orange-red corolla.

Fuchsia 'Pink Cornet' is a hybrid from *F. boliviana* distinguished by its cluster of very long flowers. It grows into a large shrub suitable for a sunny, sheltered place in the garden. Its leaves are large, wavy and velvety. The colour of the tube graduates from creamy-white at one end to light pink at the other and the corolla is bright red.

Fuchsia x speciosa (Van Delen) is a cross between two Central American species: F. fulgens and *F. splendens.* It grows into a large shrub with large velvety green leaves and

Fuchsia 'Fuji San'

Right: *Fuchsia* 'Pink Cornet'
Below: *Fuchsia* x *speciosa*

clusters of wide tubular flowers which are deep-red. The green-tipped sepals hardly open.

Fuchsia 'Stella Ann' is a typical Triphylla hybrid with wide, salmon-pink tubular flowers which open just enough to show the orange corolla.

Fuchsias for 5°C (41°F) to 10°C (50°F)

The species and cultivars listed below do not tolerate being stored in a clamp but they can endure fairly low temperatures in winter (5°C (41°F) or more).

Fuchsia 'Baby Face' grows into a dwarf shrub with relatively small cream-coloured flowers flushed with red. The plant does not like the sun.

Fuchsia 'Danny Kaye' has "comical" flowers with pink sepals and a flamed corolla in hues of red and pink. It was developed in 1992 by crossing F. 'Bicentennial' and F. 'Waltz *Mandoline'*. It can tolerate the full sun.

Fuchsia microphylla var. *hemsleyana* originates in the mountainous border region between Panama and Costa Rica. The compact shrubs have small, dark green leaves and very small red flowers.

Fuchsia 'Melanie' was bred in 1987 and is a cross between F. 'Grusz aus dem Bodethal' and F. 'Foolke'. This shrubby plant likes semi-shade. Its tube and sepals are glossy red and its corolla is plum-purple.

Fuchsia 'Baby Face'

Fuchsia 'Danny Kaye'

Fuchsia 'Melanie'

Fuchsia 'Red Rain' has wide, scarlet-red tubular flowers (it is a Triphylla type). It can be grown as a hanging plant or small shrub and requires a very light or sunny position.

Fuchsia 'Sunray' is cultivated especially for its variegated foliage which is green with creamy-white and flushed pink when young.

Fuchsia 'Waltz Jubelteen' is an easy growing plant with erect amber-coloured to pink flowers. It was bred in 1990 and is a cross between F. 'Toos' and F. 'Prince Syray'. In a sunny position it will flower for a long time.

Fuchsia 'Zet's Alpha' is a new cultivar (1993)

with clusters of very long flowers. It is a robust, upright shrub whose flowers have a carmine tube and sepals and orange corolla.

Fuchsia 'Red Rain'

Fuchsia microphylla x *hemsleyana*

Fuchsia 'Zet's Alpha'

Hardy fuchsias

The wild fuchsia species from cold regions are used more and more to breed cultivars which can remain in the garden in winter. The above-ground part of the plant dies off and the roots benefits from being covered with leaves, straw or some other insulating material. The plants

Fuchsia 'Corallina'

Fuchsia 'Sunray'

can also be grown in pots but in that case they have to be brought inside.

Fuchsia 'Corallina' is a very old cross (1843) between *F. magallenica globosa* and *F. splendens*. It flowers profusely but late and produces carmine to purple blooms. It is a spreading shrub which can also be used as a hanging plant. It likes a sheltered position away from direct sunlight.

Fuchsia 'Monsieur Thibaut' grows vigorously. Each flower has a large cherry-red tube and calyx and a magenta corolla.

Fuchsias for the clamp

The majority of available fuchsias can be kept through the winter by a process called "clamping". The plants are pruned hard and taken out of their pots as soon as the first frosts arrive. The root clumps and leafless stems are heeled in to a hole in the garden. Some keen amateurs also use redundant freezers kept in sheds for this purpose. They put the plants (each of them labelled) in the old freezer and cover them with peat.

Fuchsia 'Alison Ryle' was bred in 1968 by crossing F. 'Lena Dalton' and F. 'Tennessee Walz'. It is a freely branching shrub with bright pink and lavender-blue flowers which

Fuchsia 'Gift Wrap'

likes a light or even very sunny position.

Fuchsia 'Berba's Fleur' looks very similar to 'Alison Ryle' and has a signal-red calyx and purple-blue corolla.

Fuchsia 'Gift Wrap' grows tall and flowers

Fuchsia 'Alison Ryle'

Fuchsia 'Glenby'

Below: *Fuchsia* 'Juni May'   Right *Fuchsia* 'Multa'

Fuchsia 'Berba's Fleur'

Fuchsia 'Whiteknight's Pearl'

profusely its flowers having a white tube and calyx and a variable corolla. The petals are purple to begin with but turn red during flowering.

Fuchsia 'Welsh Dragon'

Fuchsia 'Glenby' branches out in a regular manner and flowers "mildly", the tube and recurving sepals being madder-red. The corolla is purple turning to pink.

Fuchsia 'Juni May' is a spreading plant and is therefore suitable as a hanging plant. It has a white tube and calyx with a corolla underneath which turns from mauve to pink.

Fuchsia 'Multa' has a bright-red tube and calyx with a bright-purple corolla. It is a hanging shrub and produces a profusion of small flowers.

Fuchsia 'Welsh Dragon' has noticeably bulbous buds and flowers, reddish-pink on the outside with a magenta corolla. It is a shrub for a sunny position.

Fuchsia 'Whiteknight's Pearl' flowers profusely with slender, delicately pink flowers which have the same shape as those of *Fuchsia magellanica*. This bushy shrub likes a sunny position.

Fuchsia. Most of these plants are sold unspecified in garden centres. They are often multi-hybrids whose exact name has been lost. Fuchsias which are grown outside in pots like a sheltered place. Some like a position in full sun but most like semi-shade. They need a lot of water in the summer and regular feeding.

It is very easy to propagate fuchsias. Take cuttings in spring by cutting off young shoots through a node. They can be put in water or in a mixture of coarse sand and peat. Heat from underneath to a minimum of 15°C (59°F) helps the cuttings to root quickly. Fuchsias can be sown in late season as soon as the seed is ripe, or in spring. The seed quickly looses its power to germinate.

Fuchsia

Fuchsia boliviana luxurians 'Alba'

See: *Fuchsia boliviana* 'Alba'

Pelargonium

GERANIUM

Geranium is the scientific name for the crane's bills which can be grown in the garden throughout the year. The popular name "geranium" is used for *Pelargonium*, of which there are more than 250 species. They grow chiefly in South Africa and cannot tolerate frost.

It is only the cultivars of geraniums which are usually available on the market. Their range is enormous and they can be classified as follows: scented geraniums, Regal hybrids, Zonal hybrids and Peltatum hybrids (ivy-leafed geraniums).

Scented geraniums

Pelargonium capitatum

ROSE-SCENTED GERANIUM

The foliage of the rose-scented geranium produces the smell of roses when rubbed. Leaves and stems are covered with white hairs. The plant has a creeping habit and is very suitable for a hanging basket. Small flowers rise from the numerous leaf axils. They are bright-pink and have darker veins, a characteristic of this group of geraniums. For maintenance see *Pelargonium graveolens*.

Pelargonium capitatum 'Snowflake'

Pelargonium crispum

LEMON GERANIUM, PRINCE RUPERT GERANIUM

The lemon geranium has a smell of lemon which is enhanced when the leaves are touched. The foliage is hairy and a rather sticky. The nomenclature of this easily grown plant is an insoluble problem. Plants which are sold under the name "lemon geranium" are usually crosses between related species of *Pelargonium* from southern Africa. They are often sold under the name *Pelargonium* graveolens, but the hybrid shown in the picture looks more like *Pelargonium crispum* 'Variegarum'. See *Pelargonium graveolens*.

Pelargonium x domesticum

See: *Pelargonium* Regale hybrids

Pelargonium crispum 'Variegatum'

Pelargonium graveolens

ROSE GERANIUM

Plants offered under this name are sometimes hybrids (see *Pelargonium crispum*). Rose

Pelargonium graveolens hybrid

geraniums are problem-free as regards their maintenance. They will grow well in the full sun as long as they are not allowed to dry out. If many leaves start to wither they need more water or fertilizer. Re-pot regularly in loose, sandy soil preferably with some clay.

In winter they will produce lanky shoots unless they are kept in a cool, light place with hardly any water. They will then loose their leaves but they branch out beautifully again in spring after being pruned.

In time the plants will become woody and bare at the base. They can then be propagated by taking semi-ripe cuttings which can be rooted in water or damp compost.

Pelargonium fragrans

NUTMEG GERANIUM

A group of geraniums with soft leaves is to be found under the name *Pelargonium fragrans*. When touched a plant gives off any of a number of different herbal scents. When buying a plant, rub the leaves and choose with your nose. There are countless cultivars of this South African species. The names refer to their scent: 'Old Spice' and 'Snowy nutmeg'. Variegated forms are on offer under the name 'Variegata'.

The maintenance is the same as for *Pelargonium graveolens*, but protect the softer and thinner foliage of the nutmeg geranium against the hottest afternoon sun.

Pelargonium fragrans

Pelargonium Grandiflorum hybrids

FRANSE GERANIUM

These are large-flowered geraniums for the living room. balcony or terrace. They are crosses between South African species such as *Pelargonium grandiflorum* and *Pelargonium alchemilloides*. The leaves are relatively fleshy and funnel-shaped. The plants flower in bright colours throughout the summer.

Give them a sunny location in the house and protect slightly from the hottest summer sun. Water moderately and feed regularly. The leaves will wilt if the plant lacks water.

Put in a cool place and keep nearly dry in winter. Prune back in early spring, re-pot if necessary and gradually increase watering and temperature. Propagate by taking cuttings of the juicy stems, preferably in summer. Put the cuttings in mildly warm, sandy compost. Keep the soil evenly moist. Too much moisture causes basal rot.

Most regal pelargoniums are on offer according to colour. Named cultivars are: 'Grand Slam' (pink-red), 'Lavender Grand Slam' (lavender-pink) and 'White Glory' (white).

Pelargonium x *hortorum*

See: *Pelargonium* Zonale hybrids

Pelargonium Peltatum hybrids

IVY-LEAFED GERANIUM

Ivy-leafed geraniums have ivy-like, fleshy leaves. The thin stems are trailing which makes this geranium particularly suitable for window boxes and hanging baskets. They can flower from May until well after late summer. They can tolerate slightly more water and fertilizer than the Zonal hybrids but make sure the compost dries out between waterings.

While some geraniums have been bred to produce particular flower characteristics, the decorative value of others lies in their foliage. A beautiful Peltatum pelargonium is *Pelargonium* 'L 'Elégante' with simple white flowers with purple stripes. Its leaves are fleshy and grey-green with a creamy-white to light pink margin. For further maintenance see *Pelargonium* Zonal hybrids.

Pelargium Grandiflorum hybrid

Left and below: *Pelargonium* Peltatum-hybrid

Pelargonium Regale hybrids

See: *Pelargonium* Grandiflorum hybrids

Pelargonium Zonale hybrids

These are the best known geraniums. They are sometimes called *Pelargonium x hortorum.* They are hybrids of *P. inquinans* and *P. zonale*, both from South Africa, and others. The round stems are fleshy and green at first, later turning woody. The plant grows into a small shrub. The leaves are usually more or

Pelargonium Stellar hybrid

Pelargonium Peltatum hybrid 'L'Elégante'

313

less rounded and have a marking in the shape of a horse shoe. The flowers are large, single or double, often pink, red, purple or white.

The plants are very suitable for window boxes or in containers on the balcony or terrace, preferably in a sunny, sheltered position. Grow them in relatively small pots so that the soil can dry out well in between waterings. Be sparing with nitrogen because this fertilizer encourages leaf growth but inhibits flowering. Keep the plants dry in winter and put them in a cool but frost free place to stop active growth. It does not matter if the leaves drop off during this period. Pick off the withered leaves to prevent the occurrence of grey mould. Prune back hard in late winter and pinch out the tips of the new shoots in spring to produce compact little shrubs.

The pinched out tips can be rooted easily in spring. Cut them off immediately beneath a node. Let the wound dry off in the shade for a day and pull off all the leaves (except the new ones at the top). Put the cuttings in sand or a mixture of sand and peat. Keep the compost mildly moist (never wet, to avoid basal rot). Give the cuttings a temperature of at least 15°C (59°F) and keep them out of direct sun light.

As well as the nameless hybrids and the more compact F1-hybrids, there are sub-groups with clear characteristics such as: Stellar hybrids which have star-shaped leaves. The flowers are usually white or pale and have ragged or fringed upper petals.

Startel hybrids are compact F1-hybrids, bred from the Stellar hybrids, with colourful flowers.

Pelargonium Startel hybrid 'Bird dancer'

Pelargonium Zonale hybrid

Index

319

Acknowledgements

The editor and author thank the following persons and institutions for their assistance with this volume which could not have been produced without their help:

Arboretum Poort-Bulten, De Lutte
Botanical Gardens University of Utrecht
Horticultural research station, Delft
The Priona gardens, Schuinesloot
Hortus Botanicus Amsterdam
Hortus Botanicus Leiden
Hortus Botanicus "Vrije Universiteit", Amsterdam

J. Hummel, Zevenhuizen
Castle gardens Arcen
Nursery "De Bloemenhoek", De Bilt
Nursery Hartog, Peize
Mrs. Dekker, Veere
Mrs. Roozen, Haarlem

We are especially indebted to Intra Garden in Groningen where many of the photographs in this book were taken.